A Critical Biography

A. E. HOUSMAN

A Critical Biography

A. E. Housman by Francis Dodd
(*National Portrait Gallery*)

A. E. HOUSMAN

A Critical Biography

Norman Page

Schocken Books · New York

92
H842 p

First American edition published by Schocken Books 1983
10 9 8 7 6 5 4 3 2 1   83 84 85 86

Published by agreement with The Macmillan Press Ltd, London

Library of Congress Cataloging in Publication Data

Page, Norman.

A. E. Housman, a critical biography.

Includes index.
1. Housman, A. E. (Alfred Edward), 1859–1936.
2. Poets, English—19th century—Biography.
3. Classicists—England—Biography.   I. Title.
PR4809.H15P33   1983   821'.912 [B]   83–4510

Manufactured in Hong Kong
ISBN 0–8052–3872–7

To Ben

Contents

List of Plates

The publishers wish particularly to thank Mr and Mrs G. Symons, Mr Robert Symons and the Society of Authors, as the literary representative of the Estate of A. E. Housman, for their patience during the illustration research.

Acknowledgments

One of the most pleasant aspects of engaging in scholarly research is the amount of friendliness, generosity, and kindness beyond the call of duty that one encounters; and it is as no mere matter of form that I acknowledge some of my debts to those who have assisted me in a wide variety of ways. Professor Edward Griew and Mr John Sparrow read a draft of this book; without their scrupulous, expert and patient criticisms the final version would contain many more inaccuracies and infelicities. Mr Henry Maas, the editor of Housman's letters, generously placed at my disposal his files, including those of letters he had collected but not included in his edition. Mr Paul Naiditch has been, on many occasions, a mine of precise and accurate information. Among the many institutions whose staffs have come to my help I should like especially to mention the Library of Trinity College, Cambridge (Mr Trevor Kaye and Miss Rosemary Graham); the Library of Magdalene College, Cambridge (the Pepys Librarian, Mr R. C. Latham, and Mrs Coleman); the London Library; the Library of University College, London (Mrs J. Percival); the British Museum (Miss K. Janet Wallace); Ramsgate Library (Mr C. E. Busson); and, by no means least, the Manuscripts Division of the Library of Congress. I am also grateful for information and assistance to Professor Robert Ackerman; Mr Frederick B. Adams, Jr; Professor D. R. Shackleton Bailey; Professor William M. Calder III; Mr Stephen Calvert; Professor Glyn Daniel; Professor Leonard Findlay; Mr Martin Higham; Mr David Newsome; Mr Richard Palmer; Dr L. Pars; Mrs Margaret M. Phillips; the Rt Hon. J. Enoch Powell; the late Professor I. A. Richards; Mr Jeffrey Weeks; Mr L. P. Wilkinson. I owe a considerable debt of gratitude to the John Simon Guggenheim Memorial Foundation for a fellowship that enabled me to concentrate on writing this book in 1979/80, and to the University of Alberta for providing me with leisure and with financial and research assistance; also to Mr William Barclay for assistance with the notes and the index, and to Mrs Marguerite

Meyers and her staff for cheerful and expert typing services.

Grateful acknowledgment is also due to the following: the Syndics of Cambridge University Library, for permission to quote from the manuscript of Housman's Leslie Stephen Lecture (Add. 7734) and from his report on an edition of Fronto; Faber & Faber Ltd and Random House Inc., for W. H. Auden's 'A. E. Housman', from W. H. Auden, *Collected Poems*, ed. Edward Mendelson (copyright 1940, renewed 1968); Granada Publishing Ltd, for the extracts from *The Letters of A. E. Housman*, ed. Henry Maas; the Master and Fellows of Magdalene College, Cambridge, for the extracts from the diaries of A. C. Benson; the Society of Authors as the literary representative of the Estate of A. E. Housman, Jonathan Cape Ltd, and Holt, Rinehart and Winston, Inc., for the quotations from Housman's *Collected Poems*; the Society of Authors for the quotations from unpublished manuscript material by A. E. Housman, © 1983 The Estate of A. E. Housman; the Master and Fellows of Trinity College, Cambridge, for the quotations from manuscript material in Trinity College Library; the Library, University College, London, for the quotations from the Appointment Committee Report on the University College School Headmastership (AM/D/92); the University of Minnesota Press for the quotation from *The Manuscript Poems of A. E. Housman*, ed. Tom Burns Haber (copyright 1955 by the University of Minnesota). I am particularly grateful to Professor D. Shackleton Bailey, who has generously allowed me to quote extensively from his broadcast talk on Housman originally published in the *Listener*.

Notes on the Referencing System

An asterisk after a word or phrase in the text indicates that there is a note at the end of the book, where page-references are given for the notes.

A list of abbreviations will be found on p. 209.

Introduction: 'All that need be known'

Most writers envisage an ideal readership of the living; or, damning the age, write for posterity. The biographer alone writes for an audience that includes a dead man, his subject, and can hardly escape the sense of a ghost, gratified or resentful, at his elbow. Housman would not have applauded very loudly the attempt to write his biography, but I think he would have viewed it more tolerantly than is often supposed. He was a man of deep reserve whose instinct for secretiveness was now and then overcome by the impulse to reveal himself: the appearance of *A Shropshire Lad* prompted one member of his family to exclaim that Alfred had a heart after all. He remarked in 1931 that 'all that need be known of my life and books is contained in about a dozen lines of the publication *Who's Who*,* but that meagre sop to curiosity leaves even the most casual enquirer unsatisfied: it does not, for instance, name his parents, it lists no recreations, and it contains such remarkable understatements as 'St John's Coll. Oxford (M.A.)'. It is about one-third the length of the entry provided by Laurence Housman, himself a not uninteresting figure but not three times as interesting as his brother.

If Housman usually declined to indulge the inquisitiveness of his contemporaries, however, there are signs that he was eager for, and indeed provided for, posthumous truth-telling. Near the end of his life he wrote that 'I have sometimes thought of depositing in the British Museum a few pages to be published fifty years after my death';* he repeated the idea at least once; idea became rumour, rumour hardened into 'fact' and was duly enshrined in *The Times* obituary. But the few pages never reached the British Museum, and probably were never written. Still, the very notion is significant as suggesting that, towards the end, Housman was thinking of making amends by posthumous candour for a lifetime's dissimulation – as did, for example, John Addington

1

Symonds (in the manuscript memoirs which became generally
available only in 1976 and are still unpublished)* and
Goldsworthy Lowes Dickinson (in the autobiography published
in 1973, in which he states his object as being 'to tell what is
usually not told').*

What Housman actually did was to appoint his brother
Laurence as his literary executor. Laurence earned the gratitude
of posterity by bungling the job with considerable thoroughness,
as Housman must have known he would and perhaps intended
that he should. (Laurence later admitted that he had made a
'dreadful mistake'* in selling rather than destroying portions of
his brother's poetical notebooks.) Henry Maas shrewdly notes
that it was an odd choice, for Housman had little respect for his
brother's literary judgment: he 'must have guessed that
[Laurence] would fail to carry out his instructions. Had he
wanted an obedient executor he could easily have found one'.*
The explanation must be that the last thing Housman wanted was
a too-scrupulous executor who would efficiently burn the in-
discreet verses he had declined to publish in his lifetime: Laurence
could be relied on not to discharge his task too punctiliously. He
was struck by the fact that among his brother's papers were fair
copies of two 'doubtful' poems: one urging a sampling of 'stolen
waters' (*MP* XXII); the other, beginning 'Oh who is that young
sinner with the handcuffs on his wrists?' (*AP* XVIII), prompted
by the Oscar Wilde case. Laurence concluded that the intention
was that they should be given to the world (of the 'young sinner'
poem he wrote that 'it says something which A.E.H. very much
wished to say but perhaps preferred not to say in his own
lifetime');* and he was surely right. He came to realize that, as he
put it, his brother's purpose was 'to let me know the secret of his
life, and to give me liberty to make it known'.* It was, after all, a
neat arrangement: the dead man's wishes would be gratified, but
the blame for any lapse of judgment or taste would fall on
Laurence, whose long career of unconventionality left him in any
case with both a vested interest in frankness and little to lose by
indulging in it.

Housman never spoke of his homosexuality to Laurence,
though he would certainly have received a sympathetic hearing;
but Laurence wrote after his death that 'I have known for many
years what Alfred's tendency was. He knew that I knew . . .'.*
During Housman's lifetime some readers interpreted the poems

as a record of homosexual feelings, and more than one corres-
pondent wrote to him to say as much in circumspect phraseology.
In a letter expressing his admiration for *Last Poems*, Goldsworthy
Lowes Dickinson wrote that

> what they say appeals to something very deep in me. And deep
> calls to deep. It does not follow that surface calls to surface, and
> I am not trying to intrude myself. I wanted to say just this and
> leave it there.*

And very soon after Housman's death in 1936 the secret of his life
began to be more widely known. Laurence's memoir, published in
the following year, contains some discreetly worded hints which
were not wasted on at least some of his readers; reviewing it in the
New Statesman, Desmond Shawe-Taylor asked: 'Is it a coincidence
that the greater part of *A Shropshire Lad* was written in the year,
almost in the month, of the Wilde trial?'* Even earlier, Laurence
had quickly put together a posthumous collection of his brother's
verse and had published it as *More Poems*. With the eighteen
further poems included in his memoir, this raised the number of
Housman's published poems from 104 to 170 (excluding light
verse and parodies), and among the posthumously published
ones were poems more revealing than anything that had appeared
during the poet's lifetime. (Andrew Gow, Housman's colleague
and memoirist, wanted the 'colour of his hair' poem left out; but
Laurence ignored his advice, commenting that 'I have a queer
feeling that he would like that to be known; he suffered so much
himself'.)* Only six months after Housman's death, Desmond
MacCarthy was able to reflect in the sedate columns of a Sunday
newspaper:

> It is strange . . . how often he saw the emblem of his own
> emotional life in an outcast, a youth condemned by other men
> to die in shame, and yet not strange once we suppose intense life
> came to him in the guise of 'the love that dares not speak its
> name'.*

The Times Literary Supplement reviewer of Laurence's memoir
quoted and drew attention to his comment on the significance of
the 'colour of his hair' poem. But not all were able to recognize the
truth when it stared them in the face. As late as 1939, H. W.
Garrod could write:

> That Alfred's heart bore no wounds of the conventional kind,
> that he was never in love, that he was, indeed, what his brother
> calls him, 'a born bachelor', we must now, I think, take as
> certain . . . It is only known certainly that, whatever
> unhappiness there was [during Housman's early years in
> London], there were no unhappy loves. I have sometimes
> wondered whether there were no unhappy friendships . . .*

He might well wonder: one envies Garrod's assurance in judging
where love begins and ends. Twenty years later, Laurence was
still industriously propagating the truth that he believed his
brother wished to be known to the world.

Still, to urge that Housman would not have scorned a
biographer's attention may be to claim victory in a battle that no-
one is interested in fighting; and there remain more vital questions
– whether the task is worth doing, whether it can be done.
Housman's overall achievement may well be unique in scope if
not in scale: a scholar of the very first rank, and the last great
textual critic in the tradition of Bentley; a minor poet of distinctive
voice who was deeply admired by a whole generation (that of
Auden and Orwell), whose influence was considerable, and who
wrote a handful of the finest short poems in the language; a prose
stylist whose elegance and brilliance are not widely enough
appreciated (though he has been called 'one of the wittiest writers
in the English language')* – there is no need to apologize for
wishing to know more about such a man and to come closer to an
understanding of the perplexing pattern of his life and the
apparent contradictions of his mind and sensibility: it is a deeply
moving human story, and to strive to know it is to follow that
craving for knowledge which, as Housman insisted, makes us
human. And we are in a better position now than even a very few
years ago to know all that can be known about Housman; if his life
cannot be written today, it can probably never be written. Much
of the material in this book has never appeared in print, and some
of it has become available only very recently. (Two examples: the
death in 1978 of Andrew Gow, the last of Housman's close friends,
placed many fresh papers at the biographer's disposal; and the
release, after a fifty-year embargo, of Arthur Benson's diaries
makes available a first-hand account of Housman that has not
hitherto been drawn on.) There are gaps in the record, and one
would happily exchange a whole loaf of anecdotes from the

Cambridge years for a few crumbs from the silent, undocumented years of youth; but the gaps are likely to remain for ever unfilled.

The problems of a Housman biography are those of any biographical undertaking, with the addition of others peculiar to the special case. Among the normal hazards is the temptation to over-simplification: the reduction of a life to a simple pattern, the tidying up of a personality so that one is left not with the moving and teasing complexity of a human being but with the flavourless clarity of one of those exercises that old-fashioned English teachers used to prescribe ('write a character-sketch of Hamlet'). Part of the attraction of biography for readers and writers is that it creates the illusion of making sense and wholeness of a life and places it under our control: as readers we can make time pass as slowly or quickly as we wish, we hold birth and death simultaneously in our hands. But there are dangers in making *too* much sense of a life. 'How mean a thing a mere fact is,' wrote Coleridge, 'except as seen in the light of some comprehensive truth.'* The biographer has a responsibility to both, but there are many times when a comprehensive truth must defer to mere fact.

A biography, boiling down a lifetime to a few hours' reading, cannot avoid reductiveness; but Housman, perhaps because the paradoxes of his career are so arresting, seems to have fallen an especially easy victim to over-simplification. An extreme example is also the most familiar piece of biographical writing about him and short enough to quote in full:

> No one, not even Cambridge, was to blame
> (Blame if you like the human situation):
> Heart-injured in North London, he became
> The Latin Scholar of his generation.
>
> Deliberately he chose the dry-as-dust,
> Kept tears like dirty postcards in a drawer;
> Food was his public love, his private lust
> Something to do with violence and the poor.
>
> In savage foot-notes on unjust editions
> He timidly attacked the life he led,
> And put the money of his feelings on
> The uncritical relations of the dead,
> Where only geographical divisions
> Parted the coarse hanged soldier from the don.*

Who would have supposed that the life of a textual critic would turn out to be so tuppence-coloured? Auden has done an extraordinary amount in fourteen lines, about the same length as the *Who's Who* entry. The paradoxes are there – the poet-don, the emotional over-reactions of scholarly controversy coexisting with the seemingly passionless nature, worldly success of a highly conventional and approved kind masking crude unsatisfied appetites. There are even notes for a biographical outline: North London, Cambridge, gastronomy, pornography. But of course, like *Who's Who*, it leaves almost everything still to be done. The third and fourth lines, where syntax is made to carry the burden of a psychological theory, are too easy (it takes more than a broken heart to make a great scholar). Elsewhere Auden implicitly defended the summary treatment he had meted out to Housman:

> I have always thought that Housman would make an admirable model for a novelist to use for a fictional character, because the essential structure of his personality was so unusually clear. He was one of those rare people whose skeleton, so to speak, was always showing . . .*

But nobody, one wants to interrupt, is *that* simple: to make complete sense of a life, to explain everything, is at best an unrealizable ideal, at worst a hubristic snare and delusion.

It has often been said that Housman was an unhappy man; also that he was a disagreeable one. It is not the business of this introduction to provide instant verdicts on those suggestions, but they indicate the biographer of Housman is not exempt from the rule that calls for a delicate balancing-act between too much and too little sympathy for his subject. The tradition of hagiography in which modern biography has its origins is not quite extinct, nor is the much shorter tradition of denigration; and Housman has suffered from at least one biographer who loved him not wisely but too well, and from at least one who plainly disliked him a good deal. The present book is not an apology for Housman any more than it is an attempt to depreciate the impulses that drove him or the values he chose to live by. It seeks an understanding bred of willingness to see the world for the time being through his eyes, without foregoing the advantage of, as Conrad's Marlow says, seeing him as well as seeing what he sees.

Housman's biographer cannot complain of a shortage of

material, though he might wish it to have been less widely
scattered by time and chance. Collecting the evidence, though, is
only the beginning of his task: to bring into play a sympathetic
scepticism, judging how much to accept as valid, how much
allowance to make for the conscious or (more commonly)
unconscious distortions of witnesses, must be his constant
preoccupation. Only the most naive – but some of Housman's
biographers, I fear, merit the label – will treat with uniform
respect all that has appeared in print, or be duped by the delusion
of total recall enjoyed by so many memoirists and retailers of
anecdote. The abundance of material that makes the researcher's
heart glad also raises a major problem. Lytton Strachey said that
'a becoming brevity [is] the first duty of the biographer'; no doubt
he had reasons of his own for saying so, and the reaction against
Strachey set in long ago. For some years now we have witnessed a
regression to the monumental kind of biography favoured by the
Victorians (though different from theirs in some important
respects), heavy, dense and indigestible as a Christmas pudding.
The latest biography of Conrad runs to over a thousand pages; a
life of Fielding, about whom relatively little is known, is even
longer; minor figures such as Ford Madox Ford are given the full
treatment, though whether they or we need it remains open to
question. It would not be difficult to write a long biography of
Housman. A single paragraph, not to be found elsewhere in this
book, will make the point:

> Housman habitually wore black elastic-sided boots known
> colloquially as 'Jemimas'. He had very small feet. When he
> died, his 'gyp' or college servant, George Penny, inherited his
> footwear as well as receiving a modest legacy of twenty pounds.
> Unfortunately, however, the boots were too small for Penny to
> wear and too old-fashioned for him to find a purchaser . . .

And so on. Footnotes (well named) could point irreproachably to
sources, for none of the above is untrue; but none of it is worth
saying. Yet many biographies are full of such stuff, as if providing
for the distant day when someone, somewhere, may wish to test a
thesis linking foot-measurements to creative genius. Of a similar
kind is the excessive attention commonly devoted in a mandatory
opening chapter to a writer's ancestry. We know that a fifteenth-
century Housman had an interest in land in Lincolnshire, and

that a seventeenth-century Housman was a Fellow of Magdalen College, Oxford; but we hardly *need* to know such matters. There may be writers whose personalities are so magnetically fascinating that one is grateful to learn what they ate for breakfast; but they are few. It is, of course, natural, though inexcusable, that researchers who have patiently culled facts should be reluctant to let them remain in their files awaiting a call to resurrection that never comes. Nabokov's biographer tells us that he spent hundreds of man-hours checking a single point, but does not tell us whether it is worth knowing. My own policy has been anti-inflationary: I have conceived the biographer's first duty as being to discover all he can about his subject; his second duty to decide on the strictest criteria how much needs to be told, and to exclude the rest. A recent biographer of Gerard Manley Hopkins tells us that the poet was afflicted with piles; so, it seems, was Housman; but what business of ours is such knowledge, unless a connection is to be established between piles and poetry? This, persisted in, is to reduce biography from an art to a form of collecting; to offer the reader not a shaped selective narrative but a do-it-yourself kit out of which he must construct a biography as best he may. Too many modern biographies are dropsical with fact, fat books out of which slim books are seeking to escape. Let lives of Dickens and Balzac mimic their subjects' hyperactivity: a life of Housman (or Gray, or Leopardi) demands a becoming spareness. I have tried never to give a fact simply for the sake of giving a fact – a rule that has doubtless, but not deliberately, been broken.

In no life, though, and certainly not in Housman's, can fact be everything. Biography abhors a vacuum, and narrative could only proceed in bone-shaking lurches without the cushioning of surmise. With Housman (and the case is typical of many) the extent of our knowledge of the various aspects of his existence is usually in inverse proportion to their interest or significance: to go no further than the physical appetites, his tastes in eating and drinking are fully documented (he liked hock and hare, and ate hedgehog at least once: I shall not take the reader through the entire gastronomic alphabet), but his sex-life remains a mystery. Speculation there must be, and not merely in the interests of a smooth ride for the narrative: to eschew it is to shirk the responsibility of guesswork that is not random but prompted by a hard-won sense of the overall pattern of a man's mind and experience. Richard Ellmann has predicted that 'biographies will continue to be archival, but the best ones will offer speculations, conjectures, hypotheses'.* Ah yes, one murmurs; and the worst ones will do precisely the same. It is an act of the nicest discretion, continually demanded, to decide when speculation, top-heavy, sinks under its own weight from duty into self-indulgence.

When evidence is lacking, certain stylistic as well as strategic and ethical problems loom; they constitute part of what may be called the distinctive rhetoric of biography. The novelist's words, sliding or struggling from his pen, shape a truth that may have been hitherto non-existent, but the biographer is the hard-driven servant of fact (supplemented, as I have said, by a disciplined surmise). Hence the novelist can write 'he walked across the room', knowing it never happened or causing it to happen by saying it; the biographer ought not to write 'he quarrelled with his friend' if he does not know it certainly to be true, even though he may know it very likely to be true. Writing criticism, one dispenses with the need to begin every sentence with some such formula as 'I think', 'I believe', 'in my opinion', because these cautionary phrases are 'understood'. In any case the difference between fact ('Wordsworth died in 1850') and opinion ('Wordsworth is a better poet than Pope') or interpretation ('for Wordsworth, mountains were a father-substitute') is reasonably clear-cut. In a biography, some of the sentences are speculative but a great many belong to the historical narrative the provision of which is the primary purpose of the work: the danger is that statements belonging to the first category will be mistaken for those belonging to the second. Our language hardly supplies enough signals of tentativeness for tedious repetition to be avoided: the judicious 'perhaps', 'possibly', 'presumably', 'it may be'; the more hectoring 'surely', 'no doubt', 'Housman must have': these brief lists go far towards exhausting the repertoire. Long before he has done, the biographer is likely to find himself longing to write in a language whose verbs are richer in moods and aspects than English, in order to convey more precisely yet more unobtrusively the sense of what must very likely (but not quite certainly) have been, what may have been, what may possibly (but not probably) have been, what might well have been but almost certainly wasn't.

A single simple case in point: the phrase 'Housman said', less innocent than it looks, can mean that Housman made a written statement the original of which survives, or a copy of which survives (which may or may not be accurate); or that he made an oral remark once (or more often) which was immediately (or subsequently) written down by one (or more) who heard it; or that it was told by one who heard it to one who did not hear it but who then, or later, wrote it down; or— the list is not exhausted, though the reader's patience may be. Housman's latest biographer prefaces a long quotation with the phrase 'Housman remarked dryly';* a distant note confesses that the source of the 'quotation' is a letter written nearly sixty years after the time in question by the son of a man who may be supposed to have heard what Housman said (though he may have had it from another, who may have had it . . .) and who would, if he was not an exception to the human rule, have told it many times over many years with unconscious modifications, to say nothing of the transformations it may have undergone in the memory of his son. If I seem to labour the point it is because the habit is always with us. In such circumstances 'Housman remarked', dryly or otherwise, can be no more than a kind of figure of speech; on other occasions the phrase means precisely what it says. Some modern biographies seem to have been written by Humpty Dumpty. Pieces of evidence customarily presented in identical guise ought to be accorded different status, and that status ought to be properly signalled, lest biography turn into romantic fiction.

It goes without saying that I do not believe that an entirely satisfactory biography of Housman has been written: if I did, I should not be adding to their number. But one learns something from every previous attempt, even if only what to avoid; and it will save time if I indicate summarily what I take to be the merits and limitations of my predecessors in this field, to some of whose writings I shall have many occasions to refer. Four books on Housman appeared within a few years of his death in 1936, those of A. S. F. Gow (1936), Laurence Housman (1937), Percy Withers (1940) and Grant Richards (1941). None of these is a full-dress biography, and indeed the time was not yet ripe for such an undertaking: it takes longer for the dust raised by a man's earthly doings to settle, for private materials to come to light, for the sensitivities of the living to be blunted by death or time. But since each of these writers, in one capacity or another, knew Housman over many years, they deserve attention. There was a flurry of biographical activity in the late 1950s, when two books appeared almost simultaneously, by George L. Watson (1957) and Maude

Hawkins (1958); then a long silence until the appearance of Richard Perceval Graves' substantial biography in 1979 (near-simultaneity repeating itself, for my own work was under way before I knew of Mr Graves').

The short memoirs by Andrew Gow and Laurence Housman complement each other, for as, respectively, colleague and brother they were able to write of quite different areas of Housman's life. Gow's is no more than an essay but remains one of the best accounts of the professional and public Housman, who would have admired its classical economy and elegance. He and Gow did not meet until about 1909, and Gow's account of the earlier years is perfunctory; the memoir is presented as an introduction to a checklist of Housman's classical publications, and takes its flavour accordingly. It was no part of Gow's purpose to offer revelations: begun almost before Housman was cold, his essay is a worthy memorial to a great scholar but respects the privacy of one so recently dead. Gow wrote to Laurence Housman that 'his emotional life, which would be interesting, couldn't be discovered, and couldn't be published if it were';* how, if it could not be discovered, he knew that it would be interesting but unpublishable is not quite clear, but one senses that he was grateful for an excuse to leave it at that.

Laurence had the advantage of having known his subject for a lifetime; on the other hand he was six years younger and, after childhood, they were never close and saw little of each other. In many ways Laurence was an attractive personality, amiable, open-minded, tolerant, energetic and enthusiastic even in extreme old age, and quite without envy. (He was a prolific and successful writer whose play *Victoria Regina* made him rich, so that envy was not a strong temptation.) But blood, though thicker than water, is not in itself a qualification for writing a good biography; and Laurence's fluency as an imaginative writer was not auspicious, even if family piety had not been in question. Laurence, a homosexual himself and even something of a sexual as well as a political activist,* would no doubt have been more candid if he had not been reluctant to hurt the feelings of his sister Katharine. But he offers some vivid glimpses of the scantily documented years of childhood, and there is further material in his lively if unreliable autobiography *The Unexpected Years*.

Withers and Richards form another pair, for both were members of that circle of male friends drawn from outside the academic world whose company Housman enjoyed over many years but with whom his relationship remained fairly superficial. Withers did not meet Housman until 1917, and his memoir is sympathetic but slight. Richards was Housman's publisher and an ardent fellow-gastronome; he enjoyed Housman's confidence to the extent of sending him new items of pornographic literature, and they occasionally took holidays together. As was often the case with Housman, their relationship was long rather than deep, and Richards' book tells us a good deal about Housman's taste in wine but little about his inner nature. To be quite fair, of course, even if revelations had been timely as well as fashionable (and they were neither), none of those so far discussed was the best man for the job. The memoir we should most like to have, that of Moses Jackson, was never written. But their collective efforts pre-empted the field, and for long there was no biography by a literary scholar to compensate for the absence of an authorized biography.

Watson is the first of the outsiders and, a generation after Housman's death, he could afford candour. The verdict of *The Times Literary Supplement* reviewer on his book, 'a crude and falsely coloured portrait', is harsh but not unfair. One's misgivings begin very early, for in the third sentence of his foreword Watson refers to Housman's 'fussy concern about the spelling and punctuation of each edition' of his books. One wonders why anyone who can see Housman's lifelong passion for accuracy only as fussiness should want to write his life: to fail to grasp that correctness is better than error is to be ill-equipped to write the life of a scholar, or for that matter to write a biography at all; and Watson's book has no shortage of errors of fact and misuse of evidence. He is, I think, disabled by total deafness to Housman's habitual irony, finding him 'irascible' and 'neurasthenic' where I find him witty and reasonable; in an entertaining piece such as the Cambridge inaugural lecture, which the audience found brilliant, Watson can detect only a 'severe pedantic tone'. Alas, the pedantry is all his own. Significantly, he assigns to the Cambridge years, which constituted almost one-third of Housman's entire life, only one out of ten chapters; he finds them uninteresting, one presumes, because he has no notion of what the life of a scholar involves.

Lack of sympathy for his subject is evident: one wonders why Watson chose to write the life of a man he clearly disliked a good deal. Lack of sympathy is not one of Maude Hawkins' disqualifications, but she has plenty of her own: a determination to present Housman as a hero at all costs, a gross ignorance of the English social and academic scene, a disregard for accuracy that verges on inspiration (she gives – a trivial but revealing instance – the name of Housman's London landlady as Mrs Trim: an excellent name for a Victorian landlady, but she was actually called Mrs Hunter). Whilst her book was in progress she corresponded extensively with Laurence Housman, and his letters show that he was good-temperedly aware of her shortcomings.

Neither Watson nor Hawkins had come within hailing distance of even a moderately satisfactory biography, but they remained unchallenged for a further generation. Mr Graves' recent book has virtues missing from theirs: he has examined a great deal of material, and his unsentimental enthusiasm for Housman as man and poet enables him to steer between Watson-Scylla and Hawkins-Charybdis in the delicate matter of the biographer's relationship to his subject. Some of his interpretations, however, leave me so uneasy as to render it impossible to regard his book as satisfactory. His two most serious weaknesses have to do with the use of evidence. Mr Graves shows a capacity for sudden disconcerting flights in drawing conclusions from facts. Housman was circumcised at fourteen, therefore – of course – he regarded sex as 'dirty'. How do we know that he was a great Latin scholar? Well, he was clever enough to compose a dedicatory poem *in Latin verse* for his edition of Manilius; but since it is even harder to be funny in a foreign language than to be serious, it is a comic poem that he composed in Latin that really shows him to belong to the tradition of Bentley. One rubs one's eyes: can such things be? When Mr Graves encounters a gap in the evidence, he is prepared to fill it with surmise; and indeed there is no reason why he should not, but he ought not to offer his surmises as facts.

When he says, for example, at particular points in his narrative that Housman's 'affection for Moses Jackson was deepening into love' and that 'Jackson himself began to look with fresh eyes at his friendship with Alfred', he is speaking of matters concerning which neither he nor anyone else can possibly know the truth; such sentences belong not to a biography but to a romantic novel. If one were to substitute quite different sentences – for example, 'Housman fell in love with Moses Jackson the moment he set eyes on him', and 'Jackson knew right away that Housman's feelings for him were not merely those of a friend' – Mr Graves would be in no position to contradict them, though they would be equally out of place in a biography. Other instances I shall have to call in question at the proper points of my own narrative; let it suffice for the moment to mention that one such excursion into romance has been cited by reviewers who should know better and has thus passed into the common 'knowledge' of those who will never read any biography of Housman. There rings in one's ears Housman's dictum that 'the faintest of all human passions is the love of truth',* though another of his observations may be no less apt to the present discussion: 'perhaps the reader will do well to consider how far my judgment of [others'] performance may have been warped by the passion of envy'.*

My decision to separate the extended discussion of Housman as a poet and a classical scholar from the biographical chapters was not lightly taken. The biographer's dream is to integrate the life and the work so successfully that the latter can be seen and felt as flowering naturally from the process of living. With some subjects (Keats, Lawrence) the ideal can be realized; but not with Housman, for whom art was separate from daily life, a consciously different, secret activity, running in quite another direction from his public existence. In any case, the practical difficulties are insuperable: Housman published his poetry in two bursts, in 1896 and 1922, and the posthumously published poems swell the corpus; but the dating of many poems is uncertain or impossible, and many were written over long periods, an original draft being taken up and revised or completed long after its conception. Although, therefore, I have in my biographical chapters given a personal context for the most conspicuous periods of creative activity, it has seemed best to let the full discussion of Housman's poetry stand by itself. In this way, too, I have hoped to avoid the elementary but pervasive error of using the poems as biographical 'evidence'. As for Housman's achievement as a classical scholar, I have in writing on this subject drawn heavily, and gratefully, on the work of classical scholars who have described and estimated his accomplishment in this field.

The biographer lives in daily contact with his subject over a long period, reading his letters and even more private records, encountering his friends, accompanying him on his walks, sharing his meals, until his habits and attitudes become intimately familiar and one finds oneself asking, of some matter of the present moment, 'What would Housman have thought, or said, of that?'

Such intimacy has obvious perils: there are better mottoes for the biographer than *tout pardonner*, and Housman's personality and conduct are at some points such that complete sympathy must be withheld. Still, he remains, I think, a much less repellent figure than popular superstition has painted him, and a less miserably unhappy one. After his early years he had much to enjoy: a taste for pleasures – food, wine, books, looking at fine architecture, travel, agreeable company – and the ability to indulge them; a congenial occupation that enabled him to use his exceptional intellectual powers and to devote his time to doing what he knew he could do supremely well; fame, dignity, affluence, and above all the consciousness that he had been wholly successful in building the monument that his ambition desired. In some respects he was less happy than many: he never knew requited love, and he suffered from an incurable loneliness that recalls the phrase of his favourite Matthew Arnold, 'We mortal millions live *alone*.' On the other hand, he knew satisfactions denied to all but a very few, and it would be melodramatic and false to declare that they turned to ashes in his mouth; if he believed that the world was a vale of tears, he was in no great hurry to quit it, and he died of natural causes at an advanced age. I am tempted to say that there are plenty of others, dead and living, who stand in greater need of whatever pity we may have to spare; but the chapters that follow will enable the reader to decide for himself whether this view is just.

1   A Worcestershire Lad

'Every one is born a king, and most people die in exile . . .'
(Oscar Wilde)

Towards the end of March 1871, Alfred Housman was staying at the home of the Wises, family friends of long standing, in the Gloucestershire village of Woodchester. He had been dispatched there from his own home at Bromsgrove on 19 March; and there, a week later, he celebrated his twelfth birthday. Soon afterwards a letter arrived from his father to tell him that on his birthday his mother had died, and to suggest that he should stay on at Woodchester for a while. The other children, still at home, had learned the news first; they had been taken in to see their mother's corpse, and the older ones attended her funeral; but Alfred, her first-born, never saw his mother again.

The event brought to an end an enviably happy childhood: like another intelligent and sensitive child of the period, George Eliot's Maggie Tulliver, Alfred found that the golden gates had closed behind him for ever. They had not shut quite suddenly, it is true: Sarah Housman's terminal illness (breast cancer) had been protracted, and according to the custom of the day she had been nursed at home and had remained there to the end. The strain on those around her must have been intense; Alfred had borne a greater share of it than most of the others, and it may be that he had been sent to the Wises because he was showing signs of finding the ordeal intolerable. Still, the first decade of his life at least had been all that anyone could wish for.

The family background was one of solid middle-class comfort, and the Housmans, Anglican and Tory, were fairly big fish in the little Midlands pond of Bromsgrove. Alfred's paternal grandfather, Thomas Housman, was a clergyman who had married money; he had become the first incumbent of the new

16

church at Catshill, just outside Bromsgrove, and lived at Fockbury House nearby. Thomas was himself the son of a notable divine, Robert Housman, 'the evangelist of Lancaster', who earned a place in the *Dictionary of National Biography*. Thomas's wife, Anne Brettell, the daughter of a Bromsgrove attorney who had also married money, was distantly related to Herbert Spencer. The Church and the Law were both prominent in A. E. Housman's ancestry, appropriately enough for one who spent most of his working life scrutinizing texts and settling points of dispute. He was descended from prominent members of provincial society who inherited, and in due course bequeathed, substantial amounts of capital and who lived, in that age of large houses and cheap servants, in a style of unostentatious dignity. An odd feature of their family history was a fluctuation between philoprogenitiveness and an unwillingness or inability to propagate their kind; by a curious coincidence, Alfred's grandfathers both sired twelve children, of whom on each side only one left descendants, and in his own generation all but one of his father's large family were to die without issue.

As if to humanize a family almost too respectable for comfort, the Housmans occasionally found themselves harbouring a black sheep. Alfred's great-uncle William had abandoned his wife and children and run away to America with an actress; his uncle Thomas had been 'caught in his youth leaving the nanny's bedroom',* and after this enterprising start had never looked back. Edward Housman, Alfred's father, thus found himself, although the second son, in effect the head of the clan. He qualified as a solicitor, wooed and won Sarah Jane Williams of Woodchester, married her on 17 June 1858, and took her to live at Valley House, Fockbury, a Georgian house near his parents' home. Sarah's father, recently dead, had been Rector of Woodchester for twenty-four years. Of his large family only two survived into adult life, supposedly owing to 'the infected and insanitary condition of old Woodchester Rectory'. The Reverend John Williams came of Devon stock and had been at Oxford; he was a classical scholar and a poet, and his daughter Sarah, though deeply pious, was 'witty and wrote skits in verse on the people she wanted to ridicule'.* Her new home, Fockbury, was 'a tiny scattered hamlet – not twelve houses all told – on the outskirts of the village of Bournheath'.* In spite of its proximity to Bromsgrove, a couple of miles away, and to Birmingham, it must have had a timelessly pastoral atmosphere; even today, though approached over a motorway, it contrives to retain a rural flavour.

It was at Valley House that Alfred Edward Housman, presumably conceived on the honeymoon, was born on 26 March 1859. He was promptly christened by his grandfather at Christ Church, Catshill. Within a few months the family moved into a larger house, when Perry Hall in Bromsgrove became vacant on the death of Captain John Adams, a distant relative who had held the post of Government Agent for Stamps and was Edward Housman's employer. Perry Hall, the scene of Alfred's earliest memories, stood at the foot of the hill topped by Bromsgrove Church and was a marvellous place for a child to grow up in. Its gardens of nearly two acres served as a playground for Alfred and the brothers and sisters who rapidly followed him: Robert (born 1860), Clemence (1861), Katharine (1862), Basil (1864), Laurence (1865), and George, later known by his second name of Herbert (1868). There is every sign that Alfred's childhood was very happy; and with such an attractive home, a loving intelligent mother and a cheerful energetic father ready to share his many enthusiasms with his children, there was good reason for happiness. The bells of Bromsgrove Church, Laurence recalled in his old age, were a constant background to family life; and the home was strongly Christian, with family prayers before breakfast and church twice on Sundays. But the Housman children also enjoyed considerable freedom – to escape from adult society into a corner of the large garden, to play out their fantasies, quarrel and make up. Edward Housman was a man of many interests – too many for success in his profession – and it must have been partly his example that inspired the children to be always doing something. 'Was there ever such an interesting family as we were?' Alfred once said to Laurence as they discussed their childhood long after it was past; and Laurence adds:

> There were probably many; but none, I daresay, more interested in itself, when it stood compact and pugnaciously united – seven against the rest of the world. How we loved; how we hated; how we fought, divided, and were reconciled again! How we trained, and educated ourselves; and developed a taste in literature and in the writing of it, in which, until years later, our elders had no part, and with which school-hours had little to do.*

A busy, contented, comfortable, companionable childhood: there is nothing in the record of these early years that foreshadows the self-sufficient solitariness of Housman's maturity.

In some respects, though, the young Alfred was rather startlingly the father of the man. Edward Housman belonged to the Bromsgrove Volunteer Rifle Corps, and his son was fascinated by the military life. A charming photograph shows him, aged seven, with his brother Robert, both of them clutching home-made rifles; and the enthusiasm evidently persisted, since the much younger Laurence could remember battles fought in a corner of the garden and Alfred's experiments as an inventor of weaponry. 'At eight or earlier' he was writing verse, no doubt encouraged by his mother's skill in that direction. 'A little book we had in the house' led him, 'almost as early as I can remember', to develop an interest in astronomy; and Lemprière's *Classical Dictionary* 'fell into my hands when I was eight' (as he said in his old age) and 'attached my affections to paganism'.* The pre-dilections of the classical scholar whose *magnum opus* was an edition of the astronomer-poet Manilius, and of the author of *A Shropshire Lad* with its soldier-heroes, were formed very early. Somewhat later another chance discovery which may well have been formative was J. E. Bode's *Ballads from Herodotus*, in which the Greek stories were Victorianized in stirring Macaulayesque verse. 'Thermopylae', for instance, seems to anticipate *A Shropshire Lad* in style and sentiment:

> Go, take the style of glory,
> And write their names on high;
> For some have fought to conquer;
> But these have fought to die!

From Bode, too, Housman may have learned something of the emphatic power of alliteration:

> Sudden and soft o'er sea and land
> The summer night comes down;
> And hope is on the lonely strand,
> Terror in Trachis town.

Ancient Greeks did not, however, quench the boy's thirst for hero-worship, which found also a modern object. In 1923, in an

uncharacteristically autobiographical conversation, Housman
told A. C. Benson of

> his youthful adoration of Napoleon III, and that the Franco-
> Prussian War was a great shock and grief to him (then aged 11).
> He spoke with contempt of writers as opposed to men of action.
> 'Put Bismarck by Swinburne; Shelley by Napoleon III'.*

Alfred's earliest lessons had been from a governess (of whom,
according to Laurence, he drew caricatures); but soon he was sent
to a dame's school in Bromsgrove High Street, whence he
proceeded at eleven to Bromsgrove School. The scholarship he
won in July 1870 was a bright spot in an otherwise gloomy year,
for troubles now came, and came in battalions, to menace the
idyllic life of the Housman family. Sarah had fallen ill towards the
end of 1869 and was growing steadily worse. Early in 1870
grandfather Thomas Housman died. Robert, whose asthma was
causing anxiety, was sent off to a boarding-school in the kinder
climate of Bath, thus breaking up for the first time the 'seven
against the rest of the world'. Little Laurence suffered a prolonged
illness. And as Edward Housman's family life showed signs of
collapsing around him, his easy-going nature was unable to take
the strain: he became withdrawn and began to drink heavily.
Laurence's summing-up, eighty years later, has an unsentimental
cogency:

> My father was amiable, kindly, easy-going, rather vain, and
> self-indulgent. We worshipped him as children, but became
> more and more critical of him as we grew older.

Laurence remembered a revealing anecdote of his father which
'he told me himself without knowing how funny it was':

> In his early manhood, he was helping, one day, to clean out a
> fish-pond; and to do this he turned up his trousers above the
> knees – disclosing a fine pair of calves. A susceptible maiden
> lady gazed at them with awe-struck delight, and declared that
> she had 'never seen such a sight in all her born days'. His
> comment 'That was the properest compliment I ever got,' was
> followed by this: 'But what else could she expect from a man
> who was able to beget such a fine large family as *I* have!'*

Edward Housman was clearly no tower of strength in a crisis, and during this period the strain on the older children, and especially on Alfred as eldest, must have been grievous. As their mother grew worse she became bed-ridden, and Alfred and Clemence spent a good deal of time with her, witnessing the unrecorded drama of her anguish at the thought of the young family she would leave behind. She had written to her friend Mrs Wise to tell her that she would not live to see her children grow up; and seven young children were an awesome responsibility for a man who, as she must have realized by then, was not cut out for quiet heroism. Her mind ran on her girlhood in Woodchester – that family life, punctuated by frequent bereavements, in the crowded country rectory – and she talked of it to her children, as if anxious to come to terms with her own past or to rescue fragments of it from impending oblivion by giving them a place in their memories. She was also preoccupied by thoughts of religion, and her High Church leanings became more pronounced as the end drew near; she asked to see a Roman Catholic priest, but her husband refused. His state can be surmised from the fact that she poured out her anxious urgent messages not to him but to Alfred and Clemence. The latter was enjoined to look after little Laurence, and she heeded her mother so well that her dying wish was carried out until Clemence's own death eighty-five years later.

Alfred prayed to God that his mother might be spared, but she died just the same. Sent to the Wises at Woodchester, he received there, among the scenes of his mother's early life, the news of her death on 26 March 1871. The letter also told him of her dying request that he should not lose his religious faith. One can only speculate why she felt this needed saying, but the communication of it by her widower could have been more tactfully timed. Her plea adds great poignancy to her son's declaration, when he himself was near death, that 'I became a deist at thirteen'.*

It fell to the Wises to comfort the boy amid their own grief, for Mrs Wise was an old friend of Sarah Housman. Her daughter Edith was seventeen, and there were also in the household a younger son and daughter and a German governess, Fräulein Sophie Becker. Their affection and sympathy meant so much to Alfred that he remembered it for the rest of his days. He continued to visit the Wises for many years, and in his mid-seventies was still taking an interest in old Woodchester friends. R. P. Graves is probably right to stress the significance of the Wise family for Housman as a living link with his dead mother:* when he visited them he was entering her past. One must add, though, that the most potent association the Wises held for him was surely a highly specific one – the memory of their presence when he was dealt the blow of his mother's death. With unswerving loyalty he remembered them always, and to Sophie Becker in particular he retained a lifelong attachment. Though they almost certainly never met again after she returned to Germany some time before 1914, he continued to write to her until she died at a very advanced age in 1931. She was getting on for twenty years older than Alfred, a motherly, or at least an elder-sisterly, figure. Laurence wrote in 1950:

> I think the woman he loved most in the world was his mother . . . after her probably came Sophie Becker, who 'mothered' him in his great loss; I think his *mother*-love was very passionate . . .*

After his brother's death Laurence had found a letter from Sophie preserved among his papers; it began 'My dear boy' and ended 'Your affectionate friend'. It was a friendship that lasted longer than any other in Housman's life.

When he returned to Bromsgrove his home must have seemed, despite the family and servants, desolate and empty. But it was clearly important that, as the eldest, he should set an example to the other children by not giving way to his feelings in their presence; and from this period in his life dates the withdrawn, deeply reserved side of his nature that in later years was to grow dominant. His mother's death, according to his sister Kate, 'depriv[ed] him of a guide and counsellor who was never replaced. From that time he became his own counsellor, confiding to no one his mental troubles or ambitions.'* He spoke only rarely of his mother until very near the end of his life; then, as if to make up for a lifetime's reticence before it was too late, he talked freely of her to Laurence.* But he kept 'every scrap of writing that he had received from her or about her'.*

For a man as fundamentally weak and as hard hit by circumstance as Edward Housman, it was a daunting burden to be responsible for the upbringing of seven children between twelve and two years old. Even with a female relative to run the house, it must have been a black period for him and for all concerned; so it is not surprising that before long his thoughts turned to remarriage. His cousin, Lucy Housman, who had introduced Sarah Williams to him, had never married; seven years older than himself, she was now nearly fifty. Although the prospect of such a large instant family must have been sobering, when he proposed she accepted; and they were married in London on 26 June 1873. After she had been dead for more than forty years, Laurence summed up Lucy as 'a very mixed character – a tyrant, but very courageous and staunch to her duty as she saw it . . . a monument of Victorian vitality'.* Courage, staunchness and vitality were certainly in demand; as for the tyranny, it does not seem to have prevented Laurence and the others from going their own way when the time came. It is only fair to say that she seems to have made a good job of the demanding role of stepmother, and Alfred's relationship with her was a happy one.

Since the autumn before his mother's death he had been a pupil at Bromsgrove School. Before his second marriage Edward Housman had moved his family back to Fockbury – not to the old home where Alfred had been born, but to Fockbury House (also known as The Clock House), an attractive seventeenth-century building demolished in 1976. It lacked gas, running water and drainage but was a good place for children with its garden and orchard and ready access to lanes, fields, woods and streams. The spire of Bromsgrove Church, now two miles away, was still visible. So it was from Fockbury that Alfred set off every morning to walk to school in Bromsgrove.

The school,* originally the Grammar School of King Edward VI, had enlarged its premises during the forties and fifties and, inevitably, built a chapel; the then headmaster, J. D. Collis, had been one of Arnold's pupils at Rugby and had endeavoured to transplant Arnoldian principles to Bromsgrove. The transformation from tiny ancient grammar school to expanding minor public school was of course a common one in the period; the Reverend G. J. Blore, who was headmaster when Alfred arrived, was an original member of the Headmasters' Conference when it was founded in 1869. Blore was an ambitious man, and lasted only five years at Bromsgrove before moving on to King's School, Canterbury. He was succeeded in 1873 by Herbert Millington, a Cambridge man in his early thirties who was to remain at Bromsgrove for twenty-eight years. When Millington took over, the school was still small, with only seventy-seven boys (including eleven foundation scholars, Alfred among them, who paid only five pounds a year) and an average of only half a dozen in the combined classical and modern sixth forms. Millington was a snob, but within his limitations a good teacher; those limitations are indicated by Housman's own verdict on him – 'Excellent for those of good ability in the subjects he cared about'* (a cap that also fitted himself tolerably well). Another pupil wrote of him less guardedly that

> He was absolutely in love with the felicities of Latin and Greek. It thus came about that he drove us without seeming to do so. He did not appear to be saying, 'I insist on you learning'. Rather he created the feeling that Latin and Greek have to be treated in the living and intense way of which he was giving us an example.*

Again, that 'living and intense' way was later to characterize Housman's own classical teaching.

Alfred 'took no part in games or athletics', but he had a 'natural liking for book-learning',* did well academically, and won a prize for English verse. He was rather small and not physically assertive, and was bullied at first: our knowledge of the troubles at home makes it saddening to learn that the other boys nicknamed him Mouse and 'used to tread on him pretending they could not see him'.* In his quiet way, though, he showed determination and a strong ambition to excel in whatever he undertook willingly. In due season he was joined at the school by his brothers, and at one point, thanks to the system of foundation scholarships and their own brains, there were four Housman boys simultaneously obtaining a sound education at a minimal cost. During the holidays he continued to visit the Wise family, and a photograph taken in about 1874 shows a fancy-dress group: Fräulein Becker as the Queen of the Night, and Alfred as (of all things) an Archbishop, as well as his brother Basil and the two Wise sisters, Edith and Minnie.

During the Christmas holidays at the beginning of 1875 he paid what was probably his first visit to London – a reminder how self-contained provincial life could be even in the railway age. He saw the usual sights, 'but I think,' he wrote to his stepmother in his earliest surviving letter, 'of all I have seen, what has most

impressed me is – the Guards. This may be barbarian, but it is
true.'* Inside the fifth former and the promising student of
classics, the little boy who had played in the garden at soldiers was
still very much alive: too old now to play at being a soldier, too
small and physically timid to confront the world with an imposing
presence, he could find the military life, seen from a distance,
compellingly fascinating in spite of himself (there is something
attractive about the prim precocious honesty and self-knowledge
of 'barbarian . . . but true'). Another sensitive provincial boy,
John Addington Symonds, had daydreamed of 'the rough sailors
he had seen on the streets of Bristol';* no doubt Alfred
daydreamed of soldiers.

A few weeks later he wrote to Lucy Housman again; this time
the separation prompting the letter was caused by scarlet fever
raging at home, as a result of which he had become a temporary
boarder at school:

> Yesterday I went into the churchyard, from which one can see
> Fockbury quite plainly, especially the window of your room. I
> was there from two o'clock till three. I wonder if you went into
> your room between those hours . . . The house looks much
> nearer that you would expect, and the distance between the
> sycamore and the beeches in the orchard seems very great,
> much longer than one thinks it when one is at Fockbury.*

There is something striking in the sensibility of his response to this
brief exile, a dress-rehearsal for the permanent exile of adult life.
Quoting this passage, Laurence perceptively comments that the
incident 'has in it the authentic note of the "Shropshire Lad".
Even as a boy, separation from home surroundings affected him so
much that it pleased him to spend from two to three of a winter's
afternoon in viewing them from a distance.'*

Writing with post-Freudian hindsight, Laurence is also
interesting on his stepmother's attitude to bodily functions: she
taught the children that it was wrong to be seen entering or
leaving the WC, and later, when one of Alfred's friends from
Oxford (Alfred Pollard) stayed with them, she 'commented
severely upon the fact that, she being somewhere about, he had
not observed the proper secrecy of approach. "He ought to have
waited," she said. "It wasn't modest".'* Although Alfred's toilet-
training was well behind him by this time, this ought not perhaps

to be dismissed as a merely comic prudery; Laurence argues quite persuasively that this strong and all-too-easily-infringed taboo led to habits of 'evasion and untruthfulness':

> Frankness being so much discouraged, concealment and the moral sense became morbidly allied; and one grew to feel that between the individual and his social environment was a barrier which had to be defended even from those whom one loved and might naturally have trusted.

Laurence, who later resolutely flouted convention, had a personal axe to grind; in any case, nearly six years younger than his brother, he came more fully under Lucy's influence; but the suggestion is not a ridiculous one. Another episode noted by the young Laurence, a future political agitator, suggests that sexual disapproval (to the pure all things are impure) could combine with class-consciousness to form an unattractive insensitivity to the feelings of others:

> As regards work and wages, the servants got decent treatment, but very little liberty . . . We had a married cook, whose husband had work at such a distance that they could see each other but seldom. One day he came, and his wife asked leave to stay out with him for the night. It was refused, and when later it was discovered that she had gone out secretly and spent the night in the barn, her behaviour was considered most indecent.*

Lucy's 'streaks of puritanism'* naturally led her to do nothing to interfere with her stepsons' ignorance on sexual matters, but could not altogether suppress the workings of nature in the lower orders. When Laurence was sixteen, 'two of our quite "respectable" domestics came and tickled me in bed. *I didn't know what they were after*. I screamed, and they ran away.'*

Poor Lucy Housman: she was a sincerely religious woman, and no doubt believed it was all for the best. Under her reign the practice of family churchgoing did not flag, and in her old age Katharine could still recall the precise formation of the crocodile that, 'in arm-in-arm pairs',* and dressed in their Sunday best, made its way to church. At home there were daily Bible-readings in the family circle for many years,* but secular reading aloud happily also found a place.* Lucy was 'a good reader' and gave them Scott and Thackeray and Tom Moore as well as Shakespeare; Edward read *Pickwick.* In other ways the family made its own entertainments: they were fond of word-games and play-acting,* and had some skill in composing comic verse.

In all these activities, Alfred was the moving spirit. He had, his sister Kate recalled after his death, 'a way of making things he did amusing as well as interesting. Our gatherings were generally hilarious . . . '.* But the shadow cast by his mother's death sometimes fell over the fun, and Kate also recalled that he was 'subject to gloom that spread in spite of his attempts to subdue it'.* Some of the pastimes he devised made hilarity difficult: when he was about thirteen (and newly a deist) he decreed that the children should contribute one verse each to a composite poem (the precocious Laurence, aged seven, rhymed 'ever hence' with 'reverence'); the prescribed subject was 'Death'. But his sense of humour was often strong enough to exorcise gloomy thoughts: he was, said Kate, 'quick to see humour in things about him, or to give grim things a humorous turn'.* He got on well with his brothers and sisters and was a peacemaker in their squabbles – 'in a very quarrelsome family the only one with whom we never quarrelled'.* For the baby of the family, Herbert, he had a special affection; Herbert was unlike his brothers in being athletic rather than studious, winning cups at school rather than prizes; he was to become a soldier and to die in battle.

Edward Housman had never taken his profession very seriously; he enjoyed his leisure and had grown accustomed to living off unearned income. With a good deal of money in various branches of the family, he cheerfully took it for granted that some of it would sooner or later find its way into his pocket. Without the means to justify it, he had allowed himself to live the life of a well-to-do man; and during Alfred's adolescence he began to sink deeply and inextricably into financial difficulties. R. P. Graves has explored in detail Edward's chicanery over mortgages and inheritances; he emerges from Graves' account as a more unscrupulous, less endearing Mr Micawber, raising money for immediate use with no thought for the future. Towards the end of Alfred's school career impecuniosity began to press heavily upon the Housmans. If he was to proceed to a university, he would need to win a scholarship; but where he should make the attempt was not immediately obvious. One grandfather had been at

Cambridge, the other at Oxford. The record is confused: according to Laurence, Herbert Millington dissuaded his brother from attempting Cambridge, 'saying that his English was not good enough';* but another informant reports Housman himself as saying towards the end of his life that he was sent to Oxford because ' "they considered that I was good at essays and not good enough at Greek and Latin" '.* Be that as it may, to Oxford he went. The obvious choice of college would have been Balliol, which led the field academically; but his father disapproved of Jowett's liberal theological position and would not permit him to try there.

On 15 January 1877, according to Lucy Housman's diary, 'Alfred went to Oxford for the first time in his life'* and sat the scholarship examination at Corpus Christi College. He was unsuccessful; but in June he fared better at St John's College, carrying off a £100 scholarship – the most valuable of several won in that year by pupils from his school. Herbert Millington later claimed that in the examination his star pupil had written a very good essay comparing Horace and Juvenal as writers of satire without having read a word of Horace's satires.* Soon afterwards he obtained the Oxford and Cambridge Leaving Certificate and, at the annual Commemoration, was awarded prizes for Latin and Greek verse. His school career had reached a gratifying climax, and the scholarship would see him through Oxford. But it did not solve the chronic financial problems at home; and no-one could have foreseen the end of a university career that was about to begin so auspiciously. To Alfred Housman – whom we must from now on call by his surname, as he would have wished – Oxford was to bring the excitement of rapid intellectual development, the beginning of his life's work as a scholar, an increase in self-knowledge, a brief intense happiness, and a deep and lasting misery.

2 Oxford

'The great and real troubles of my early manhood . . .'
(A. E. Housman)*

Arriving in Oxford in 1874, Oscar Wilde had found it 'full of an inexpressible, an incommunicable charm'; it was, he later told Frank Harris, 'The capital of romance'.* (Wilde's final year was Housman's first; there seems to have been no contact between the flamboyant Irishman at Magdalen and the quiet boy at St John's, but twenty years later Housman sent Wilde a copy of *A Shropshire Lad* after his release from Reading Gaol.) Father Gerard Manley Hopkins, on the other hand, who during Housman's fourth term moved from the Jesuit church in Farm Street, Mayfair, to the new parish church of St Aloysius, Oxford, saw the hand of change at work in the university city, and for the worse. It was eleven and a half years since Hopkins had completed his time at Balliol, and his saddened awareness of the changes that had taken place is recorded in the sonnet 'Duns Scotus's Oxford': the frame of 'neighbour-nature' in which was set the grey beauty of colleges and churches seemed to him now to be menaced by the 'base and brickish skirt' of suburban building. A modern historian of the City of Oxford confirms Hopkins' point:

> By the third quarter of the nineteenth century, it was scarcely possible 'as the eye travels down to Oxford's towers' from any point of vantage to be unimpeded by a small suburban ring of red brick.*

Both views, that of Wilde and that of Hopkins, had some truth in them. By comparison with the modern city, in which dreaming spires fight a losing battle with chain stores and tourists, Housman's Oxford was still enviably small and quiet and unspoilt. Undergraduate dress and the minor rituals of daily life retained a formality that makes the students of 1880 and 1980 seem like different species. Sir Charles Oman, who went up to New College in 1878, recalled that 'on Sunday no self-respecting man would have dreamed of appearing in anything but a black coat and tall hat', and 'whiskers were largely worn', the favourite style being the mutton-chop.* In the extensive gardens of St John's College, archery was very popular.

But even Oxford, after energetic resistance – the railway, for instance, proposed in the thirties, had been held off until the forties – was at last yielding to the nineteenth-century spirit of change.* Nor was it only the physical environment that was undergoing transformation. The Royal Commission that resulted in the University Reform Act of 1854 had had profound effects; the revision of college statutes meant that the clerical flavour of Oxford common rooms began to evaporate, and a fellowship no longer guaranteed a lifetime's idleness. The professoriate gained in power, and new honours schools were founded. At the beginning of the decade in which Housman went up, the Test Act had thrown open 'all lay posts . . . to men of all creeds upon equal terms' and Gladstone had set up a Commission to enquire into the revenues of ancient universities. Its report in 1874 showed that the colleges, or at least some of them, were much better endowed than the university; and in the very year in which Housman began his Oxford career, the Universities of Oxford and Cambridge Act was passed, creating the prospect of real improvement in the quality of teaching and research through the establishment of a Common University Fund. Provision was also made for married fellows: the celibate don was on the way to becoming the exception rather than the rule. Indeed, in Housman's very first weeks in Oxford the Commission held sessions at the Clarendon Hotel 'for the purpose of taking information about the needs of the University'. Within the next two years the cause of female education also moved ahead briskly: the Association for the Higher Education of Women in Oxford was founded at the end of Housman's first year, the first two colleges for women were opened in 1879, and lectures for female students were provided.

The study of classics at Oxford was also changing, thanks partly to the influence of Benjamin Jowett, Regius Professor of Greek from 1855 and Master of Balliol from 1870. As early as 1849 Jowett had become a Public Examiner in Classics and had worked with his usual vigour to reorganize the Final Examination in such a way that increased stress was placed on ancient philosophy. From 1853, when the new system of finals began, Jowett's favourite Plato was prominent, and the undergraduate teaching naturally reflected this new bias. Jowett's aim was less to produce scholars than to fill the ranks of politics, the civil service and diplomacy with Oxford men in general and Balliol men in particular; if the man of affairs was also a scholar and the statesman devoted his leisure (in Max Beerbohm's phrase) to flat but faithful translations of Theocritus, so much the better; but pure scholarship had no place in the corridors of power, and Jowett's energetic views on 'the futility of conjectural emendation' were well known. Perhaps rationalizing his personal limitations, he declared that 'exact scholarship' ought not to be seen as the last reward of a classical education: it was the ideas and the moral influence of the ancient authors rather than linguistic or textual niceties that were the proper study of an Oxford undergraduate. During Housman's first year Jowett wrote in a letter that 'the time for minute criticism on the classics, or on most of them, has passed. I want to get them turned into English classics and sent far and wide through the world.'* Jowett's words amount to a dismissal, in advance, of Housman's life's work; and, the influence of Jowett on the classical curriculum at Oxford must be judged to have had a crucial effect on the young man's academic future.

Not that Jowett's views on the proper function of a university, and in particular the purpose of a classical education, did not encounter vigorous and vocal opposition. In the year before Housman came up, a volume had appeared with the title *Essays on the Endowment of Research*, to which Mark Pattison, the best known of Jowett's opponents, was a contributor. The collection also included an essay 'On the Present Relations between Classical Research and Classical Education in England' by Henry Nettleship, in which he urged that 'there is an amount of work, practically infinite, yet to be done before we can know all that is to be known of the ancient world'. An academic revolution was needed, however, before research assumed its rightful place:

It may be doubted whether an average first-class man at Oxford or Cambridge has, as a rule, any clear conception of the principles and procedure of classical research . . . At Oxford . . . a definite course of reading is prescribed to the classical student, which occupies him from the beginning to the end of his career, leaving him no time for following his own inclination in the choice of a branch of study.

Nettleship's provocative remarks give an insight into the existing state of classical studies; his conclusion, bluntly stated, is that 'if a man wishes to make himself a thorough scholar, he must go to Germany and learn method there'. Another contributor, A. H. Sayce, writing on 'Results of the Examination-system at Oxford', notes ironically that the undergraduate's 'chief business is to run from lecture to lecture, filling his note-books with scraps of knowledge to be poured out in a crude and undigested mass when the examination-day arrives'; he adds, revealingly, that Professor Max Müller's lectures were poorly attended because they were unrelated to the topics of the examination: he 'offered in vain, term after term, to read the *Rig-Veda* with any one of the 2,400 members of the University of Oxford'. A few years earlier Müller himself had said in his inaugural address as Professor of Comparative Philology that

> knowledge for its own sake and a chivalrous devotion to studies which command no place in the fair of the world and lead to no place of emolument in church or State, are looked down upon and ridiculed by almost everybody.*

With a quasi-parental eagerness that his pupils should succeed in 'the fair of the world', Jowett had his eye firmly fixed on those places of emolument. But Housman, on the occasion of his own first public appearance as the occupant of a chair many years later, was to echo Müller's championing of learning for its own sake. It was not, however, a fashionable doctrine in the Oxford of 1877, and he was to pay a heavy price for (in Nettleship's phrase) 'following his own inclination' instead of playing the examination game by the prescribed rules.

St John's, with just over a hundred undergraduates, was a medium-sized college, less than half the size of Balliol or Christ Church, but larger than Corpus Christi, Jesus, Lincoln, Oriel, Pembroke, Wadham or Worcester. A glance at the group of young men who read classics there as Housman's contemporaries* gives some idea of the social background of its students and the futures for which it prepared them. The only ones to achieve a modest subsequent fame were Alfred Pollard and William Perry. Pollard was a Londoner who spent his career in the British Museum, eventually becoming Keeper of Printed Books and an editor and bibliographer of distinction. Perry, the son of a china and glass dealer in Clapham, joined the War Office, rose to be Director of Financial Services, and was rewarded with a knighthood. Of the rest, Walter Lawrence, the son of a tailor with premises off Bond Street, obtained an athletics blue, went to the Bar, and wound up as principal of a private preparatory school; Herbert Fripp came from Clifton and made his career at the Bar; and James Marr, a surveyor's son from Pimlico, took Holy Orders. Oxford's function was to provide manpower for the professions; at St John's, it seems, its raw material was often the sons of tradesfolk and professional men, though naturally the picture would have been different at, say, New College. None of these young men came from a famous public school; as the son of a provincial solicitor and former pupil of a very minor public school, Housman would by no means have been out of his element socially.

The college had strong links with Merchant Taylors' School, and twenty-one of its thirty-three scholarships were restricted to candidates from that school. Perry, Lawrence and Marr all held awards of this kind; Housman and Pollard, on the other hand, had open scholarships. None of the Merchant Taylors' scholars subsequently obtained a first, so there may be justice in E. L. Woodward's severe observation that in Victorian Oxford 'the restriction of many fellowships and scholarships to . . . persons . . . educated at particular schools led to abuse, and filled the colleges with idle and useless members'.* And it was true that, if St John's was not a socially fashionable college, neither was its recent academic record outstanding. During the period 1875–80 it scored only four first-classes in the final examination in classics, whereas Balliol scored twenty-four and Corpus (a considerably smaller college than St John's) twelve. Balliol also dominated the lists of winners of university prizes and scholarships: in the three years 1879–81, for instance, its members monopolized the Hertford Prize, the Ireland Scholarship and the Chancellor's Prize for Latin Verse. Nearly sixty years after the event Pollard suggested that 'if the College had looked after Housman better'* his academic fate might have been very different, and another contemporary stated roundly that 'the tuition at St John's was thoroughly bad'.* It is certainly conceivable that Housman would have responded to the more bracing intellectual atmosphere of

Balliol; on the other hand, as we shall see, he had scant respect for Jowett and must have enjoyed the famous quatrain on the Master of Balliol's delusions of omniscience which was circulating by word of mouth at the time.*

Housman matriculated on 13 October 1877, having no doubt arrived at the college a few days earlier by the method described in an Oxford guide-book of the period: 'We reach this celebrated seat of learning by rail, in the north-western suburbs. Omnibuses, flys, and Hansom cabs await the arrival of every train.'* The Oxford–Birmingham line had been opened in 1852 and coaches in that direction had promptly disappeared from the roads, though they continued to run daily to London and Cheltenham until the nineties.

He was assigned rooms in the second quadrangle, on the same staircase as Alfred Pollard. His letter to Lucy Housman describing the matriculation ceremony* is in an ironic vein that was later to become characteristic. This particular eighteen-year-old firmly declined to be impressed by the solemn traditions of the ancient university, noting that its statutes forbid him, among other things, 'to trundle a hoop', and that the document recording his admission was written in 'what passes at Oxford for Latin'. Long afterwards an Oxford story was current that when the matriculation candidates were filling up their forms, one of them asked the Reverend Robert Ewing, a college classics tutor then officiating, what was the Latin for 'only son' and received the reply 'filius natu unicus' with – to Housman's intense disgust – a false quantity in the last word.* The hapless Ewing, who ended his days as a Wiltshire parson, is also the subject of another anecdote with a similar thrust: preaching a sermon in the college chapel, he made an error over the pronunciation of a Greek word, whereupon Housman declared that he would not attend the lectures of such a man. Scholars more celebrated that Ewing could also provoke the contempt of the young man from Bromsgrove: Andrew Gow reported that 'from the single lecture of Jowett's which he attended Housman came away disgusted by the Professor's disregard for the niceties of scholarship'.* (Although he was a famous tutor, Jowett seems to have been a very indifferent lecturer: one Oxford wit said that his lectures consisted of 'getting up quietly and giving a few faint glimpses into the obvious'.)* One has, right from the outset, a strong sense of a young man with considerably more than his share of the normal assurance, or arrogance, of youth, judging his seniors according to his own rigorous and precociously established standards, and, when necessary, unhesitatingly pronouncing them wanting.

The same letter to Lucy Housman records that, as well as attending nine lectures weekly in college, he was to go to 'Mr Warren at Magdalen' three times week. This was Thomas Herbert Warren, then only twenty-four and a brand-new classical Fellow of Magdalen, who within eight years was to become President of the college, and was to serve in that capacity for forty-three years.* Warren, a former scholar of Balliol, had won the Hertford Scholarship for Latin in 1873, and the intention of the St John's tutors in farming out Housman must have been to have their promising new scholar coached for this prestigious award, which had been won in their time by such men as Jowett, Conington and Nettleship. Fifteen years later Warren was to write a testimonial for Housman which gives a sharp and striking picture of the young man who had recently arrived in Oxford:

> I still cherish a most vivid recollection of the strong impression which he made upon me. He was certainly to me one of the most interesting and attractive pupils I can remember. He had even then, as quite a young student, a combination of force, acumen and taste which I shall never forget . . .*

Housman was also taught by two fellows of his own college, T. C. Snow and H. J. Bidder. Snow was a young tutor who had migrated from Corpus Christi College and whose reputation as a teacher was already high: 'promising youths from other colleges' were sent to him, and there is evidence that Housman regarded him with respect. At any rate, forty-five years later he remembered him gratefully enough to send him a copy of *Last Poems*. Bidder, described by David Hunter Blair as 'a genial but somewhat eccentric divine',* retired to a Devonshire parsonage in 1880; later he was quoted as referring to Housman as 'a man on whom he had done his best to make some impression – and failed [because] Housman refused to consider Plato's meaning except so far as it was relevant to the settlement of the text'.* Quite early on, Housman had determined to beat out a path for himself rather than to follow the well-trodden, clearly signposted road of Oxford classical studies. His decision was to have far-reaching results.

At this period the University was at an early stage of transition between the exclusively college-based teaching of the past and the fully developed system of university teaching of later generations. Apart from his contact with Warren, Housman would have received his instruction mainly from the limited resources of his own college. It is true that 'combined college lectures' had already been instituted as the first step in the changeover to a system of university teaching; but St John's did not participate in these until Housman's final year, and he would consequently have been ineligible to attend them. Their topics, in any case, indicate plainly enough the heavy bias towards ancient philosophy and history and the virtual neglect of literary and textual studies: the courses covered Plato, Aristotle, Herodotus, Cicero, Sallust, Tacitus, Political Philosophy, Logic, Greek and Roman history, as well as Bacon, Locke, Kant and the Utilitarians. A student could have attended all these lectures faithfully without ever suspecting that there are ancient poets and dramatists worth reading. Sir Charles Oman attended them and found them 'perfectly useless'.* The lectures for the School of *Literae Humaniores*, familiarly known as Greats, were given by professors and were therefore open to the entire University, but reflected a similar lopsidedness. In Housman's first year, Jowett was lecturing on Aristotle's *Politics* (and, as we have seen, Housman sat at his feet for only a very limited spell); the Corpus Professor of Latin, Palmer, on Tacitus; the Waynflete Professor of Moral and Metaphysical Philosophy, Chandler, on Aristotle. It was a system which neither encouraged nor rewarded a taste for poetry or for close engagement with an author's text – that 'exact scholarship' of which Jowett was so impatient but for which, with poetry, Housman had already developed a marked taste.

His few surviving letters of these years offer occasional glimpses of his doings and of the development of his temperament. In his first term he attended the lectures of Ruskin, then Slade Professor of Fine Art, who was offering a short course on Landscape Painting ('the Course will consist of Twelve Readings in "Modern Painters", collating the passages which the Author thinks likely to be permanently useful', as Ruskin's announcement modestly promised). Housman sent home a lively vignette of the great critic in action, visual aids and all:

This afternoon Ruskin gave us a great outburst against modern times. He had got a picture of Turner's, framed and glassed, representing Leicester and the Abbey in the distance at sunset, over a river. He read the account of Wolsey's death out of *Henry VIII*. Then he pointed to the picture as representing Leicester when Turner had drawn it. Then he said, 'You, if you like, may go to Leicester to see what it is like now. I never shall. But I can make a pretty good guess.' Then he caught up a paintbrush. 'These stepping-stones of course have been done away with, and are replaced by a be-au-tiful iron bridge.' Then he dashed in the iron bridge on the glass of the picture. 'The colour of the stream is supplied on one side by the indigo factory.' Forthwith one side of the stream became indigo. 'On the other side by the soap factory.' Soap dashed in. 'They mix in the middle – like curds,' he said, working them together with a sort of malicious deliberation. 'This field, over which you see the sun setting behind the abbey, is now occupied in a *proper* manner.' Then there went a flame of scarlet across the picture, which developed itself into windows and roofs and red brick, and rushed up into a chimney. 'The atmosphere is supplied – thus!' A puff and cloud of smoke all over Turner's sky: and then the brush thrown down, and Ruskin confronting modern civilisation amidst a tempest of applause, which he always elicits now, as he has this term become immensely popular, his lectures being crowded, whereas of old he used to prophesy to empty benches.*

In his second term he wrote a long letter, this time (and exceptionally) to his father, describing a debate of the Oxford Union and various sermons he had heard. He is evidently infected with political excitement – not a feature of his riper years, but still apparent in his account a few months later of the general election campaign; and his reports of the preaching of eminent divines show, as well as a predictable irreverence, a knack of impaling his victims with coolly observed satirical detail: the Bishop of Manchester 'commenced operations by blowing his nose, which is a rhetorical device he has apparently just found out, and which in the first ecstasy of novelty he uses with injudicious profusion'.* The embryo scourge of incompetent scholars is already to be seen in Housman's habit of seizing on the one utterance or mannerism by which an unfortunate speaker has exposed himself to ridicule. Thus, of the Conservative MP for Oxford speaking at the Union:

He said nothing worth remark, except that the Christians of Turkey hated one another with a hatred passing the love of woman. This I relished very much, especially as his wife was sitting beside him.*

'Relished' is a suggestive word, worth remembering when one considers the later and notorious fulminations against scholarly ineptitude, which seem to me not so much sour as delighted: like Jane Austen's Mr Bennett, Housman was to derive a keen enjoyment from the spectacle of human folly. But not all the young Housman's comments on Oxford preachers are in this vein: he could appreciate a good performance in the pulpit, and wrote enthusiastically to the Wise family about Canon Liddon, who preached 'the best sermon I ever heard . . . about Religion and Natural Science'.* The same letter records that 'here everyone is going over to Rome like wildfire'.

As a scholar of the college, he was required from time to time to read the lesson in chapel, and an anecdote suggests that he did not waste the opportunity of showing the limitations of his respect for academic authority or Holy Writ: Laurence Housman tells us that his brother 'used to leave out the list of names in the biblical genealogies; and the President used to cough disapprovingly'.*

There is something startling as well as refreshing about the intellectual self-assurance of this youth who, fresh from school, could speak of 'what passes for Latin at Oxford', and Housman can hardly have been an easy pupil if, as seems to have been the case, much of the teaching at St John's was second-rate. In fairness to the college, though, it should be remembered that Pollard finished in the first class, and his suggestion that the tutors failed to 'look after' his friend perhaps referred less to intellectual than to pastoral guidance. Wiser tutors would have recognized the collision course on which he had set himself and have warned him of the possible consequences. Whether he would have heeded them is another matter. It is not clear just when he began seriously to pursue in private, as an alternative to the required syllabus, the study of Propertius – a poet who would certainly have paid no examination dividend at that period. But the academic bankruptcy which resulted from Housman's unorthodox course of study was still some way off, and in the Moderations examination in 1879 he was placed, together with Pollard and Lawrence, in the first class. Three firsts out of eighteen made this an exceptionally good year for St John's classicists, who figure much less prominently, and often not at all, in the lists of first classes in the years immediately preceding and following. It seems likely, therefore, that this flash of glory, which ranked the college second only to Balliol, was the result less of superior teaching than of exceptional talents fortuitously coinciding. Since more than sixty candidates were placed in the second class, and nearly as many in the third, a first was no mean achievement. Among the examiners were S. H. Butcher, who published in that year his translation (with Andrew Lang) of the *Odyssey*, and Francis de Paravicini, a friend and Balliol contemporary of G. M. Hopkins and one of the first Roman Catholics to become, under the liberalized statutes, a college fellow. His success earned Housman an addition of ten pounds to the amount of his scholarship.

Earlier, in his second term, Housman had competed for the Hertford Scholarship in Latin. Since this was open to both first- and second-year undergraduates, it is not clear why he should have attempted it after only six months at Oxford, unless it is a sign that he was regarded as exceptionally promising. A few days after the examination he wrote to Lucy Housman that he had been placed 'among the first six'.* He must have been told this informally, for his name makes no appearance on the official announcement. No undergraduate of St John's had carried off the Hertford during that decade, and Housman must have known the form and have been wryly conscious of his own college's reputation. At any rate, he seems to have been reasonably gratified by the result, his letter making the scrupulous distinction that it was 'better than anyone else thought I should do, and better than I myself fancied I had actually done'. In his second year he had attempted the competition for the Newdigate Prize, awarded since 1805 for the best English poem on a set subject and traditionally the first hurdle in the career of an aspiring Oxford poet. Housman would have recalled that it had been won by his favourite Matthew Arnold, and probably knew that the previous year's prizeman had been Oscar Wilde.

The subject for 1879 was 'Iona', and Housman was placed third – if not exactly success, certainly not a disgraceful result. The poem was said to have been produced at an all-night sitting, presumably just before the deadline of 31 March; the next morning, according to a legend almost too neat to be true, the lesson in chapel included the words 'we have toiled all the night, and have taken nothing'. The epigraph to 'Iona' consists of the last four lines of Catullus 64 – the poem on which, fifty-seven years later, Housman was to deliver his last lecture. 'Iona'* is an unremarkable piece of versifying, the prescribed form of heroic couplets hardly fostering an individual voice; but the modest achievement of third place, with the success in Moderations, was announced by the headmaster at the Bromsgrove School annual Commemoration that summer, and to the Housman family the prospects of decent academic success must at this midpoint of Alfred's Oxford career have seemed excellent. After the term was over, Housman stayed with Pollard in London and on four successive evenings they went to see Henry Irving and Ellen Terry at the Lyceum Theatre.

Later in his life Housman told Gow that 'Oxford left little mark upon him, except in the matter of friendships formed there',* and both parts of the statement are worth pondering. Intellectually, Oxford had failed to offer him what he sought, the classical curriculum of the day satisfying neither his appetite for exact scholarship nor his love of poetry. None of the various sets into which the Oxford undergraduate of the period might be drawn – social, athletic, aesthetic, political or pious – appealed to him. Oscar Wilde had filled his rooms with blue china, hunted such Oxford lions as Pater and Ruskin (and worked on the latter's famous road at Hinksey), dazzled his contemporaries with his conversation, and dismayed his elders with his impertinence. Housman cannot have had much spare cash, but in any case he was temperamentally averse to such a way of life. 'He lived,' one of his tutors recalled, 'a quiet student's life, reading hard, and not taking any interest in the general life of the College'.* His own rebellion against complacent authority, not less deeply felt than Wilde's, took a less colourful form: where Wilde dressed to be stared at and treated the college authorities with open contempt, Housman worked away at the text of Propertius instead of getting up Plato and Aristotle. The system was such that Wilde carried away the glittering prizes, Housman only a deeply humiliating failure.

He also carried away, however, a lasting friendship that made the Oxford years the turning-point of his emotional life. In a small college it cannot have taken him very long to strike up at least a nodding acquaintance with all the men of his own year. One of them was Moses John Jackson. A year older than Housman, he had been educated at the Vale Academy,* a small private school in Ramsgate of which his father was principal and owner, and had passed on at seventeen to University College, London. From there, two years later, he had won a science scholarship to St John's. Jackson was an athlete who rowed for his college and seems to have had a hearty contempt for literature: one contemporary remembered him as 'a perfect Philistine . . . a vigorous rowing man, quite unliterary and outspoken in his want of any such interest'.* Given Housman's bookish tastes, his highly specialized interests, his lack of enthusiasm for games and his marked intellectual intolerance, the basis for friendship was not an obvious one. But the friendship was real enough, and lasting, though not equally intense on both sides. Jackson was of immense importance in Housman's life; but in the absence of even a single letter written by him he remains a somewhat shadowy figure.

We must know him, as far as we can, by his deeds rather than his words; and the exact tone of the relationship in its various phases, especially on Jackson's side, is very difficult to catch. To the end of his life he seems to have treated Housman with the detached interest and unagitating affection one brings to a relationship which includes shared memories of youth but excludes most of what is important in later life – a relationship renewed at long intervals with mild pleasure but quite without urgency. For Housman, it was the love affair of his life, and his unrequited devotion was still constant when Jackson died more than forty years later after a career of useful obscurity in the service of Empire. When Laurence Housman in his brother's later years visited him in Cambridge, he noticed a portrait hanging over the fireplace in his Trinity rooms and asked whose it was. 'In a strangely moved voice he answered, "That was my friend Jackson, the man who had more influence on my life than anyone else".' A Cambridge girl who knew Housman well towards the end of his life wrote of him that he

> would not tolerate the idea that it was possible for a man truly to love more than one woman in his life; anyone who considered that he had done so had simply never really loved at all.

Man, according to the old jest, embraces woman; in this case 'more than one woman' includes 'more than one man'.

A photograph of the young Moses Jackson shows him as good-looking, with particularly fine eyes. Pollard remembered him as 'often lively, but not at all witty', and added: 'I think it was the simplicity and singleheartedness that attracted Alfred'.* Jackson was an able scientist, but his subsequent career was not brilliant and there is nothing to suggest that he was anything but a decent commonplace man who worked hard and married and begat children and died. But we cannot wonder at the appeal of his ordinariness without wondering at the nature of love itself. The attraction was exerted not by shared qualities or interests but, in part at least, by attributes Housman knew himself to lack: like some other scholarly and unathletic men – Goldsworthy Lowes Dickinson and E. M. Forster, among others, come to mind – he was attracted by a strongly masculine type. To despise athletic pursuits (largely on the grounds of one's own incompetence) is not to rule out being attracted to athletes; and Laurence Housman once made the surprising comment that his brother 'admired athletes greatly and cared about the boat-race'.* Indeed, the type of the 'vigorous rowing man' exercised a perennial fascination for Housman, whose later friendships included a Thames oarsman and a Venetian gondolier. In his rooms at Trinity there hung, somewhat incongruously, a photograph of the St John's College eight of which Jackson was a member.

There is, indeed, something fitting in Housman's association of Jackson with the schoolboy and undergraduate world of games, for their relationship embodied an element of permanent immaturity. On one of their infrequent reunions in later years one of them made an apple-pie bed for the other; this ingredient of banter survives to the very end, and Housman's last letter to Jackson offers the epistolary equivalent of the apple-pie bed in its tone of laboured facetiousness. It is different from any other of Housman's letters that I have seen in its curiously juvenile, or at least dated, language: the crude pedantic irony seems to belong to the world of Kipling's schoolboys and suggests a relationship in which it was possible for men in their sixties still, as it were, to roll together on the floor like boys. If their relationship was of this kind throughout life, it must have been so from the start; and this most important friendship evidently offered the intellectually precocious and arrogant Housman the relief of a relapse into the undemanding, irresponsible state of boyhood – the stage of life at which masculine friendships are all-sufficient.

Of the other friendships Housman formed at this time, the only one which lasted was with Pollard, who sixty years later could still remember their walks and talks. Housman's favourite poet was Matthew Arnold and he recommended *Empedocles on Etna* as containing 'all the law and the prophets'.* Another contemporary recalled that he knew Arnold's poetry by heart and 'would challenge us to cite a line the continuation of which he could not give. We never caught him out':* early evidence of the superb verbal memory that was to be one of his qualifications as a scholar of the first rank. He read, on or soon after publication, a now-forgetten book, W. H. Mallock's *Is Life Worth Living?* (1879), the title of which may be said crudely to summarize his later poetry. He was also writing: in his second year he contributed frequently to an undergraduate periodical, *Ye Rounde Table*,* under the pseudonym of 'Tristram', and later he published two poems in another Oxford magazine, *Waifs and Strays*, edited by Wilde's friend Harold Boulton. Both were signed with his initials, and though he did not see fit to republish them, one of them, 'Parta Quies', is one of the best poems he ever wrote.

In their fourth year (1880–1), Jackson and Pollard and Housman all moved out of college and took five rooms in 'a picturesque old house in St Giles' nearly opposite the college and now swept away'.* This was the intended setting for the hard reading that traditionally led up to Finals. Jackson was regarded as certain of a first-class degree (less a tribute to his outstanding brilliance, one suspects, than to the modesty of the required standard in Natural Science, for in the event the first he duly secured was one of ten out of only sixteen classified candidates). As a result he had no need to work particularly hard. Housman's case was quite different, however, and he obviously spent time with his friend that should have been spent on making good his deficiencies in ancient philosophy and history. He 'enjoyed idling'* with Jackson, recalled Pollard, who blamed the friendship for Housman's failure. This does not in itself, however, seem to explain the full extent of the disaster in the early summer of 1881. Over-confidence bred of contempt for the Oxford establishment may also have contributed: this at any rate was the explanation favoured by those, including Gow, who were disinclined to probe for more deeply personal causes. Housman had pursued a course of studies of his own devising rather than that laid down by authority: as Percy Withers reports, 'He did once in talk spontaneously refer to the "Greats" episode, merely commending that his interest had gone in directions not required by the Schools . . ."* In ancient philosophy his work for his tutors had been so 'ludicrously bad' (according to one of the dons of his college) as to suggest that he was treating it with contempt. More sympathetically, Pollard pointed out that the Finals papers involved translation and discussion of Greek and Roman historians and philosophers, and added: 'I rather think that Housman was really more interested in Propertius than in all these eminent prose-writers put together.'*

The Second Public Examination in Literae Humaniores in 1881 began on 27 May. Candidates were required to sit fifteen papers, and opportunity to display a detailed knowledge of the text of Propertius was signally lacking. Even so, many of the required exercises involved translation, and one would have expected anyone who knew as much Greek and Latin as Housman to have made a tolerable stab at them – sufficient at least to have obtained a pass, if only at the lowest level. But there is evidence that he did not put up a fight: on some papers, Pollard reports, he wrote 'practically nothing'.* On one day he went up for a fresh supply of paper, and when congratulated on having so much to say merely 'replied a little gruffly that he was tired of sitting still'. One of the examiners recalled long afterwards that his answers on the philosophy papers were 'short and scrappy, and practically no answers at all'.* Pollard's view was that the fiasco was the result of miscalculation, Housman having underestimated the standard of the examination. This makes sense; but it is hard not to believe that something more radical than foolhardiness was behind such a complete act of academic suicide.

The answer may lie partly at least in the deeply disquieting news that had very recently arrived from Bromsgrove. Edward Housman was 'terribly ill for weeks'* in the early summer, and Alfred received the tidings of his father's state on 21 May, six days before the examination began. Katharine Symons, summarizing the account given in her stepmother's diary, refers to the illness as a 'break down' and notes that it 'lasted till end of July'. She elsewhere recorded that 'the doctor told our stepmother that my brother ought to be warned that recovery was unlikely'. The warning came, with effects no less sure for being unintended. As the eldest son, Alfred knew that a heavy responsibility, moral and financial, would devolve upon him if his father died or were incapacitated. As he turned up for the fifteen papers, the far-reaching results of failure must have been vividly apparent to him; and those blank sheets must have been handed in not so much out of bravado or arrogance as in deep despair; distress at an impending family tragedy compounded with a consciousness of inadequate preparation may well have produced a paralysis of the will. The blow had fallen without warning: a letter written to his sister Kate early in April* is full of high spirits and extravagant humour. If one chose to play the dangerous game of quarrying Housman's poems for personal allusions, one might suspect that, of all the Mays he lived through, it was that of 1881 which he had in mind when he wrote:

> May stuck the land with wickets:
>   For all the eye could tell,
>   The world went well.
>
> Yet well, God knows, it went not,
>   God knows, it went awry;
> For me, one flowery Maytime,
>   It went so ill that I
>   Designed to die.
>   (*MP*, XXXIV)

The examiners to whom Housman's answers, or blank sheets, were delivered included Ingram Bywater, Herbert Richards, and Bidder of St John's. Bywater, the subject of R. W. Chapman's *Portrait of a Scholar*, later succeeded Jowett in the chair of Greek; in his 'exact, profound, and laborious scholarship', his brilliance as a textual critic, his conservatism in politics and his love of France, he had much in common with the man Housman later became. Richards was the uncle of Grant Richards, subsequently Housman's publisher and friend. In later life Housman was on good terms with both scholars and bore no resentment. Their decision to fail him outright must have been reached only after considerable discussion; but, as the system stood, they had no alternative. Rumours of what had happened spread quickly in the college, perhaps thanks to Bidder; tongues must have wagged excitedly at that momentous time, for Housman had been regarded as 'exceptionally able',* and Pollard heard of the failure before the class-list omitting his friend's name was published. (He, like Jackson, obtained a First.) But it must have been

Housman's painful task to deliver the news to Bromsgrove, thus adding to rather than mitigating his family's anxieties.

He took no degree with him when he left Oxford. It was an Oxford professor, Sir Walter Raleigh, who once observed of the imperfections of the examination system that 'the nightingale got no prize at the poultry show'; and it was not the only occasion on which Oxford failed to recognize original genius – Matthew Arnold and J. H. Newman had got Seconds, W. H. Auden was to take away a Third. But there was something shockingly total, and apparently final, about Housman's failure. In two ways, though, the Oxford years were crucial. He had developed as a scholar, but according to a model of his own choosing rather than one prescribed and rewarded by the university. His academic failure was to motivate his outward life for the next decade, perhaps for the next half-century. Writing of his own unhappy schooldays, Graham Greene has wondered 'if those years of humiliation had not given me an excessive desire to prove that I was good at something'; and that same desire born of humiliation, whether excessive or not, was also Housman's. He had also fallen in love, in every sense hopelessly; and that was to colour his inner life, and his poetry, for the rest of his days.

3 The Years of Penance

'He very much lived in water-tight compartments that
were not to communicate with each other.'
(Katharine Symons, Housman's sister)*

For Housman, as for others, the four years at Oxford had been in
many respects a prolongation of schooldays. Oxford had given
his life a regular pattern of comings and goings, objectives and
challenges, and had placed at his disposal a small but important
circle of friendships in a society in which roles were clearly defined
and considerable individual freedom existed within a framework
of institutional authority and discipline. When he returned home
in the early summer of 1881, all this was left behind. The present
was deeply disquieting, for his father's 'break down' lasted until
the end of July; the future was bleakly uncertain. As for the
financial difficulties which beset his family, these must have been
felt as a keen reproach as well as a source of immediate anxiety
and discomfort. 'We were frightfully poor at the time',* Laurence
recalled. Housman's depression, natural enough in the
circumstances of his failure, must have been increased by feelings
of guilt and intensified by his proud and lonely refusal to find
solace in human relationships. Fifty-five years later his sister Kate
still remembered his mood during this period as 'very morose . . . I
saw little of him except at meals';* and Laurence confirmed this:
'he withdrew into himself – very taciturn and ungenial – and
showed nothing'.*

One source of help in this time of trouble was Herbert
Millington, the headmaster of Bromsgrove School, who had
already expressed his concern at Housman's collapse and had
assured Lucy that, in the event of her husband's death, 'he would
see that the boy's education did not suffer'.* Now he came forward
again and offered his former pupil occasional employment at the
school, teaching classics to the sixth form. It was not much, and it

47

could be no more than a stop-gap; but it was timely and thoughtful. From the summer onwards Housman seems to have put in a little time at the school, but in October he returned to Oxford in order to satisfy the requirements for a pass degree. Technically his scholarship still had a year to run, but in view of his failure it was suspended after the end of 1881 and he then left Oxford for ever. That final term, in the absence of his friends and in the unenviable role of one reading for a pass degree, can hardly have been exhilarating. His stepmother's diary records that he arrived home on 13 December and the next day 'returned to Oxford to fetch his things'.* The simple phrase stands as a monument to the end of an epoch in Housman's life and the beginning of a ten-year exile from the academic world.

In the early part of 1882 his time was divided between occasional work at the school and study at home. The latter was conducted on the dining-table after the breakfast things had been cleared away, and had two objectives: the completion of a pass degree at Oxford, and preparation for the competitive examination for entry into the Civil Service. The motives which led him to contemplate a Civil Service career are not far to seek: Moses Jackson had been appointed an Examiner of Electrical Specifications in the Patent Office in London, and a Civil Service post might convert into reality the fantasy of rejoining his friend and taking up again, in new surroundings, the daily intimacy of their college life. It was, in any case, a sensible and realistic enough goal for one whose ambitions had necessarily been so abruptly reduced in scale.

Housman's movements during the early summer are recorded in Lucy Housman's diary. On 29 May and again on 6 June he made brief visits to Oxford to take his pass degree examination, and was duly successful (though he nearly came to grief in political economy). It was another ten years, however, before he troubled to go through the formality of receiving the degree. On 26 June he travelled to London to sit the Civil Service examination, and again was successful – though any gratification he felt at these successes must have been moderated by a painful sense of the modesty of his new aims. A post in Dublin was offered him, but Housman turned it down. The prospect of Irish exile held no charms, and though a beggar he was too proud not to be also a chooser. London was his goal: it would give him (his public but not insincere reason) access to the British Museum Library, where he could continue his classical studies; and it would give him (the unspoken reason) access to Moses Jackson. His refusal of the Dublin post was not well received at home, and Lucy delivered an ultimatum: he must take the next job offered. As it turned out, he was perfectly willing to do so, for it was a clerkship in the Patent Office. (If this was a lucky coincidence, it ought to have converted him to a belief in a kindly Providence; more probably he had had the opportunity of expressing a preference for a particular branch of the service.) Lucy's laconic diary entry for 26 November, 'Alfred has his appointment', seems to be accompanied by an audible sigh of relief. Within a week or two he was installed in lodgings at 15 Northumberland Place, Bayswater, and was travelling daily to the Patent Office in Chancery Lane. He spent Christmas at home but on New Year's Day of 1883 returned to London to begin the first of ten new years that he was to spend as a Higher Division Clerk in the Trade Marks Registry. And if, put like that, it sounds a little like a retributive sentence, that may have been just the light in which it struck Housman – except, of course, that he cannot have known at the time that the sentence was not for life.

The Trade Marks Registry was a fairly new department of the Patent Office, having been created by the Trade Marks Act of 1875. Its creation and rapid growth testify to the importance in the mid-Victorian period of trade, technology and invention. Housman became one of a team of clerks whose task was to scrutinize and record applications for the registration of trade marks; his specific duty was 'investigating the claims of new marks applied for as compared with those already registered' under the supervision of a colleague, Ralph Griffin, and then 'communicating with the applicant about any objections'.* The work must have been both fussy and tedious, and it made him the servant of a competitive business world utterly remote from his classical studies; and yet in its mundane way the close comparison of similar but not necessarily identical trade marks resembled a bizarre travesty of the process of editing a classical text. Soon after Housman arrived, Parliament passed another Act designed to simplify the bureaucratic process of registering trade marks and patents. This came into force on 1 January 1884 and its effect, partly as a result of a reduction in the fee charged, was to increase enormously the volume of applications. Delays led to public criticism of the new Act, and the staff was expanded, so that by

1886, on the patents side alone, where Moses Jackson was
employed, there were three examiners and fifty-two assistant
examiners. Jackson had a responsible and well-paid job, greatly
superior in status to that of his friend. Housman's salary was £100
a year, adequate but not much more even for a single man. The
few voices that speak to us from this period of his life seem to evoke
an atmosphere of shabby respectability, office camaraderie and
prickly sensitivity about inferior status, with a background of long
hours and monotonous, eye-wearying work – not much different,
in fact, from the clerk's world evoked by Dickens and Gogol.

Whatever disgruntlement or even bitterness Housman felt with
his lot was not allowed to interfere with the performance of his
duties, which was notably efficient and conscientious. Colleagues
later recalled in particular the distinction of his style in official
correspondence. But he chafed under the constraints of the
bureaucratic hierarchy, and 'was an outspoken critic of his
superiors'.* He became private secretary to Reader Lack, the first
Comptroller-General of Patents, Designs, and Trade Marks,
which suggests that he was marked as a young man of exceptional
promise; but he did not survive long in a capacity that made
excessive demands on his limited supplies of tact and
subservience. On the other hand, his relations with his fellow-
clerks were happy. Griffin said long afterwards that he and
Housman 'lived on most friendly terms' together, and added –
somewhat strikingly, in view of Housman's later reputation– that
'nobody could possibly not love him'.* As with all post-mortem
recollections of the distant past, some discount may have to be
deducted from this one for piety and nostalgia; still, the residuum,
suggesting genuine affection in the fifty-year-old memory,
commands our respect. Some of the office friendships were
pursued after hours. Another colleague recalled that 'his most
familiar friends were rowing men',* and we know two of these by
name, John Maycock and Ernest Kingsford. Maycock is
described by yet another contemporary:

> His most intimate friend was a man named Maycock, a Thames
> oarsman, and I think a *bon vivant* . . . Maycock was an excellent
> fellow – but his literary output took the shape of occasional
> verse contributions to the weekly comic papers – so the
> friendship was rather a strange one.*

But the friendship need cause us no surprise: Housman was always inclined to keep his social life distinct from his intellectual and creative life, recognizing that relief from the scholar's ineluctably solitary lot can best be found by temporarily casting it aside, if needs be concealing its existence, and entering into some quite different world. 'He neither looked nor talked like a poet',* said William Rothenstein years later; and we may be sure that, in the company of Maycock and others, he took pains not to talk like a scholar. Revealingly, Griffin, who worked by his side for years, had no notion that he was a scholar and, when Housman left the Patent Office, was 'astounded' to discover that his fellow-clerk enjoyed a considerable repuation for his classical publications. With Maycock and a third man called Eyre he would go for long Sunday walks. The other two lodged in Putney, and their rambles took the three young men into rural Surrey, usually winding up with dinner at an inn and a train home. As a very old man Eyre recalled Housman as a 'most delightful companion'* who had a notable sense of humour.

The Patent Office years, then, were not all gloom. But underlying Housman's life during this decade must have been the nagging sense that examining trade marks was not the business in life for which his education or his abilities best fitted him. If he was making the best of a bad job, that is what after all it remained. Such speculation is hardly wild: it would have been extraordinary if he had felt otherwise. But it has to be said that the early eighties represent the most striking hiatus in the documentation of Housman's adult life. No letters survive from the years 1880–5, and scarcely any from the entire decade. It follows that the narrative of his existence at this period must be brief and must proceed in lurches if it is not to be padded and cushioned by fantasy. Fifty years later, in an unwontedly autobiographical moment, Housman referred to 'the great and real troubles of my early manhood'.* 'Early manhood' is not a very exact phrase, but it may reasonably be taken as referring to the epoch that began with the Oxford failure, or perhaps a year earlier, in 1880, when at twenty-one he came of age.

Shortly before his death he wrote to his sister, 'I abandoned Christianity at thirteen, but went on believing in God till I was twenty-one, and towards the end of that time I did a good deal of praying for certain persons and for myself.'* More succinctly, he had told an earlier correspondent that he 'became a deist at thirteen and an atheist at twenty-one'.* The reference to 'twenty-one' is consistent and precise. If he went through an intellectual crisis in 1880–1, that would have been a common enough late-Victorian experience, familiar from a hundred autobiographies; but he was an intellectually precocious youth and the reference to 'thirteen' suggests that the major crisis of faith came earlier, in the aftermath of his mother's death. Among the persons for whom at twenty or so he had done 'a good deal of praying', Edward Housman was probably one; but Moses Jackson was surely another, and it seems probable (one can put it thus strongly, though not more strongly) that this was the period at which he recognized his own homosexuality. Faith in a loving and caring God revealed through the Incarnation had been abandoned after his mother had died in spite of his prayers; the existence of God was finally rejected when the love of man – love for a man – was acknowledged to himself.

Those 'troubles' of early manhood, therefore, included the ones evident to the world – the family poverty, his father's breakdown and deterioration, the Oxford failure, his settling for a mediocre career with limited prospects and his consequent inability to replace his father as breadwinner. But they also included the secret love for Moses Jackson; and the inner drama of Housman's life in the eighties is of an unrewarded quest for a permanent and satisfying relationship. That it was ever otherwise we have no reason to suppose: from what we know of it, Jackson's nature seems to have been thoroughly 'normal', and his temperament was not of a kind to view sympathetically, even in a friend, what he would no doubt have regarded as 'spooniness' if not actually 'beastliness'. The tragic dénouement comes with Jackson's emigration and marriage at the end of the decade. Housman was a romantic who fell in love once, once only, and for ever: sexual love had for him the permanence that his mother's love had failed to offer. If it was not only unrequited but forbidden by God and man, so much the worse: that did not lessen the strength of his feelings, though it denied them expression or fulfilment, and that without hope of reprieve.

He must, then, have brought with him to London the dream of a renewed life with Moses that would prolong the happiness of the Oxford years without the sense of impermanence that necessarily underlies the undergraduate experience, and for many people turns Oxford (and not only Oxford) into an Eden on the wrong side of whose gates they spend a lifetime loitering. The chronologically conscious reader will have noted that my eager narrative has raced ahead and must be sternly called back: although they cannot be dated, the clerkly friendships and Sunday rambles already described seem likely to belong to the later eighties, for during the early years at the Patent Office Housman enjoyed the steady companionship of the Jackson brothers. Once in London he was soon in touch with Moses again, and within a few months they had decided, economy no doubt conspiring with friendship, to share lodgings at 82 Talbot Road, Bayswater. We cannot know whose idea it was; perhaps Housman simply moved in with Jackson; but the scheme certainly involved a third man, Moses' younger brother Adalbert, who was a classics student at University College.

Adalbert remains an even more shadowy figure than his brother, not even a photograph of him surviving; but he played a role in Housman's life between 1883 and 1892. How important that role was must be a matter for conjecture, and those with a taste for conjecture find their appetite sharpened by some statements made, very near the end of his long life, by Laurence Housman. He wrote on 19 June 1958 that although Moses Jackson '*shied away* from the full implication [of Housman's love for him], knowing he could not share it "in kind" . . . [Housman's] attraction to the *younger* brother *was* reciprocated . . . I doubt whether Moses ever kissed AEH: but I have no doubt that AJJ *did*.'*

How far are we to doubt Laurence's 'no doubt'? Old men forget, but they are also very good at remembering the distant past, and Laurence is speaking here of impressions some seventy years old; on the other hand, he can never have known the Jackson brothers at all well or have seen more than a very little of them in Alfred's company, and he admits elsewhere that Alfred never explicitly acknowledged to him his own sexual nature, so there is no question of confidence or confessions. In another letter a month later he wrote: 'I have *no* doubt whatever that A.E.H. was in closer and warmer physical relationship with A.J.J. than with his brother Moses.'* His conviction seems, if anything, to have grown stronger with the passing of a few weeks, but it is still not necessarily to be taken at face value, for Laurence was ninety-three and elsewhere admitted his failing memory as well as giving clear evidence of it in other statements that are demonstrably untrue. All of this does not of course mean that the two young men did not make love: simply that there is no real evidence that they did.

From Housman himself we have two poems, three very brief diary entries, and the fact that Adalbert's portrait hung beside that of Moses over the fireplace in Housman's rooms in Trinity College half a century later. The diary entries lack the charged intensity of those referring to Moses: two of them are identical and merely record that Adalbert called at the office and that they went out to lunch together (17 January and 28 March 1888); the third mentions Adalbert only because he has received a letter from Moses (22 December 1889), and this may well indicate the young man's main interest for Housman. He was evidently still seeing 'Add' after his brother's departure, but not frequently; Adalbert would, though, have possessed some importance as a source of information about Moses and as someone to whom Housman could speak of him. As for the poems referring to the young man (*MP* XLI and XLII), these seem to me to express real affection but not passion: even at their most explicitly admiring, in the penultimate stanza of 'A.J.J.', they are on an entirely different emotional level from the ravaged, desolate cries torn from him by his love for Moses.

But (yet again) none of this precludes a physical relationship, especially during the time they had been living under one roof; all one can say is that it remains not proven, and indeed that to be the brother of Moses was in itself sufficient basis for Housman's interest and affection. After Adalbert's death, Housman wrote a letter of condolence to the Jackson family; it was seen by one of the sisters, and although the letter disappeared she remembered years later one of its phrases – that Adalbert's was 'the most amiable nature he had ever known'.* She also remembered Adalbert receiving a letter from Housman and 'roaring with laughter over it'. It sounds like a good relationship, happy and relaxed, rather than a grand passion or even an infatuation.

The Bayswater threesome lasted for something less than three years, during which the record is all but silent. A couple of letters to Lucy Housman in 1885 chat lightheartedly about politics, the weather, the boat race, the new vicar. Housman has served on a coroners' jury and found it 'rather amusing' – his account is very much in the style of the comic verse he liked to write for his family:

We sat on five bodies: one laundryman who tied a hundredweight to his neck and tipped over into the water-butt; one butcher's man who cut his throat with a rusty knife and died a week after of erysipelas (moral: use a clean knife on these occasions); one old lady who dropped down in a fit; one baby who died in convulsions; and one young woman who died of heart disease after eating spring onions for supper . . . The butcher's man had a brother-in-law: he looked radiantly happy; a member of his family had distinguished himself, and he was revelling in the reflected glory.*

Of the Jackson brothers there is no mention in these letters, and the inference must be that he gave them little if any place in the version of his life in London that was relayed to Bromsgrove. This fits with the rest of the evidence, for he was always averse to bringing together his family and his friends: the tendency to divide his life into 'watertight compartments' manifests itself at this time and became an enduring habit. Early in 1883 Laurence and Clemence had arrived in London to study art. Their brother met them at Paddington and took them to their lodgings: 'as we parted, he said I don't want you to come and see me at my lodgings; I shall be out or too busy.'* About two years later, Laurence and Clemence met Alfred at the home of the Pollards: 'he introduced us to Jackson. Jackson expressed surprise at meeting us' – as well he might; it must have been a socially awkward moment for all concerned. Laurence had, long afterwards, an explanation: 'AEH held us at arm's length when my sister and I came to London partly because his pride had not recovered from the blow of his having failed in "Greats".'* Partly, perhaps; but surely also because he felt a possessive urge to keep the Jacksons to himself, a disinclination to mix Bromsgrove and London, the worlds of innocence and experience, as well as a prudent reluctance to expose to those who knew him well a relationship in which they might detect more than he cared to have them know.

If he was happy in Bayswater, there must also have been an element of strain in living alongside a man who could offer only friendship in return for passionate love; and the break-up seems to have been dramatic. It came towards the end of 1885. That, curiously enough, was also the year of the Criminal Law Amendment Act, with the notorious Labouchère Amendment which made all homosexual acts illegal between males. (Hitherto only sodomy had been punishable; now, Victorian penal progress grinding momentarily into reverse, acts of 'gross indecency' became punishable with a maximum of two years' imprisonment with hard labour.) How readily could the romantic novelist, whose mantle sits so much more lightly than that of the biographer, invent a powerful scene! – guilt and panic, reproaches and declarations, sparked off by *The Times* reports and cut short by the slamming of a Bayswater door. Less dramatically, but more plausibly, the public discussion of homosexuality and the growing intolerance of it may have produced in Housman a shock of recognition of his situation. The subject had until that time been so little talked about, only the most gross or the most evasive vocabulary being at the disposal of anyone who wished to do so, that he may now have realized for the first time how his romantic feelings might strike an unsympathetic observer. Be that as it may, he is said to have disappeared for a week; and he did not return to the Jacksons. But before the end of the year he was writing from fresh lodgings to Messrs Macmillan with a proposal that they should publish his edition of Propertius. It looks as though he had resolutely opened a new chapter in his life: if he could not have Moses' love, he would at any rate show them . . . – the pronoun including posterity and the Oxford examiners as well as Moses Jackson. That he was able to send so promptly 'the first book [of Propertius] with its apparatus criticus'* to the publisher as a specimen indicates that his classical studies had not been entirely in abeyance during the Jackson years. There was an appropriateness in his working during the Bayswater period on a great poet of unhappy love, as there was also in his subsequent abandonment of Propertius in favour of the aridities of Manilius; but of course the commitment to Propertius dated from his Oxford days, and in any case his primary interest was in the problems of the text.

Macmillan turned his proposal down, and the edition of Propertius never appeared. The manuscript, in an exquisite hand, was destroyed after Housman's death. Probably he realized that it was unworthy of the standards he quickly came to set himself. But his earliest scholarly publications belong to this decade; indeed the first of them, 'Horatiana', had appeared as early as 1882, before the move to London. It presumably represents some of the fruits of that undergraduate preoccupation with textual criticism that had contributed to the failure in Greats; but he must also have found time, amid other preoccupations at home, to prepare and submit it. That he did so at all suggests that his despair was not complete: the idea of excelling as a scholar, and of demonstrating his excellence to the world in self-justification and revenge, was born very early. The editors of the *Journal of Philology* can scarcely have guessed that the paper they accepted was by a man of twenty-three who had failed in his Finals; its style is vigorous, self-confident and individual. In his twenties Housman assumed that magisterial tone and (what is more impressive) the habit of relating specific scholarly issues to a moral view of life that were to signalize the style of his classical papers and prefaces for the next fifty years. One example, from an 1888 paper on the *Agamemnon*, will suffice for the moment:

> The time lost, the tissues wasted, in doing anew the brainwork done before by others . . . are in our brief irreparable life disheartening to think of.*

It is hardly the conventional language of scholars, or of youth, this unmistakably personal manner which transforms the dryasdust into an urgent moral issue and seems designed to shake the intellectually slothful out of their complacency.

In 1883 there followed a paper on Ovid's *Ibis*, then a four-year silence which more or less corresponds to, and is explained by, the companiable period with Moses and Adalbert. For the rest of his days Housman was to court solitude, recognizing it as a necessary condition of his scholarly productivity. The record of publication is resumed in 1887 – for the previous year or two he has had no temptation not to go regularly to the British Museum Library after leaving the Patent Office – and in the following year no fewer than eight papers appear; some, it is true, are only brief notes, but one is a fifty-page article on Aeschylus. At this time Housman was still dividing his time between Latin and Greek: it is only a little later that he recognized that, in the late nineteenth century, no man could become pre-eminent in both. By the end of the ten-year period 1882–92 (the significance of the latter date will soon become apparent), this Civil Service clerk who had never held an academic post had a list of twenty-five papers to his credit – more than many dons could show in a lifetime.

Another change of residence quickly followed: perhaps

Bayswater held too many and too painful associations. Housman found lodgings at 17 North Road, Highgate: his new home, Byron Cottage, was opposite Highgate School and handy for walks in London's semi-countryside. He was to spend nineteen years there and to remain faithful to his landlady, Mrs Hunter, as long as he stayed in London. He was good at remaining faithful.

It seems likely that he continued to see Moses Jackson from time to time after they ceased sharing a home, but there are no records until the beginning of 1888. During the previous year Jackson had taken the bold decision to strike out into another career in another continent. Like Housman, he had contrived to combine his Patent Office duties with spare-time study, and in 1883 had received the D.Sc. degree from London University. Armed with this impressive qualification, he obtained the Principalship of Sind College, Karachi. The job was a little less imposing than its title, but it represented an exciting challenge and must have gratified the ambitions of a man still in his twenties. Moses made his farewells and sailed for India at the end of 1887.

At this point Housman's record (not quite a diary, though written *in* a diary)* takes up the tale in its own heartrendingly laconic terms. From 4 to 27 January 1888, Jackson's movements across the globe are traced: one visualizes Housman despairingly looking out the movements of shipping reported in each day's *Times* at the distance between them steadily increased. The *Bokhara* touched at Gibraltar, Naples and Port Said; then Jackson transferred to the *Mongolia* for the latter part of his journey. Later Housman added a few details from private sources to this scrupulously precise record. Towards the end of the year he received a letter: Jackson, who had reached his destination before the end of January, seems to have been in no hurry to write to him, and there must have been aching months of disappointment constantly renewed for Housman until the letter arrived at the end of October. Even more woundingly, a Patent Office colleague, one Nightingale, heard from him in July. Housman saw the letter and set down in his diary the form of salutation, 'My dear Nightingale': every detail of the pathetically scanty evidence of Moses' feelings, slighting or reassuring, came under his loving jealous scrutiny. In the diary the name of Moses, Jehovah-like, is never used: lesser men are called by their names, but he is simply 'he'. The correspondence hardly flourished: Housman wrote in December, and again six months later, but no replies are noted.

There is some comfort in noting that 'Nightingale has not heard from him a long while', but not much.

In October 1889, however, came something more than a letter: Jackson arrived in England for a visit of about seven weeks. After less than two years he had hardly earned a home leave; and in any case, in those days of slow travel, such a long journey for such a short stay would seem odd if there were not a good reason for it. He had in fact obtained permission to return – it may even have formed part of his original agreement with the College – in order to marry. The lady was a widow, Mrs Rosa Chambers, and the ceremony took place on 9 December; immediately afterwards Moses set off with his bride for India. He must have met, and had probably proposed to, Mrs Chambers before his first departure; it would be natural for her to wait until he had a home in Karachi ready to receive her and had settled into his new work. She may even (speculation edging farther along the limb) have been the source, or a source, of whatever disagreement ended the shared home in Bayswater. None of this is surprising: Jackson was ready to marry, and did so as soon as circumstances permitted. What *is* rather surprising is that, although he was in London for most of his stay, he seems to have seen Housman only twice during the seven weeks; and what is very striking is that Housman not only was not invited to the wedding but knew nothing about it until it was over and the couple were far away (the diary for 7 January 1890 notes: 'I heard he was married').

That his old friend left him in ignorance of this landmark in his life surely speaks volumes. One sympathizes with Jackson's predicament, for Housman's reaction to the news would hardly have been such as to augment the joy of his homecoming. As Housman must have realized after the event, Moses shirked seeing him on account of the painful or at least embarrassing memories that lay between them. On one of the two occasions they met it was for a lunch party with two friends, Jackson taking his leave afterwards with one of the others; on the second occasion 'he came to me at the Office' and there is no mention of their walking or dining together. It looks as though Jackson was prudently anxious to avoid a *tête-à-tête* that might have taken a very awkward turn. The episode stongly suggests that Jackson was well aware of Housman's feelings for him but – whatever his earlier sentiments may have been – now preferred to pretend they did not exist.

The diary entries of this period, succinct, mainly monosyllabic, entirely factual, are almost more moving than any poem Housman ever wrote, though their real-life drama is played between the lines. A less taciturn writer who suffered a somewhat similar experience provides words that may come close to expressing Housman's unexpressed feelings. Of the marriage of his friend Alfred Le Poittevin, Gustave Flaubert wrote: 'I experienced, when he married, a very deep stab of jealousy, it was a rupture, a tearing away. For me he died twice.'* Housman's diary entries for the rest of 1890 add little. He wrote to Jackson on 9 January, presumably a letter of congratulation on his marriage which must have made painful writing and perhaps uncomfortable reading. He wrote again on 7 November, this time to offer congratulations on the birth of a son, announced 'in the paper'. There are no references to replies from Jackson. There the diary, such as it is, comes to an end – except for a single two-word statement eight years later. But that, if far from being another story, belongs to another phase of Housman's life, and must await its turn. Whatever the sense of inner desolation caused by Jackson's departure and marriage, that life took before long a more hopeful direction.

Housman was now in his thirties, and it would have been odd if his impatience to quit the monotonous and in every sense unrewarding work of the Patent Office had not grown, even though his leisure was sometimes enlivened by the company of Maycock and others. He had long been eligible to take a pass degree at Oxford, and with his record of publications he could no doubt have landed some more or less congenial educational employment. Characteristically, though, he preferred to wait until a post worthy of him turned up: if he was to be readmitted to the academic world, it should be with as much éclat as possible. His opportunity came early in 1892. Alfred Goodwin, who held the combined chairs of Latin and Greek at University College, London, died on 7 February while still in his early forties. He had been appointed Professor of Latin in 1876, four years later had exchanged the Latin for the Greek chair, and from 1889, when the two posts were merged, had done two men's work. His death raised both the problem of a successor and the question whether the two positions should again be separated. On 15 February Senate set up a committee to consider the teaching of Latin and Greek in the College; its recommendation was 'to return to the rule of having two Classical Professors',* and it also urged an increase in the salaries in question. The decision recognized that there was an urgent need to raise the standard of classical teaching in the College.

The two chairs were advertised on 15 March; the salary for the Latin post would be of the order of £436. The chairman of the selection committee was W. P. Ker, a Scot who had become Professor of English in 1889 and was to remain there for thirty-three years. A notable scholar who made a major contribution to the development of English studies in his generation, he was a life-long bachelor, 'conservative in politics and in every habit of his daily life',* immensely learned, with a keen wit and a love of nature, walking and wine. He thus had much in common with Housman, and they came to enjoy a mutual respect. Not long before his death, Ker was one of the friends to whose judgment Housman submitted the manuscript of *Last Poems*.

Nineteen applications were received, Housman's among them. His letter, written (somewhat defiantly, perhaps) from the Patent Office and dated 19 April, came before the committee at two meetings in May, and on the 24th of that month he appeared in person as one of the four short-listed candidates. The field was impressive, several of the applicants being fellows or former fellows of Oxford or Cambridge colleges. Of the other men interviewed, one had been a scholar of Trinity College, Cambridge, had taken a double first, and had 'a future of distinction' predicted for him by Professor Jebb; another was a fellow of a Cambridge college with, again, a double first and experience of lecturing; the third, William Wyse, was yet another Cambridge man with a first-class degree and a string of university prizes to his credit. Housman's succinct statement of his own academic record stands in curious contrast: after noting his college scholarship and his first class in moderations, he adds that 'in 1881 I failed to obtain honours in the Final School of Litterae Humaniores. I have since passed the examinations required for the degree of B.A. ... .'*. Although he was the oldest of the four, his career had taken him right outside the academic world. So far, not so good. But his letter was accompanied by copies of a printed booklet containing no fewer than seventeen testimonials,* and he must have taken a quiet pleasure in the knowledge that it presented the selection committee with an extraordinary and perhaps an unprecedented problem.

For the seventeen letters were from some of the leading classical scholars of the day, and most of them spoke of him in superlatives. Nettleship, Professor of Latin at Oxford, said that 'his perculiar gifts seem to me to deserve, in an especial way, public recognition in England'; Tyrrell, Professor of Greek at Dublin, said 'I regard him as holding a place in the very van of modern scholarship, and as worthily carrying on the best traditions of the great English school of classics'; and Palmer, Dublin's Professor of Latin, said 'Mr Housman's position is in the very first rank of scholars and critics.' These were tributes that no committee not blinded by prejudice could afford to ignore, and Ker and his colleagues had the wisdom to give them due weight. Further support came from J. E. B. Mayor, whose chair at Cambridge Housman was later to occupy; Henry Jackson, who as an editor of the *Journal of Philology* had published his first paper; A. W. Verrall of Trinity College, Cambridge (later, like Jackson, a colleague); and others, including scholars in Germany and America. Pollard praised Housman's general literary culture and his sense of the relationship between the classics and English literature; and Robinson Ellis, somewhat implausibly, referred to him as 'an amiable and modest man . . . [who] would conciliate the esteem of his pupils'.

Housman had presented himself for either chair, with a preference for the chair of Latin. The committee's report, in Ker's handwriting, conveys a sense of the discussion that took place when it found itself confronted with this far from straightforward case: the applicant least qualified – in fact quite unqualified – in terms of his academic record had a reputation based on published scholarship that placed him in a category entirely by himself. He was, the report concedes with ambiguous donnish caution, 'the most remarkable of all the candidates'; his published work was 'the product of his leisure, and unconnected with any professional duties'; as for the Oxford failure, obviously a great stumbling-block for any committee, it 'may be attributed to his exclusive interest in scholarship, and his want of interest in some of the other subjects of the School of *Litterae Humaniores*'. At the interview the committee were 'strongly impressed . . . by his evident interest in teaching, as well as by the good sense and strength of character shown by him on that occasion'; they believed he would 'attract students' and might 'help to form a brilliant classical school' at the College. At that stage in the College's academic fortunes, the final point may well have been decisive. At any rate, he was offered the Chair of Latin, that of Greek going to Wyse.

It was a momentous day for Housman, that 24 May, eleven years almost to the day since the beginning of the fateful Oxford Finals; and he must at once have recognized it for what it was – a turning-point in his life. 'During the last ten years', he had written in his letter of application, 'the study of the Classics has been the chief occupation of my leisure.' The stilted phrase concealed vast and patient labours; during those years he must have known some hours of delight and exhilaration, and many others of depression; but it was sheer pertinacity that had carried him through the frustrating decade as part-time scholar and full-time bureaucrat. Now the professorial title constituted formal recognition of his achievements; the failure of 1881 had been made good. It was a period when success in an academic career could come very early to the brilliant: in 1889 Gilbert Murray had become Professor of Greek at Glasgow at the age of twenty-three. Housman's entry into the company of professional scholars had been long delayed, but at thirty-three he had come into his kingdom.

Many of his colleagues at the Patent Office knew nothing of his scholarly alter ego, but one had been taken into his confidence, and Jack Maycock wrote Housman a letter of congratulation which shows very touchingly that the years of penance had not entirely lacked the consolation of friendship:

As a rule English people never allow themselves to say or write what they think about anyone, no matter how much of a pal he may be. Well, I am going to let myself loose. I like you better than any man I ever knew. There is, as far as I could discover, absolutely no flaw in your character as a man . . . Dear old pal, I'm as pleased as if I'd done something good myself.*

Housman treasured this affectionate tribute, and after his death it was found in the privileged company of Moses Jackson's last letter.

4 'Picked out of the gutter'

'He said in his farewell speech to us that we had picked him out of the gutter . . .'

(R. W. Chambers)*

The transition in 1892 from clerk's stool to professor's chair sounds, and was, dramatic: it permanently changed the course of Housman's life. Nonetheless there was something inevitable about it: given his strength of will and powers of self-discipline, the years of penance seem in retrospect no more than an interruption of his real vocation, though there must have been hours and weeks when it was hard for him to believe that he would not grow old in the Patent Office, as Maycock and others were destined to do. What was really remarkable was the quiet drama of his scholarly activities during the preceding decade – the heroically patient succession of evenings in the British Museum, the publication of papers of outstanding brilliance and authority, and the growth of an international reputation for one who held no academic post or even degree.

Still, without wishing at all to diminish the impressiveness of Housman's achievement in self-rescue, it has to be said that a chair at University College at that period was not quite the academic plum that it might nowadays be thought; and it was to be almost another twenty years before Housman's ambitions could be said to have been fully satisfied. The College, opened in 1828 to provide a university education for those debarred by religious tests from Oxford and Cambridge, was still small when Housman arrived. In the 1891–2 session there were altogether 928 students, of whom 361 were in the Medical School, the remaining 559 being divided between the faculties of Arts, Sciences and Laws. In the years that followed there was steady growth but no sudden explosion of numbers, and it was not until 1905–6 that the non-medical students topped the thousand mark. One-man departments were the rule: the Professor of Latin *was* the Department of Latin, and only in his last few years there did Housman have even the part-time assistance of a junior colleague. As a result the teaching load was heavy – Housman seems never to have taught for less than ten hours a week, and sabbatical leaves were unknown – whilst much of the work was of a very elementary standard. The Lower Junior class (three hours a week) studied for the London Matriculation examination, doing exercises in translation and composition and getting up the set texts of such elementary authors as Ovid and Sallust. The Junior class (two hours) worked for the Intermediate BA examination, roughly equivalent to the A level papers taken by today's school-leavers. The Senior class (five hours) aimed at the Pass BA.

It would not be unfair to say that much of the work at University College at that time was of a standard we might associate with a sixth form college (or American junior college), and it cannot have been much more intellectually taxing than the work Housman had done as a schoolboy at Bromsgrove. Much of it must have been monotonous and repetitive, though not more so than the duties of the Patent Office, and there was virtually no scope for him to relate his teaching to his researches; only in his last four years there was he able to offer courses in textual criticism. The committee report which had recommended to the Senate that two classical professors be appointed included a minority report by one member which makes the revealing suggestion that a single professor was all that the situation called for, since the work was mostly 'pass' work, Oxford and Cambridge offering 'scholarships enough to tempt all, and more than all the young men really likely to profit by higher classical teaching'.* With the abolition of religious tests at the ancient universities there must have seemed a real possibility that University College would lose its *raison d'être*, attract only mediocre students, and sink into obscurity.

But the calibre of the college staff was high, and some of Housman's colleagues offered an intellectual stimulation which his work and his students can have provided only intermittently. Apart from Ker, there was the Professor of Comparative Literature, J. P. Postgate, who had recently invited Housman to contribute to his monumental *Corpus Poetarum Latinorum*, and, from 1894, Arthur Platt, who succeeded Wyse as Professor of Greek when the latter, finding himself unable to adjust to the very different academic climate of Gower Street, scurried back to Trinity. Platt was an attractive personality as well as a good scholar; he was a man of wide literary culture, had a phenomenal memory and was a brilliant conversationalist. R. W. Chambers speaks of his 'scholarly gaiety',* and Housman composed a couplet on him:

> Philology was tame, and dull, and flat;
> God said, 'Let there be larks', and there was Platt!*

He and Housman became friends for life; Housman visited his home and, when he died, wrote a touching obituary.

Ker, Housman and Platt formed a notable triumvirate. Chambers (who was in Housman's first Latin class, returned to the College as a junior teacher in 1899, and eventually became Quain Professor of English there) has said that by about 1890 morale was at a low ebb in the Faculty of Arts at University College: 'the students in Classics had become in very great measure mere birds of passage – boys who had left school, and were putting in a few terms before going to Oxford or Cambridge' (Chambers himself was only sixteen when he went there). He adds that 'there seemed a danger that in some important departments of the Arts Faculty, professors and students alike might come to regard themselves as merely filling in time till they could pass to a real university'.* The appointment of Ker in 1889 and of Housman and Platt within the next five years changed all that: between them they set the humanities on their feet again, restoring morale and raising intellectual standards. At first, however, as Chambers notes, there was a 'strange incongruity between those two mighty scholars, Platt and Housman, and the tiny and, I fear, immature classes they had . . . to teach'.

Housman owed a debt of gratitude to University College for picking him out of the gutter, and he paid it: he gave nearly twenty years to the College and must take some of the credit for the revival of its academic fortunes. An inspection by Treasury officials in 1897 found it 'a place of learning of some considerable prestige and tradition', and their report added that 'in no college has the advancement of knowledge for its own sake as the ideal of University work been more distinctly kept in view'.* (The buildings, it noted less enthusiastically, were 'adequate for their purpose, though not at all more than adequate'.) Standards continued to rise: another visitation in 1906 reported that 'the work of the College, especially advanced work and research, has been greatly strengthened during the past five years'* and there had been a significant rise in the qualifications of students on entrance.

For Housman, at thirty-three, it was an abrupt change of occupation. His only teaching experience had been the brief spell with the sixth form at Bromsgrove a decade earlier. Now, leaving behind the masculine world of the Patent Office with its bureaucratic routines and established procedures, he found himself facing classes of boys and girls for ten hours a week. He was also quickly caught up in college affairs, finding himself Vice-Dean of Arts and Laws in his second year and Dean a year later. He was to prove a capable administrator, notably in the financial crisis that later confronted the College.

His duties began in the autumn of 1892, but he had been busy during the summer not only preparing his lectures but writing the Introductory Lecture which he delivered to the Faculties of Arts, Science and Laws on 3 October. In spite of its timing, this was not strictly an inaugural but an annual lecture given by a member of staff to launch the new academic session. So far as is known, Housman had not spoken in public before, and the task was in every way an exacting one. His execution of it was a minor triumph, and the College's decision to print the lecture* (not its usual practice) must be seen as an acknowledgement of the impression he had made. The lecture, privately printed but not published for a wider audience until after his death, was described by Housman long after its delivery as 'rhetorical and not wholly sincere'. It is rhetorical in the sense that it was consciously devised for a specific purpose: brilliantly provocative, incisive and entertaining, it was skilfully adapted to the occasion that called it forth, and must have sent its audience away murmuring appreciative comments on the new Professor of Latin. But its central argument, though perhaps overstated, is serious enough, and it declares a professional and moral position with an uncompromising boldness not often to be found in inaugural or commemorative lectures.

Housman begins by asking what is the value of learning, and then proceeds to demolish the claims traditionally made for both scientific and humane studies, his specific targets being Herbert Spencer's argument that the object of scientific knowledge is utility and Matthew Arnold's conviction that the study of humane letters, and especially of the classics, will 'transform and beautify our inner nature by culture'. Housman saw it as no part of his business to reassure his audience with platitudes, and seems indeed to come close at one point to questioning the value of the professorial duties on which he was embarking:

> I do not believe that the proportion of the human race whose inner nature the study of the classics will specially transform and beautify is large; and I am quite sure that the proportion of the human race on whom the classics will confer that benefit can attain the desired end without that minute and accurate study of the classical tongues which affords Latin professors their only excuse for existing.

What follows shows him equally unafraid to attack sacred cows, from Shakespeare ('who at his best is the best of all poets, at his worst is almost the worst') to the whole tribe of classical scholars ('as a rule the literary faculty of classical scholars is poor, and sometimes worse').

The latter part of the lecture moves from the attack on received ideas to the positive and even passionate statement of a creed. He quotes Aristotle to the effect that 'all men possess by nature a craving for knowledge', and argues that curiosity, 'the desire to know things as they are', must be good because 'happiness . . . attends its gratification':

> Let a man acquire knowledge not for this or that external and incidental good which may chance to result from it, but for itself; not because it is useful or ornamental, but because it is knowledge, and therefore good for men to acquire . . . For knowledge resembles virtue in this, and differs in this from other possessions, that it is not merely a means of procuring good, but is good in itself simply: it is not a coin which we pay down to purchase happiness, but has happiness indissolubly bound up with it.

That hedonism which Housman was to declare in his replies to Maurice Pollet more than forty years later is, we can see, already an essential ingredient in his system of beliefs. And there is, too, a hint of that aristocratic disdain of quotidian standards which was to become more pronounced in later years when he says that he will not demean himself by suggesting that knowledge is useful: it must be worthwhile because it is 'part of man's duty to himself'. Even painful knowledge is worth having:

> It is and it must in the long run be better for a man to see things as they are than to be ignorant of them; just as there is less fear of stumbling or of striking against corners in the daylight than in the dark.

'To see things as they are': it was the creed of a man who spent his life in the pursuit of knowledge, truth and certainty. The more striking, then, that he should have become identified, not at all unreasonably, as a poet of romantic day-dreaming and self-delusion.

Housman's praise of learning is not that of a man unaware of, or indifferent to, the other pleasures that life offers. He concedes that the pleasure of knowledge is not the keenest of human pleasures: those of 'sense' and of 'the affections' give more immediate delight; but it is 'the least perishable of pleasures; the least subject to external things, and the play of change, and the wear of time'. It is a view of the 'affections' that not all will share, but one that grew directly out of Housman's own experience.

His final point is the logical outcome of what has gone before but also the most disturbing part of the lecture. Since all knowledge is good, he argues, it matters not what a man studies – let him study what specially attracts him and not seek to vaunt his own chosen pursuits or to devalue those of others, for (with a graceful gesture towards the occasion of the lecture) 'there is no rivalry between the studies of Arts and Laws and Science but the rivalry of fellow-soldiers in striving which can most victoriously achieve the common end of all, to set back the frontier of darkness'. Although he does not say that all knowledge is equally good – his position rests firmly on the gratification of the individual concerned – this last part of his argument is bound to strike many as disconcerting if not repellent; it perhaps helps, however, to render less baffling the thirty-year dedication to Manilius.

The peroration conveys in eloquent and moving terms the excitement of the scholar's life. The lecture as a whole, the first extended piece of Housman's non-technical prose that has survived, is a fine example of his prose as well as a key to his faith as a scholar. A final quotation will show both the Johnsonian influence upon the prose and the characteristic but always remarkable habit of advancing boldly from a specific issue to an acknowledgment of the nature of human existence:

> Existence is not itself a good thing, that we should spend a lifetime securing its necessaries: a life spent, however victoriously, in securing the necessaries of life is no more than an elaborate furnishing and decoration of apartments for the reception of a guest who is never to come.

Such reflections, delivered with such sober assurance, are not often the fare provided for those who attend commemorative lectures: it can have taken no more than an hour for Housman to make his mark at University College.

Exactly one week after delivering the Introductory Lecture, Housman received the BA and MA degrees at a Congregation held at Oxford. To take up a professorial appointment before receiving a degree, and then to receive both degrees on the same day, were two more events in an academic career that up to this point seems determined to have nothing to do with the conventional. Yet outwardly conventional – in his appearance, his demeanour, and the circumstances of his daily life – was precisely what Housman was and remained. His comic verse combines the highly decorous with the outrageous; in his own person a startling capacity for virulent controversy – and, on the other hand, for passionate or sentimental verse – underlay a public manner of aloof and even glacial severity. The latter furnished most of the anecdotes and legends; and even though, as usual, the stories lost nothing in the telling, they were not without foundation. Of the caustic, unapproachable Housman there is, however, very little evidence up to the point at which he migrated from the Patent Office to University College – the testimony of Maycock and others, indeed, suggests a genial sociability – and one must assume that entry into the academic profession inaugurated a change in Housman's outward manner that, over a long period, deepened into second nature. To be a professor is, after all, to make a profession (in both senses) of knowing more about something than most, with the attendant risks of arrogance, intolerance, and impatience at the failings of lesser men; to be a scholar on the scale that Housman's ambition prescribed is to be condemned to long hours of solitude. To teach is also to enjoy the opportunity, or to run the risk, of forming personal relationships and attachments; if Housman did not escape the snares of intellectual superiority, he took care to minimize this last risk by maintaining an inviolable distance between himself and his pupils.

By the students at University College he came to be regarded, as Chambers recalled, with 'admiration, tempered by awe'; his remarks were

so caustic as to paralyse the female section of his class. But what, I think, hurt them more was that, having reduced Miss Brown, Miss Jones and Miss Robinson to tears, Housman professed, when he met them next week, not to know which was Miss Brown, which Miss Jones, and which Miss Robinson. When . . . Housman . . . left us, he apologized to his essembled students, past and present, for this lack of memory. A certain Dartmoor shepherd had, just at that time, attained a place in history by getting into prison and out of it. This Dartmoor shepherd knew the faces of all his sheep. Housman ruefully admitted that *he* did not. But then, he said, if I had remembered all your faces, I might have forgotten more important things – not, he hastened to explain, things more important in themselves, but more important to him; had he burdened his memory by the distinction between Miss Jones and Miss Robinson, he might have forgotten that between the second and the fourth declension.*

There is clearly some affectation here as well as some mildly sadistic leg-pulling; but the motives of his refusal to advance beyond the most formal kind of relationship were real and serious. He had been deeply and permanently hurt by his ventures into personal relationships and did not lightly risk a renewal of the experience; as one who was aware of his own nature he may have wisely hesitated before befriending young men.

One of his students, Miss Gundred Savory, remembered him as 'a tall, slender, serious-faced man, who never seemed to see his class. There was an occasional flash of humour, sometimes so dry that we might easily miss it; there was never a moment wasted or misspent'.* She adds the revealing detail that 'a favourite phrase of his was "really and truly". He said it hundreds of times', and it is clear that his concern as a teacher was not with exerting a personal influence upon his students in the Jowett tradition but with disseminating 'accurate learning', that which is 'really and truly' true and real, to those fit to receive it; it was not to Miss Savory and her like but to the Latin authors that his ultimate responsibility was due. Another of his women students later said that 'we did not mind him making us cry, because we knew he was just';* and Miss Savory acknowledged that 'we thoroughly appreciated, and were inspired by, his attitude towards truth and scholarship'.*

Mortimer Wheeler, later well-known as an archaeologist, began his studies at the College in 1907 and found Housman 'professing Latin on the "take-it-or-leave-it" principle; as one with his mind elsewhere, though liable to rally unexpectedly in caustic comment'.* Richard Aldington was at University College during Housman's last year; he records that, though student-professor relationships were in general 'friendly and cordial', Housman 'never addressed a word privately or publicly to any student . . . It was as if he were enclosed in an invisible envelope of frigidity.'* By that time, the envelope had had nearly twenty years to form and harden. Aldington adds, however, that he later came to realize that shyness as well as pride was responsible for Housman's ungenial manner. And the verdict is in any case not unanimous: a woman student who attended his classes from 1897 to 1900 found him 'very kind and helpful' and 'as a teacher . . . unsparing in his efforts to help others';* she herself kept in touch to the end of his life.

Obviously memories of student days forty or more years in the past may be affected by the natural tendency in each of us to rewrite his own history in more vivid colours than it actually possessed, as well as by the subsequent public legend which comes to overlay the personal recollection. Still, the majority verdict seems to be that Housman's classroom manner, even in an age when formality was the rule, was of more than average frigidity. The enforced confrontation of teacher and taught in the classroom presented a challenge to his social gifts that he was unprepared or unable to take up: he remained the professor 'with his mind elsewhere', 'who never seemed to see his class'. With colleagues, however, he was more genial, and in the social life of the college as a whole he was surprisingly active: it seems to have been the curiously exposed intimacy of the classroom that put him at a disadvantage. Lawrence Solomon, who taught in the Department of Latin from 1904, remembered him as 'always friendly and considerate, and on a few well-remembered occasions genial'.* Housman became treasurer of the professors' dining club and, according to another colleague, 'was at his best at the dinner table',* winning general respect for his gastronomic expertise. When it was proposed to admit women members of the teaching staff to the club, however, his geniality was not in evidence, and his opposition effectively killed the suggestion.

He was, on the testimony of Professor F. W. Oliver, 'an incomparable after-dinner speaker'.* It seems an unlikely talent in a man chronically shy and reserved, and precisely when and where it was discovered and developed is uncertain; but the gift did not desert him, and we shall find further confirmation of it in his later years. In March 1895 he spoke at short notice at a dinner held to celebrate the part played in the discovery of the gas argon by the Professor of Chemistry, William Ramsay (later Sir William and a Nobel Prizeman). Housman seized the opportunity, in a manner which maintained a delicate balance between jocularity and seriousness, to ridicule science and scientists. It was 'definitely the speech of the evening', says Oliver, and 'by his incisive chaff he almost made Ramsay sorry that he had ever discovered argon!'. 'Incisive chaff': the phrase suggests a manner in which wit and good humour render socially acceptable the expression of convictions held with a certain passionate intensity.

He was also prominent in the College Literary Society, where the tradition was to follow a deliberately provocative paper on a literary topic with hard-hitting but good-tempered discussion. Housman's Johnsonian manner and devastating retorts often managed to 'lay an adversary low'* (the phrase is Chambers'); no doubt students turned up eager to see what tossings and gorings good fortune might offer. On various occasions he gave papers on Arnold, Burns, Swinburne, Tennyson and other poets.* Some were later repeated to Cambridge audiences, but at least one perished before the fascinated eyes of his audience: during the delivery of a witty and entertaining paper he was observed to tear up each sheet after it had been read, thus ensuring that nothing that failed to reach his self-imposed standard of excellence would survive and find its way into print. One listener to his paper on Burns later caught the blend of seriousness and donnish banter in the Society's meetings:

Housman's reading of

> Now a' is done that men can do
> And a' is done in vain

can never be forgotten by anyone who heard it. There were of course the usual jibes at Scotchmen, intended to provoke W. P. Ker to discussion. Afterwards W. P. Ker rose and said, 'Forgiveness is the last refuge of malignity. I will not forgive Professor Housman.'*

It was presumably the same paper that Housman gave in about 1924 to the Martlets, a discussion society at Pembroke College, Cambridge. 'Towards the end of it', says Sir Sydney Roberts, 'Housman delivered some caustic comments on Scotsmen in general', no doubt delightedly aware that the president of the society was 'a fervent Scottish patriot.'* The paper on Arnold included a disrespectful reference to Tennyson, Housman remarking that the argument of *In Memoriam* was that 'things must come right in the end, because it would be so very unpleasant if they did not'.* It may have been these occasions that led Chambers to recall 'the feeling we had for him, and . . . the way he condescended to join in our discussions, never resenting our breaking a lance discreetly'* – a remark which suggests that in some of his students at least Housman was capable of inspiring both respect and something warmer than respect.

During these years Housman continued to lodge with Mrs Hunter. When, near the end of 1905, she moved from Highgate to Pinner (a considerably greater distance from Gower Street), Housman moved with her, deeming it less trouble to do so than to find and become accustomed to another landlady. (As an example of the legends that grew up so freely about him, it was said that he moved on account of a severe shock he had suffered and which he did not wish to have repeated: as he stepped one morning into his usual train, a fellow-passenger spoke to him.) His new address was 1 Yarborough Villas; the house was one of a pair in Devonshire Road on the Woodridings Estate, built in the fifties, and was fairly convenient for the station, the Metropolitan Railway having been extended through rural Pinner in the eighties.

Although his circle of acquaintance grew steadily, very few were invited to his lodgings. Laurence and Lucy Housman visited him 'once and once only' at Highgate, but were never asked to Pinner. When he entertained, it was in a restaurant; a typical evening out (2 December 1904) finds him dining with his publisher and fellow-gastronome Grant Richards at the Café Royal, a favourite haunt, followed by a music-hall and supper at the Criterion Bar. It must have been during these years (it can scarcely have been earlier) that Housman began to acquire an expert knowledge of food and wine. Heredity may have helped, for Edward Housman had been an enthusiastic cook, famous for his salads, and on occasion would whimsically sign his letters 'Cordon bleu'. To the study of gastronomy Housman applied himself with the same concern for exact knowledge and passion for excellence as he brought to the business of textual criticism.

The don's life is apt to have a high degree of predictability, and the regular rhythms of the academic year are not often dislocated by high drama; but drama there was in the summer of 1900 when University College found itself in the throes of a financial crisis. Debts had been mounting, disaster threatened, and rescue came only through prompt and drastic measures, including the replacement of some of the top administrators. In all this Housman played a notable part, displaying a 'power of leadership and decisive action'.* Summoned from Henley, where he was attending the Regatta with friends, he went to an emergency meeting and recorded the minutes. He was, according to Professor Oliver, 'in effect the spokesman and leader' of the body of professors, though he later and characteristically played down the importance of his own role.

He kept in touch with his family and from time to time visited Worcestershire during the vacations. During the Gower Street years four deaths occurred in his immediate family circle. Of his father's death in 1894 more will be said in a moment. In 1901 his youngest brother, Herbert, was killed in the Boer War at the age of thirty-three. As a young man he had studied medicine in Birmingham for a time, but at twenty-one he had enlisted in the ranks, serving in India and Burma and rising to the rank of sergeant. According to a fellow-soldier, his corpse 'lay on the open veldt all night in the pouring rain . . . with only his under-clothing – the Boers . . . having stripped him of everything'.* Housman himself noted that he was 'buried on battlefield'.* Four years later, another brother, Robert, died at the age of forty-four. He had qualified as an engineer and is said to have caught a fatal chill while standing in a stream in order to take a photograph. Neither brother had married. Lucy Housman died in 1907 at the age of eighty-four; thereafter the nearest Housman enjoyed to a family home, or any home at all, was the house of his brother Basil, a school medical officer who married in 1894 and settled at Tardebigge just outside Bromsgrove. In his later years he visited Basil and his wife Jeannie regularly and enjoyed a happy, comfortable relationship with both of them.

In June 1897 Housman was in Worcestershire for the Diamond Jubilee celebrations, and in August he left England for a month's holiday abroad, visiting Paris, Rome and Naples – his first trip to the Continent and a sufficiently predictable itinerary for one who was both classical scholar and gourmet. On 22 September, the day after his return, he wrote Lucy Housman a long letter which might have been penned by almost any conscientious sightseer ('When I got into Italy the weather was very hot, and remained so all the while I was there',* and so on) – which is to say no more than that he wished to give her pleasure and took considerable trouble to do so, but was not prepared to open his heart to her. Housman's best letters are to his male friends, with whom his sardonic wit can be given full play; but even with them there is no spontaneous outpouring of impressions, no sense for the reader of a pen racing to keep up with the flow of thoughts and impelled by the urge to share them. The vein in which he excels is ironic reflection of lapidary polish and succinctness: the words are chosen with as much care as the letters are formed in the elegant, dignified hand he wrote until very near the end. The burst of confidence, the garrulity generated by the act of writing, the revealing implication and the Freudian slip, are almost entirely absent.

From the turn of the century continental holidays became a regular feature of Housman's tidily ordered life, with thirty-three trips over the next thirty-five years. France and Italy remained his favourite holiday destinations, though in 1904 he took the Orient Express to Constantinople. For references to his travels less stilted than the somewhat schoolboyish epistles to his stepmother, we have to turn to the letters written to Grant Richards and other friends. Architecture and gastronomy were the main objectives of his explorations: the systematic inspection of cathedrals and churches and the critical sampling of local foods and wines (his verdicts on restaurants being recorded in a little black notebook) took him on a series of tours of most of the regions of France. Much time was spent in Paris, where he usually stayed at the Hotel Normandy; Venice was another favourite destination in the earlier years.

If these usually solitary expeditions sound a little bleak, their methodical pursuit of pleasure rather chilling, that may be because surviving references to them observe Housman's strict canons of decorum and reticence. If he had had a correspondent with whom he was on terms of close intimacy and candour, or if he had kept a diary, the picture might be very different, though on the other hand it might not. In any case, it would be presumptuous to feel regret that things were not otherwise than they seem to have been: his vacation letters often convey an impression of high spirits, even when he is old and ill, and there are no grounds for supposing that he did not plan his expeditions with enthusiasm and look back on them with pleasure. There is evidence, as we shall see, that in the later years he was not without companionship even when he set off alone; and he occasionally revealed in his letters a sharp eye for the human scene. In 1913 he wrote to J. G. Frazer, the anthropologist, recalling his visit to Capri seven years earlier. He had been there for the Feast of the Nativity of the Virgin on 8 September, and offered a small contribution to Frazer's collection of materials on fire festivals (later utilized in Book X of *The Golden Bough*):

> just after sundown the boys outside the villages were making small bonfires of brushwood on waste bits of ground by the wayside. Very pretty it looked, with the flames blowing about in the twilight; what took my attention was the listlessness of the boys and their lack of interest in the proceedings. A single lad, the youngest, would be raking the fire together and keeping it alight, but the rest stood lounging about and looking in every other direction.*

For once Housman, whose interest in boy-watching was evidently stronger than his anthropological curiosity, seems to give away more of himself than he intended.

Holidays such as this punctuated the years of teaching, examining, and administration. Of the more enduring memorials of these years, Housman, unlike posterity, would have given first place to his scholarly work. During these nineteen years, in addition to many papers in classical journals, he brought out his edition of Juvenal (1905) and the first fruits of his long involvement with Manilius, his edition of Book I appearing in 1903. He also contributed editions of texts by Ovid and Juvenal to the two volumes of Postgate's *Corpus* in 1894 and 1905. But it was not these publications that, in the early years of the twentieth century, made his name familiar to an increasingly wide public. *A Shropshire Lad* was not quick to find a publisher and, once published in 1896, created no immediate sensation: the first edition of five hundred copies took two years to sell, and the second was no larger. But within a few years its popularity was growing.

When the poems were written, and why they were written at that time, or at all – these are questions to ask and to try to answer, though much harder to answer than to ask. The most startling sentence in the whole unexpected reply to Pollet's questionnaire in 1933 states that

I did not begin to write poetry in earnest until the really emotional part of my life was over; and my poetry, so far as I could make out, sprang chiefly from physical conditions, such as a relaxed sore throat during my most prolific period, the first months of 1895.*

Shortly afterwards the linking of creativity and health was repeated and enlarged upon in the Leslie Stephen Lecture. In the printed text, the famous statement runs:

I have seldom written poetry unless I was rather out of health, and the experience, though pleasurable, was generally agitating and exhausting.

But the manuscript shows that Housman originally wrote:

I have hardly ever written poetry except when I was rather out of health or mentally agitated, and I can trace the greater part of it to a relaxed sore throat which lasted about five months.*

The reference to mental agitation, and its deletion, seem significant.

'A relaxed sore throat'; 'the first five months of 1895' – when someone as secretive as Housman makes personal details public with such exactness, we are bound to suspect his motives. The autobiographical explanation, if that is what it is, came nearly forty years after the event; but although there was some mellowing in Housman's very last years, at no time in his life did he show any great eagerness for the confessional mood. He had both frivolous and serious reasons for presenting the world with an 'explanation' that was at best only a part of the truth. His mischievous sense of humour would have delighted in the sensation caused by his provocative linking of poetic creation and bodily sickness – and his gambit worked: T. S. Eliot quoted the relevant sentence in his review of the 1933 lecture, and years later F. R. Leavis was still making disapproving use of it in his practical criticism lectures at Cambridge. But Housman's impulse to keep his privacy inviolable would have been satisfied because the explanation, striking and circumstantial as it is, was no more than a smokescreen. His reticence, one must quickly add, was entirely understandable: to have told the whole truth was unthinkable as involving too many explanations of too intimate and painful a nature; but I do not think we need take very seriously the alleged creative effects of the sore throat. Housman had other, more potent reasons to be spurred into song at that point in his life.

At least as early as 1911 Housman spoke of 'the first five months of 1895' as his main period of creative activity: he told Sydney Cockerell then that 'nearly everything in the Shropshire Lad was written in the first five months of 1895 when he was 36, and the rest in 1894'.* Although this was certainly a period of poetic activity, it was only part of a more sustained period. Tom Burns Haber probably exaggerates when he says that the 'continuous excitement' must have begun as far back as September 1890: it is hard to imagine what conception Haber entertained of an 'excitement' that could be kept up for five years or so. But he is right to warn us not to take Housman's own chronological limits too literally. (Haber suggests that 'about one third'* of the volume belongs to the period *before* 1895, and another third *after* the crucial five months, with August 1895 as the richest month of all – presumably because Housman then had more leisure for composition.) The chronology of individual poems is a vexed matter and likely to remain so.* What is important for the moment is that Housman did not suddenly begin to write poetry in January 1895; nor was his poetry precipitated by a temporary indisposition. To gain some sense of the deeper springs of creativity, we need to look at the ways in which the fates of four men impinged on his life during the years 1892–5. These men are Adalbert and Moses Jackson, Edward Housman, and Oscar Wilde.

The Bayswater ménage had, as we have seen, broken up long before, and Moses had departed for India at the end of 1887. Housman and Adalbert continued to see something of each other: the former's skeleton diary shows that on 17 January and again on 28 March 1888 Adalbert called at the Patent Office and they went to out to lunch together. When Moses sailed back to India after his home leave in 1889, he wrote to his brother from near Perim in the Red Sea; Adalbert must have received this letter early in 1890 and, since Housman knew of it, they must again have been in touch at this time. Adalbert died in hospital of typhoid fever on 12 November 1892 at the age of twenty-seven, and was buried in the family plot at Ramsgate. More than forty years later he was not forgotten: his portrait hung beside that of his brother over the fireplace in Housman's rooms in Trinity College. His seaside grave is curiously foreshadowed in a poem Housman may have read in 1890 or soon afterwards (he certainly knew it a few years later). He admired Christina Rossetti's work, and 'One Sea-side Grave', published in her *Poems* in 1890, is written in an unusual five-lined stanza that Housman used in 'Bredon Hill' and other poems. Laurence Housman dates 'Bredon Hill' July 1891, and if Housman had read Christina Rossetti's poem by then and was sufficiently impressed by it to imitate its form, it may well have returned to his mind when Adalbert died the following year. The second stanza, indeed, could almost have been written by Housman:

> Cold as the cold Decembers,
>   Past as the days that set,
> While only one remembers
>   And all the rest forget, –
> But one remembers yet.

(The 'cold Decembers' suggest a possible link with the dead

young man in 'The night is freezing fast' and with other dead in other poems.)

Of the more obvious poetic responses to Adalbert's death, 'A.J.J.' is a moving memorial to their friendship and suggests an intimacy and ease of communion that were uncommon in Housman's life; the untitled poem about the street-beggar whose chance resemblance brings Adalbert sharply to mind is a more distanced tribute to the friend buried at 'the sea's brim'. If the dating of February 1893 for these two poems or their early versions can be accepted, it looks as though the creative reaction to loss may have been fairly prompt (Housman would not necessarily have heard immediately of Adalbert's death). The fact that he did not include them in *A Shropshire Lad* suggests that Housman may have regarded them as too personal to print. Yet there is in these short poems an ambiguity that forbids confident biographical deductions:

> The head that I shall dream of,
> And 'twill not dream of me

may be Adalbert's but could well be that of Moses, indifference rather than extinction being in question; and the breeze sighing

> from a lost country
> To a land I have not known

seems to be making its way from Shropshire to India. Perhaps the explanation is that his feelings for the two brothers were not entirely distinct: the permanent loss of one made the all-but-complete loss of the other the more poignant; the death of Adalbert intensified the sense of separation from the friend with whom he had been a link.

Writing to Andrew Gow soon after her brother's death, Katharine Symons said that she was convinced that the cause of the '1895 disturbance' was 'not erotic' but that 'the history of our father is at the root of it all'.* She makes no mention of sore throats. Her protective attitude towards her brother's memory (protecting also her own feelings from shock) is apparent and very natural. Still, the phrase 'the history of our father' is not precisely what one would have expected in the circumstances. Perhaps without quite intending to, Mrs Symons seems to suggest that it was not only his father's death that affected Housman but the accumulated painful memories of years which bereavement caused to surface at that time. Edward Housman died on 27 November 1894 at the age of sixty-three, and Grant Richards suggests a connexion between that event and the flow of poems. His analysis, shrewd and realistic, is worth quoting:

> Its emotional effect on Housman need not be exaggerated; it cannot be compared to the effect produced on him by the death of his mother in his boyhood. Yet it could not have fallen lightly on one who was ever strongly affected by the deaths of those he knew, even if they were not closely connected to him.*

In one of the last letters he wrote, Housman – then a dying man himself – observed that 'my family are tough and long-lived, unless they take to drink'.* The context is grimly jocular, but Housman's jests are often not merely jests and he may have had his father's fate in mind as the exception that proved the family rule. Edward's long-drawn-out deterioration must have been a painful process to witness: although only in his early sixties, he was 'broken and infirm'. Laurence's summing-up, fifty-six years later, that 'the poor man managed to outlive the respect and appreciation of everybody but himself'* sounds a tartly convincing note, and Housman's reaction must have been less of shock or grief than of an aching mixture of pity and contempt at the spectacle of human weakness, mingled with what his sister Kate called 'the inevitable poignant memories of youth'.

According to Richards, 'his short Christmas holiday [in 1894] was spent helping his step-mother with all the business preliminary to breaking up the old home and dispersing everything in it'; it can scarcely have been an enlivening or even a restful vacation, and no wonder that in the early part of the next year Housman was 'ill and depressed',* his state not improved by bitterly cold weather. The poems ascribed to this period (including *ASL* IX: 'On moonlit heath and lonesome bank') are gloomy enough; one of them, 'The Welsh Marches', contains a couplet to gladden the heart of the Freudian interpreter:

> When shall I be dead and rid
> Of the wrong my father did?

Housman's condition in the early months of 1895 was, then, not just a matter of a 'relaxed sore throat', though that may have been real enough, but one of chronic tiredness and depression, and a protracted involvement in scholarly controversy over the manuscripts of Propertius cannot have helped matters. A modern scholar has said that the recovery of three important medieval manuscripts 'touched off a process of textual reappraisal which . . . was often bitterly acrimonious'.* And alongside his private and professional troubles ran the public drama of the Wilde case.* Queensberry's famous message was handed to the porter at the Albermarle Club on 18 February, and Wilde applied for a warrant on 1 March; the Marquess was arrested and charged the next day and committed for trial a week later. The matter now, of course, became public knowledge and was fully reported in *The Times*. Queensberry's trial at the Old Bailey ran from 3 to 5 April; immediately after its conclusion, Wilde was arrested at the Cadogan Hotel, and *his* trial opened on 26 April. Problems over the jury caused delays, and a fresh start was made on 20 May; five days later Wilde was sentenced to two years' hard labour and taken to Wandsworth.

The coincidence of these events with 'my most prolific period' may be no more than fortuitous, and since the flow of poems began before the scandal broke, it can in any case have been no more than a contributory or reinforcing cause. But the effect of all this upon Housman, as upon thousands of others, must have been shattering: it is hardly too much to say that the Wilde case radically altered the self-image of the homosexual for two or three generations. The men involved were of Housman's own genera-tion (Wilde was forty and Taylor, 'places at the bar' with him, thirty-three); his own name, Alfred, was oddly prominent in the proceedings, being borne not only by Lord Alfred Douglas but by Taylor and by Wood, another man named. Two poems attest to his reaction to these events: the 'young sinner' poem published after his death, and the less familiar but even more significant fragment (dated July or August 1895 by T. B. Haber) which seems vividly to present the scene of Wilde's arrest:

> The Queen she sends to say
> That I must ride away:
> So farewell, friends; my sovereign sends
> And I must not say nay

> She lends me a coach to ride
> With a man in blue outside
> Such need of me, good soul, has she
> She will not be denied. . . .

As often with Housman, the rhythms of a light-hearted song or dance (in this instance a music-hall ditty) express a grim and ironic meaning. Where the 'young sinner' poem makes an ostensibly objective plea for rational tolerance, the fragment offers a nightmarish vision of guilt and retribution from the point of view of the arrested man. The plunge from the normal world to handcuffs, the dock and the Black Maria which had been Wilde's experience must have been shared imaginatively during those weeks by many others for whom the Criminal Law Amendment Act had turned the 'man in blue' into a figure of fear; and Housman – whether technically guilty or not is relatively un-important – may well have been one of them. As Desmond Shawe–Taylor perceptively suggested as early as 1938, 'from Wenlock Edge he could see as far as Reading Gaol'.* After his release from gaol, Wilde received a copy of *A Shropshire Lad* from the author; confirming this long afterwards, Housman added with what seems to be a touch of pride that Wilde's friend Robert Ross had learned some of the poems by heart and recited them to Wilde when he visited him in prison.

A sad pendant to the Wilde affair belongs to August of the same year, when an eighteen-year-old Woolwich cadet committed suicide in despair at his own homosexual condition.* It is hard to believe that he too was unaffected by Wilde's fate. He left a long letter explaining his action; part of it was quoted in a newspaper account of the inquest, and after Housman's death Laurence found the cutting lying in his brother's copy of *A Shropshire Lad* alongside XLIV ('Shot? so quick, so clean an ending?'). Parts of that poem come close to paraphrasing the boy's letter, one sentence of which expresses exactly his own predicament: 'There is only one thing in this world which would make me thoroughly happy; that one thing I have no earthly hope of obtaining.'

Just as we must reject that famous sore throat as the single or main precipitating cause of Housman's poetic activity, so we must also reject the first five months of 1895 in favour of a more extended period of composition. He had his own reasons for wishing to distract attention from the period before January 1895;

and the emotional experiences which lay behind the creative burst were profound and multiple – the prolonged pain of the 'disastrous love' for Moses Jackson (I take the phrase from another fragment in the poetic notebooks); the grief at the two very different bereavements of 1892 and 1894; the guilt and anxiety provoked by the Wilde scandal. A later chapter will explore the way in which, in his poems, Housman devised a mythology to express the feelings prompted by experiences of which a direct account could not be given.

Housman's original title for the collection of verse he put together in 1895 was 'Poems by Terence Hearsay'. The odd name invites speculation: Terence is the anglicized form of the name of the Latin writer of comedies who was a freed slave; his home was in Carthage, so Rome was for him a place of exile; and he died at little more than thirty. Hearsay is experience at second hand, recounted rather than undergone, and suggests a deliberate distancing and disclaiming. Servitude, exile, early death: unless we make the improbable supposition that the name is random and pointless, some at least of these associations must be relevant to Housman's choice; the use of a mask reminds us that Housman's original intention was not to let his own name appear on the title-page. Pollard is credited with encouraging him to publish and also with proposing the title eventually adopted. The more attractive label, however, was not enough to convince Macmillan, to whom Housman sent his manuscript, that the collection was publishable. Housman gathered that their refusal was on the advice of their reader, John Morley, and it rankled enough for him to include Morley's name in the brief autobiographical summary he wrote nearly forty years later. He had to wait nearly thirty years for his revenge upon the firm, but it came at last in 1924, when it was suggested to him that Macmillan might be willing to publish his edition of Lucan. He wrote to them then:

As in 1895 you refused to publish another book of mine, *A Shropshire Lad*, under similar conditions, I did not think this likely; but he [Charles Whibley] assures me you are now less haughty.*

The collection was next offered to Kegan Paul, whose reader was Arthur Waugh (father of Evelyn). They promised to publish it at Housman's expense, a common enough arrangement with little books of verse, and it appeared in March 1896 in an edition of five hundred copies at half-a-crown. It was two years before the edition was exhausted, and at that time Housman was persuaded to change his publisher. Grant Richards, a man of twenty-six, had recently set up in business and welcomed Housman enthusiastically, not less so because he desired no royalties but merely stipulated that his share of any profits be applied towards reducing the price. The second edition was issued in September 1898; it sold 115 copies in the first month and almost 400 (of 500) by the end of the year. In 1900 Richards published a sixpenny edition designed to fit the waistcoat pocket, and this bid for popularity was not in vain, for the fame of the poems grew steadily. That a new edition in 1902 was of two thousand copies speaks for itself.

As we have seen, Moses Jackson came home from India to marry Rosa Chambers in 1889. He was home again in 1894; for a long leave of some eighteen months in 1897–8; and in 1902, 1905 and 1908. There seems to be no way of ascertaining whether the visit in 1894 may have had any connexion with the 'continuous excitement' of the following year. In her summary of her brother's career, Miss M. A. Jackson says that 'during these periods there were constant meetings with Housman',* but the only evidence that survives is of a parting rather than a meeting. Though we cannot know whether the two of them met in 1894, we know that they did so four years later; for in an old diary Housman recorded a date and time with the same precision that belongs to his nature observations: Sunday, 22 May 1898, 10.45 p.m. Just two words are added: 'said goodbye'.* Any special significance the moment may have had cannot be recovered; it was another landmark in a relationship that seemed to be made up of partings. But Housman kept his note of it, as a day to be annually recalled, as long as he lived.

The watertight compartments of his life did not often spring a leak, but later in 1898 there occurred a curious and poignant intrusion of his most private associations into his profesional duties. In that year the headship of University College School fell vacant. The school, established in 1832, had been conceived as an offshoot of the college, to which its ablest boys would pass on, the founders believing that it would 'confer great benefit on the University, by training Students up for it upon a uniform system of Instruction'. At first the academic links held fast, and for a long period the headmaster doubled as a professor in the College; but by the early nineties numbers were declining and most of the pupils were proceeding into 'commercial life' rather than pursuing higher education. An inquiry in 1894 sought to restore the fortunes of the school by moving away from the traditional classical curriculum and winning a new reputation based on a strong 'modern' side (English, Science, Mathematics, Modern Languages) – in other words, by facing the realities of the scholastic market rather than competing unsuccessfully with more famous schools. The appointment of a new headmaster was, therefore, a crucial step.

Twenty-two applicants presented themselves, among them the Principal of Sind College, Dr Moses Jackson; and Housman found himself convenor of the committee of seven professors which met to consider the applications. The eighteen-page report in his handwriting is dated 3 November 1898 and records its deliberations in detail.* Four men were shortlisted, Jackson among them; the three who were in England appeared for interview. Housman's summary of his friend's claims stresses his strong points (his scientific background and his connection with the College, of which he was a former student, doctoral graduate, and since 1894 a Fellow) but does not attempt to conceal his weaknesses: 'his experience in these matters is not actually experience in a *school*', and he 'is personally known to only one member [of the committee]'. He recalls, with what unexpressed feelings we can well imagine, that 'Mr Jackson in his youth was something of an athlete, and won the Quarter-Mile Members' Challenge Cup at the London Athletic Club in 1885'. (Some may like to juxtapose this sentence and the reference to a 'challenge-cup' in the poem 'To an Athlete Dying Young'.)

The document gives a clear picture of the nature of Jackson's work in India. Sind College, 'a University College, forming part of the University of Bombay', was evidently not as grandiose as these phrases suggest. Only two years old when Jackson took over, it numbered about 120 students in Arts, Science, Engineering and Law; Jackson himself was something of a Pooh-Bah, combining administration with teaching in both science and arts subjects and even 'design[ing] and superintend[ing] the construction of all the furniture and fittings of the laboratories and class-rooms'. But his testimonials speak of his 'zeal and ability' and of the 'steady growth and success of the college'. Still, while he was clearly in the running, his candidature was not sufficiently outstanding for an *in absentia* appointment to be made, and another man got the job.

It must have been an odd experience, ironic and bitter-sweet, for Housman to preside over the discussion of his friend's qualities and inwardly to contemplate the difference that the appointment might make to his own life. His role was a delicate one since, as the only member of the committee with any personal knowledge of Jackson, he was both the pleader of his cause and one of the judges of it. An uncharacteristic blunder seems to hint at the tension he felt even after the unfavourable decision had been made: in writing the account of Jackson which forms part of his report, he finished the twelfth sheet and then continued on the verso instead of taking up a fresh sheet, discovering his error only when he reached the bottom of the page and then, perforce, cancelling and recopying it. That cancelled page is, it seems, the nearest he came to a confession of how much the episode had meant to him. The report contains the implication that this was not the first time that Jackson had applied for a new post, and it seems likely that one of the aims of his long leave in England in 1897–8 had been to secure a position that would enable him to bring his wife and children home. If so, his disappointment must have been fully shared by Housman.

'Friend' was a word in Housman's vocabulary to which Jackson enjoyed virtually sole rights, and, with few exceptions, to speak of Housman's friendships after the early years is to use the word in a somewhat qualified sense: a relaxed intimacy and informality and the relief of self-revelation were not among the pleasures with which he often indulged himself. The formal attire he donned even for a country ramble had its psychological counterpart. Perhaps he had become incapable of casting aside the armour of self-containment: his love for Moses Jackson had brought – was still bringing – more pain that joy, and he had taken the lesson to heart. In any case, in a period which ostracized the known homosexual and threatened his impulses with social and legal sanctions, the holding of a part of oneself in reserve, the habit of secretiveness and self-censorship, would long have become second nature to the middle-aged homosexual unwilling to forfeit or forego a place in society. A Professor of Latin was denied the bohemian freedom of a free-lance author such as Laurence Housman. But he did enjoy quite a wide circle of diverse relationships; they were not all with scholars or literary men, and many of them endured. Four which developed during this phase of Housman's life – with a publisher, a scholar, an artist and an American – will suggest their range and their varying nature.

Grant Richards has already been mentioned as taking over publication of *A Shropshire Lad* in 1898. Son of one Oxford don and nephew of another (that Herbert Richards who had been one of Housman's Finals examiners), he was thirteen years younger than Housman and at eighteen had gone into journalism. At twenty-four he founded his own publishing firm, and Housman's book was one of his earliest titles. Later he brought out work by Shaw, Bennett, Wells, Chesterton and others. He enjoyed food, wine and travel, and these shared tastes formed the basis of a friendship in which Housman permitted himself, if not self-disclosure, at any rate an exceptional degree of candour. It was Richards, for instance, who helped to keep him supplied with pornographic literature, or at any rate what was then deemed to fall within a category which included in due season *Ulysses* and *Lady Chatterley's Lover*. Their friendship lasted for nearly forty years, and was obviously based on temperamental congeniality as well as on their common interests as author and publisher. Richards' account notes that they dined together 'a couple of hundred times',* and Housman was also a visitor to his home. In his letters to Richards, which survive plentifully, Housman's manner is relaxed and good-humoured; Richards was bookish, but not an academic, and after the move to Cambridge in 1911 their meetings in London and elsewhere provided Housman with an escape from the narrow world of college and lecture-room. Richards was gratifyingly proud at having captured Housman for his list, and made no secret of it. All in all, his company was good for Housman.

Gilbert Murray on the other hand was a front-rank scholar, though not a rival, since his field was Greek rather than Latin and his wider fame was based on translations of Greek tragedy into English verse. Seven years younger than Housman, he too had been at St John's, where his career had been as conventionally brilliant as Housman's had been unconventional. He had carried off a string of prizes, culminating in a first-class degree and a New College fellowship; at twenty-three he obtained the Chair of Greek at Glasgow. When in 1908 he went back to Oxford as Regius Professor, Housman wrote him the kind of letter he was so skilled at composing, in which congratulations are no mere routine but based on a scrupulous sense of the precise nature of the merit involved:

> I think you are now well on your way to take that place in the public eye which used to be occupied by Jowett and then by Jebb; and as you are a much better scholar than the one and a much better man of letters than the other, the public will be a gainer without knowing it, and good judges (by which I mean myself) will be less at variance with the public.*

The relationship was not a close one, but his letters to Murray suggest a congeniality which did not exclude intellectual candour. That of 23 April 1900 is particularly memorable, providing as it does a prose gloss to *A Shropshire Lad*:

> I rather doubt if man really has much to gain by substituting peace for strife, as you and Jesus Christ recommend. Sic notus Ulixes? do you think you can outwit the resourceful malevolence of nature? . . . When man gets rid of a great trouble he is easier for a little while, but not for long: Nature instantly sets to work to weaken his power of sustaining trouble, and very soon seven pounds is as heavy as fourteen pounds used to be. Last Easter Monday a young woman threw herself into the Lea because her dress looked so shabby amongst the holiday crowd: in other times and countries women have been ravished by half-a-dozen dragoons and taken it less to heart. It looks to me as if the state of mankind always had been and always would be a state of just tolerable discomfort.

Less predictable was Housman's friendship with the artist William Rothenstein. Rothenstein, the son of a Jewish business-man, had left Bradford for Paris while still in his teens to pursue a career as an artist; by the time he was twenty-one he had 'cata-pulted himself into the very centre of the artistic life of Europe',* and he came to number among his friends Degas, Lautrec, Whistler, Beardsley and other artists. The first of his portraits of Housman was made in 1906 and by the following year they were meeting socially for Housman's favourite kind of evening out in London – dinner at the Café Royal followed by a music-hall. It may be significant that, like Richards and Murray, he was younger than Housman: a masculine relationship in which he could play the elder brother or simply the knowledgeable senior seems to have afforded Housman some gratification. He knew and corresponded with Rothenstein's wife Alice, visited their home, and wrote comic verse for their children; but he 'discouraged any show of affection towards himself',* and in his letters to the artist one catches the atmosphere of a jolly but slightly detached bachelor chumminess in which feeling is kept at bay partly by an element of teasing mock-insult. He was fond of saying that Rothenstein could not produce a likeness of him, and even contrived to gain possession of one drawing only in order to destroy it. Although another portrait hung in his rooms in later years, he 'never failed to tell me how repellent he thought my records of him to be!'.* (Rothenstein had the last laugh, however, for the drawing of Housman in the National Portrait Gallery is his.) When Rothenstein wanted to paint the distinguished group, Housman among them, who had acted as pall-bearers at Thomas Hardy's funeral, he was told that 'you are much too great an artist to catch a likeness'.*

But the most surprising of these relationships, superficially at least, was with the youngest member of the group, the American Witter Bynner. In 1903 Bynner, who later became known as a poet, was a twenty-two-year-old journalist working as poetry editor for *McClure's Magazine*. His enthusiasm for *A Shropshire Lad* led him to print some of the poems in the magazine and to write to the poet. Not only did he receive a reply but thirty years later they were still exchanging letters. Housman usually had little time for Americans ('I am told that Americans are human beings, though appearances are against them,'* he observed to Grant Richards), and his friendly replies to Bynner's overtures make one wonder why this was an exception.

It was not the only exception: another young American, the seventeen-year-old Houston Martin, wrote to Housman in 1932 and received an unexpectedly genial response. The correspondence flourished, and Housman not only kept Martin's letters but wrote to him only a few days before his death. The answer may be partly that he was touched and even excited by the attentions of a young man – 'such infatuation as yours', he told Martin, 'is quite intimidating'* – and partly that in both instances there was little danger that he would ever come face to face with his correspondent. (He never did.) When a young Englishman actually asked to *meet* his poet-hero, the hero-worship was accepted ('I value the good opinion of those young men for whom . . . my poems were written'*), but the interview firmly declined.

Housman refused to risk involvement in even the most casual personal relationship with his own students, and it is not for us to say that his rule, self-denying rather that misanthropic, was anything but prudently realistic; but he welcomed the epistolary attentions of the young, though he preferred a stretch of water to lie between him and them. Even the English Channel was better than nothing – hence the astonishing reply in 1933 to Maurice Pollet. The correspondence with Bynner obviously gave him satisfaction, and the blend of irony and kindliness in his letters is very attractive. They have, too, a relaxed quality that is fairly rare, and a single sentence in his very first letter to Bynner reveals more than years of correspondence with some of the acquaintances of his own country and generation:

> My chief object in publishing my verses was to give pleasure to a few young men here and there, and I am glad if they have given pleasure to you.*

The zigzags of biographical narrative have brought us to 1911, which saw the crowning of a new king. It was also a year of change for both Alfred Housman and Moses Jackson. At fifty-three, after twenty-three years' service in India, Jackson retired and moved halfway round the world to a new home in British Columbia, where he was to spend the rest of his days. If Housman had cherished any hope that he and his friend might see more of each other in their old age, it was disappointed: Moses was still separated from him by thousands of miles, and indeed the separation was more complete, since there were no more periods of leave in England. They continued to correspond, but there is no reason to believe that they met again after Jackson's retirement. Housman's own move was counted in miles rather than in hemispheres. He migrated from London to Cambridge, but not into retirement, for there lay ahead of him an active quarter-century which included the most productive years of his scholarly life.

The Cambridge Professor of Latin, J. E. B. Mayor, had died on 1 December 1910 at the age of eighty-five. He had held the chair for thirty-eight years and was still lecturing in the Michaelmas term of 1910, compulsory retirement for professors being still a thing of the future. Mayor was an amiable and eccentric scholar who seemed to have survived the Victorian age by some oversight; Herkomer's portrait shows him heavily bearded and side-whiskered, and he was fond of lamenting the intellectual poverty of the new race of Cambridge undergraduates – some of them, he feared, 'had libraries of less than two thousand books'. T. R. Glover has described Mayor's lecturing style in his later years:

> I once attended a course of his lectures. His subject was Tertullian, whom I was then reading. He took the *Apology*, translated a chapter or two rapidly, and then dictated a series of references, taking word after word and telling us in what authors (with chapter and verse) these words occurred. It had very little bearing on the mind or character or theology of Tertullian . . .*

The chair had been founded as recently as 1869 (those of Greek and Hebrew went back to the time of Henry VIII). It had been established in honour of Dr Benjamin Hall Kennedy, known to generations of schoolboys as the author of a Latin primer, and a famous headmaster of Shrewsbury School. Both the previous occupants of the chair, Munro and Mayor, had been pupils at Shrewsbury.

Housman had already been longer at University College than might have been expected, and a move was the most natural thing in the world. Possibly he would have preferred to return to Oxford; certainly the triumphant reappearance there of the stone rejected by the builders in 1881 would have gratified his taste for irony, and Robinson Ellis, who had occupied the Latin chair since 1893, was in his late seventies and could not live for ever. (He died in 1913.) However, when Housman was encouraged to apply to Cambridge, he did so. No account of his deliberations is available, but they cannot have taken long, since little more than a month elapsed between Mayor's death and the last date for the submission of applications.

The electors or selection committee included Henry Jackson, the Regius Professor of Greek; Robinson Ellis of Oxford; E. J. Rapson, the Professor of Sanskrit; and Leonard Whibley of Pembroke College. Jackson had known Housman for about twenty years, and as editor of the *Journal of Philology* had accepted for publication his first classical paper in 1882. Later he said that 'he had been zealously active in arranging for [Housman] to be elected, and was highly pleased with his success'.* Robinson Ellis had been a victim of Housman's published savageries; not unreasonably, it was supposed that he would vote against him. Indeed Herbert Richards remarked that Housman 'hadn't the ghost of a chance'.* But his prediction was unsound. Whibley later gave a vivid account of the scene:

> I remember Robinson Ellis – senile and drivelling at his nose, which he looked down – saying no word about Housman, but murmuring ineffectually that he thought Mr Oliffe Richmond a very good scholar. I forget whether we had more than one voting, but Housman got it easily, I think.*

Whibley also recalled another member of the committee remarking over lunch that 'Housman was the best Latin scholar in Europe since Madvig' (the Danish scholar had died in 1886).

The Chair was offered, and accepted. Immediately afterwards, presumably at Jackson's instigation, Housman was offered a Fellowship at Trinity College, and his letter of acceptance notes that.

> Macaulay used to rank a Fellow of Trinity somewhere in the neighbourhood of the Pope and the Holy Roman Emperor: I forget the exact order of the three, but I know that the King of Rome was lower down, and His Most Christian Majesty of France quite out of sight. Platt will no longer be able to despise me.*

(Another gratifying recognition of Housman's stature followed on 1 May, when he was elected an Honorary Fellow of his old college, St John's.) Within a couple of weeks he was admitted Master of Arts *honoris causa* at Cambridge, and formally elected a Fellow of Trinity. The choice was widely approved, except among those scholars who had been turned into enemies by Housman's uncompromising mode of controversy. The Cambridge correspondent of the *Oxford Magazine* wrote that 'satisfaction is general, particularly among the younger classical scholars, at Mr Housman's appointment to the Professorship of Latin',* and the unspoken reference to the older classical scholars is expressive.

Housman still had the best part of a term to serve at University

College, his translation to the new Chair being timed for Easter. On 23 March he gave the Annual Foundation Oration at University College, lecturing on Thomas Campbell. His performance was evidently in the iconoclastic style that his audience had come to expect and to relish. One student who was present remembered 'the jokes that kept his audience chuckling and laughing the whole time'* and it was on this occasion that another student, Mortimer Wheeler, produced a caricature for a student magazine. It shows a very slim and dapper Housman ('smallish' and 'dapper' were epithets used of him by his sister Katharine*); near him hovers the abashed ghost of the poet Campbell, and the caption runs: 'Mr Thomas Campbell begins to wish he hadn't'. At about the same time a farewell dinner was given for him by his colleagues, and the speechmaking engendered a *mot* that has been repeated many times in slightly different forms and attributed to different occasions; probably, indeed, Housman produced it more than once, with appropriate adjustments to fit the occasion. It followed a reference to the well-known abstemiousness of his Cambridge predecessor, Mayor, a teetotaller and vegetarian – a man who drank like a fish, as Housman remarked on another occasion, 'if drinking nothing but water might be so described':*

Cambridge has seen many strange sights. It has seen Wordsworth drunk and Porson sober. It is now destined to see a better scholar than Wordsworth and better poet than Porson betwixt and between.*

R. W. Chambers commented long afterwards on what the move meant to Housman in terms of private happiness:

We felt the loss of Housman when he left us in 1911, but I felt very strongly, when I saw him in Trinity a year ago [that is, in 1935], that you had given him the happiness – I don't think that is too strong a word – which we could never have done. He said in his farewell speech to us that we had picked him out of the gutter – an unkind way of describing the Patent Office. That was true, and due, I suppose, to W. P. Ker. But London and U.C.L. could never have contented him, as it did Ker.*

Elsewhere Chambers adds that no-one who saw him at Cambridge could doubt that he was at last 'in his right setting'.*

5   Cambridge I

How much reluctance Housman felt at leaving London for Cambridge in the spring of 1911 it is hard to say: probably not much. According to R. W. Chambers, he had never 'identified himself' with University College 'in a way which would have made it difficult for him to leave it';* Chambers may also be saying between the lines that Housman's evident ambition was not likely to let him remain in Gower Street for ever. In a note of thanks for congratulations on his appointment, Housman said that 'joy does predominate over sorrow, as I am fond of money and fond of leisure; but as I am also fond of solitude, and shall not have it at Cambridge, there is some sorrow mingled with the joy; apart from leaving friends and the College'.* The sorrow at quitting Gower Street sounds like an afterthought and cannot have been profound; he certainly did not haunt its purlieus after his departure, and although he asked to be allowed to continue his membership of the professors' dining club this may have been no more than a courteous gesture, for he reappeared only once, and then by special invitation.

But to someone so conservative in temperament and habits, the uprooting – after nearly thirty years in London and nearly nineteen at the college – must have caused pangs. Grant Richards believed he was sorry to leave Mrs Hunter and his old rooms; she for her part told Platt on the one occasion he visited the house that 'she could not entirely regret his going, for at Cambridge he . . . would have other men's society forced upon him'.* For a man in his fifties the revision of daily routine was a substantial one, since he now exchanged the role of metropolitan commuter to a day college for that of resident fellow in a small, university-dominated town. His professional role was also drastically altered, and for the better: the heavy teaching load, much of it with elementary students not specialising in classics, gave way to a very much lighter load – he lectured twice a week at Cambridge, where the terms were in any case shorter – and his courses were on topics close to his research interests. As the occupant of a chair, indeed, his primary obligation was to pursue his own researches and to contribute to the advancement of knowledge: of all things, precisely what he would have chosen to do. Gastronomically, too, the change can only have been for the better: without disrespect to Mrs Hunter's cooking, it can scarcely have competed with that of the Trinity chefs. With his characteristic self-disparaging brand of jocularity, Housman told Richards that he was 'mostly satisfied' with the Cambridge appointment 'because at Trinity . . . I shall, I hope, be a member of the Wine and the Garden Committees'.*

Housman was no stranger to Cambridge. He had been elected to the Philological Society there as early as 7 November 1889, well before the end of his time at the Patent Office. (Curiously enough, the notice of his election in the Society's *Proceedings* bestowed on him the degree of MA, though the University of Oxford was not to do so until nearly three years later.) He attended a number of meetings soon after his election, and was prompt to take an active part in the Society's discussions: in May 1890 he replied to Postgate's criticisms of one of his articles on Propertius, in October of the same year he read a paper on Euripides, and in May 1892 a paper on Virgil. During these brief visits he was afforded glimpses of the world into which, twenty years later, he was to be welcomed as an honoured member: the meeting in October 1890, for instance, was held in Magdalene College, where Housman was on many occasions to enjoy Arthur Benson's hospitality.

The society of Trinity College, Cambridge, in 1911 and the years immediately following, was a remarkable gathering of brilliance in diverse fields of intellectual activity. Perhaps nowhere in the world at that time was there regularly assembled such a company of front-rank scholars and scientists as sat nightly at Trinity high table. One list of eighteen members in that golden age includes eleven holders of the Order of Merit, seven Nobel prizewinners, and four presidents of the Royal Society. When Housman arrived, the fellows included G. H. Hardy, the mathematician; J. G. Frazer, the anthropologist; A. S. Eddington, the physicist; A. N. Whitehead, the philosopher; and J. J. Thomson, the discoverer of the electron. J. M. E. McTaggart was lecturing in Moral Sciences, G. M. Trevelyan in History, and Bertrand Russell in Logic and the Principles of Mathematics. The classicists included F. M. Cornford, J. D. Duff, D. S. Robertson and A. W. Verrall. During the next few years this company was jointed by (among others) E. D. Adrian, W. L. Bragg, Ernest Rutherford, G. E. Moore, C. D. Broad, and Ludwig Wittgenstein, who became a neighbour of Housman's in Whewell's Court. The Master until 1918 was Henry Montague Butler; he was succeeded by J. J. Thomson.

Housman arrived in Cambridge just in time to savour the last years of the golden age that ended in 1914. But in spite of the upheavals caused by the war and its aftermath of reform, Trinity's intellectual leadership continued in the twenties, and a high proportion of the most distinguished English scientists and philosophers of the period were fellows of the College, which offered Housman a bachelor existence of splendour and dignity – all very different from the quiet evenings at Pinner and the 'small, crowded, smoke-laden cell'* which was the professors' common-room at University College. He knew that the social demands made upon him would be heavier: to another correspondent he wrote that 'to have less work and more pay is always agreeable, and that will be the case with me. The drawback is that I shall be obliged to be less unsociable.'* If he was not radically altered by the changed circumstances of his life, his clubbability certainly increased by a few degrees in the ensuing years, and he often undertook social engagements which went beyond the call of duty. Trevelyan may not be a quite disinterested witness, but there is no reason to doubt his statement that, although Housman 'was notoriously not easy to please . . . he let himself be pleased in our society' and for twenty-five years 'very contentedly' made Trinity College his home.* It is revealing that Housman's prediction a few days after his appointment to the Cambridge chair that 'I shall most likely spend some part of each year in London'* was not fulfilled.

During the Easter term of 1911 he had no teaching duties in Cambridge, but a substitute was found to take over his work at University College and he soon settled in Cambridge. Term began there on 18 April; towards the end of the month he was still in Pinner, but by the middle of May he was writing to Witter Bynner from Trinity, though for the time being living in lodgings at 32 Panton Street, near the Fitzwilliam Museum, presumably until his Trinity rooms could be made ready for him. On 26 May he wrote to Sir Sydney Cockerell, Director of the Fitzwilliam, that 'the only professorial function I am discharging this term is that of residing',* and a couple of weeks earlier he had told Laurence that he was busy with 'social duties'.* But one professorial function had, in fact, already been discharged: the delivery of his Inaugural Lecture on 9 May.* Remembering how many pains prose composition gave Housman, and how much time he devoted to such tasks, one is a little surprised by his promptness in producing this lecture. It was not published during his lifetime (he was troubled by being unable to trace and verify a textual point concerning one of Shelley's poems), and the manuscript was destroyed after his death in accordance with his wishes and in the company of other unpublished prose manuscripts. In 1968, however, a typescript copy turned up among various papers of Laurence Housman which had been sent for sale at Sotheby's, and the lecture soon found its way into print.

It was given to 'a crowded and curious audience',* and was well received. Cockerell noted in his diary for 9 May:

> Splendidly fine and warm . . . At 5 went with Pollard and Greg to A. E. Housman's inaugural lecture in the Senate House as Professor of Latin – a brilliant performance.*

Another member of the audience, J. M. Image, gives a glimpse of Housman's manner:

> Brilliant is the only epithet – flashing and scintillating with dry humour (admirably enhanced by his solemnity of face) and 'delicious irony'.*

Henry Jackson, the Regius Professor of Greek, wrote to Platt:

> Housman's discourse was excellent. He smote with all his might two tendencies of modern scholarship – on the one hand, aesthetic criticism; on the other hand, the slavish, mechanical, methods of the Germans . . . And the manner was perfect . . . And, personally, I was much pleased with what he said about Munro and Mayor. He was kind, just and truthful.*

Jackson's last remarks refer to the opening portion of the lecture, in which Housman pays tribute to the two previous occupants of the chair as well as to Kennedy, in whose honour it was founded. The reference to Kennedy ('the greatest classical teacher of his century') strikes an unexpectedly personal note, for it was Housman's acquisition as a schoolboy of his *Sabrinae Corolla* that 'first turned my mind to these studies and implanted in me a genuine liking for Greek and Latin'. On Munro he is even more self-revealing: he recalls how, as an undergraduate, he used to 'molest him with letters' and even tried – in vain – to obtain a photograph of him from a firm of Cambridge photographers. He never met his hero (Munro died in 1885), but he treasured and still possessed the replies received to his letters. He described Munro as 'the greatest scholar in Cambridge and the foremost English Latinist of the century'; it was a mantle that Housman inherited, and his encomium suggests that hero-worship took the form of imitation, for the words he uses of Munro are words that might be used of Housman himself:

> he wrote English so well that most scholars do not know how well he wrote it; and he was surely the most entertaining controversialist that ever redeemed these studies from the reproach of dullness and dustiness.

Munro, the first occupant of the Latin chair, was succeeded by Mayor; and though the tribute cannot be either so warm or so personal, Housman praises the latter's erudition. His kind of scholarship was not Housman's, being that of 'the antiquarian and the lexicographer', and the implication that it is an inferior kind is plain; but in his own field Mayor excelled.

After this graceful and generous opening, Housman turns to his main purpose. The 1892 'Introductory Lecture' at University College had set forth a defence of the scholarly vocation; the Cambridge Inaugural sought to define the proper business of a student of the classics as Housman conceived it, and in the process to expose 'two current errors' which enjoyed wide acceptance. To declare, however unfashionably and provocatively, the truth, and to denounce perversions of that truth: it was a characteristic undertaking which could leave no-one in any doubt as to how the new Professor of Latin proposed to occupy himself. 'The study of Latin is a science conversant with literature': it ought not, therefore, to be pursued either as if it were one of the natural sciences (for its subject-matter is not the physical world but a product of the mind of man), nor as 'a branch of literature' (for that would be to treat it as if it were 'no science at all'). (One notes in passing that, in the context of 1911, the study of literature meant no more than a hazy, undisciplined attempt to communicate 'appreciation' or aesthetic response: the revolution in literary studies wrought by the founding of the Cambridge English School was still a few years away.) 'Scholarship is not literary criticism; and of the duties of a Latin Chair literary criticism forms no part.'

There is no reason why a scholar should not appreciate the literary qualities of the texts he works on, just as a botanist may enjoy the beauty of flowers and an astronomer be struck by the grandeur of the heavens; but it is not part of his proper business. Indeed, it may be a threat to the exercise of his peculiar function: 'literature is so alien from science that the literary temper in himself is a peril against which the scholar must stand on his guard'. To illustrate the dire results of succumbing to this danger, Housman considers an example based on the text of one of Shelley's lyrics. He quotes Swinburne's panegyric – an extreme but not unique instance of 'literary appreciation' – and reveals triumphantly that it turns out to be based on a misprint. Such are the things that are liable to occur when 'the literary mind . . . with its facile emotions and its incapacity for self-examination . . . invades the province of science'.

In England 'the literary attitude' has become 'the scholar's besetting sin'. (It had not always been so. In mid-nineteenth-century Cambridge, scholarship 'simply meant science with no nonsense about it'; in Oxford, on the other hand – and here, perhaps, painful personal associations lent force to the contrast – the literary fallacy was already predominant.) In Germany the prevailing error was precisely the opposite of that to be found in England, and consisted in treating 'the criticism and interpretation of the classical texts' as if these tasks constituted 'an exact science'. To complete the symmetry of his argument Housman cites the example of a gap in a Latin dictionary representing a monumental effort of Germanic scholarship. The point at issue is the failure to recognize that Juvenal ought to be mentioned in an article on the use by Latin authors of the Greek word for a cat. To the uninitiated this does not sound like a very serious crime, and Housman surely selected his example with an eye to its comic and mock-heroic aspect. For him, however, it is symptomatic of a whole cast of mind, 'this nonsense of orthodoxy and this propensity to servitude at the present time' which 'impede the advancement of learning and even set it back'. What is really impressive in Housman's argument is the way it moves from the local and specific to the far-reaching, from a minute point of classical learning to a moral indictment with ethical and political overtones (the date, we recall, is 1911). One sees why Housman's admirers came away from his Cambridge lectures on textual criticism feeling that they had undergone a significant *moral* experience.

In August 1911 Housman was still living in Panton Street. When in September he moved into Trinity it was to a set of rooms high up on K staircase in the heavy Victorian Gothic setting of Whewell's Court. Did he find some satisfaction in the thought that the building of this part of the college had been begun in the precise year of his own birth? Certainly, something seems to have been necessary to compensate for the lack of comfort, convenience and aesthetic appeal in his new home. Whewell's Court stands apart from the rest of Trinity College, which has to be reached by crossing Trinity Street. His three rooms, which had earlier belonged to J. G. Frazer, are up forty-four stairs; and Housman was to continue climbing them until very near the end of his life. The view of the busy junction of Sidney Street and Jesus Lane was unappealing, and the rooms themselves were chilly, ill-lit and conspicuously cheerless: 'stark and comfortless quarters',* as Percy Withers noted. William Rothenstein's epithet for them was 'bleak';* A. C. Benson found them 'bare and grim';* Housman's bedroom, according to Grant Richards, was 'narrow and austere in the extreme'.* Almost any other part of the college would have been more convenient and would have afforded a prospect of great beauty and elegance; yet Housman not only chose but clung to this depressing outpost. As Sydney Cockerell remarked in a letter to Richards,

> I often wondered how anyone so indifferent to any kind of beauty or grace in his personal surroundings and content to abide in the ugliest and noisiest and slenderest section of a great College, in which quite insignificant Fellows were able to secure ample and dignified quarters, could really understand fine architecture at home or abroad.*

But Cockerell rather misses the point. Although Housman made no pretensions to taste in painting or music, his enthusiasm for architecture (ecclesiastical rather than domestic) was genuine enough, and his knowledge of it considerable; but in the selection of rooms other considerations were overriding. As often, one feels there was something wilfully self-lacerating, or at least stubbornly contemptuous of the motives that prompt most men, and perhaps also some element of affectation, in his choice of this depressing situation and his retention of it for a quarter of a century. It possessed one merit, however, which must have weighed heavily with him: it was unlikely to encourage casual callers. The room in which Housman worked contained a large office-desk and came in time to be filled to overflowing with books; it also held, among its less predictable contents, a pair of dumb-bells with which he would exercise when drowsiness threatened to interrupt his labours, the carapace of a turtle ('one of several which he presented to furnish soup for Audit Feasts'*), and the portraits of Moses and Adalbert Jackson.

If the silence of Housman's unlovely rooms was rarely broken, the life of a Cambridge don provided continual opportunities for sociability, or at least for eating and drinking in company on a lavish scale; and Housman did not reject them. By the end of 1911 he was writing to his sister that 'being a new-comer, I was much asked out to dinner. People here are very hospitable and friendly';* to Grant Richards he wrote more graphically that 'I also have over-eaten myself this term (being asked to so many College feasts) and drunk too much of that noble but deleterious wine Madeira.'* This sounds cheerful enough, but the comments of others suggest that his manner was not always easy, and he probably took a little time to adjust to the peculiar social climate of the Cambridge colleges. Andrew Gow later commented that 'when he first came to Cambridge he was sometimes apt, from shyness, to suspect a liberty where none was intended and to be sharp-tongued in answer'.* One of his earliest engagements was a feast at Pembroke College, where he sat next to A. C. Benson of Magdalene. Afterwards Benson wrote in his diary: 'sat next to A. E. Housman, who is famed as an acrid controversialist. I did not care much for him – he was polite and finished in manner, but he did not expand, was courteously withdrawn from everything. I dare say he is shy, but he repelled my advances.'* Before the end of the year, however, Benson was finding him 'far more genial and amiable' and voicing a common puzzlement: 'Who would think that this rather elegant, dry fellow was the *fiercest* of controversialists and the author of the Shropshire Lad?'*

Apart from the regular society of Trinity and frequent invitations to other colleges, Housman dined in private homes and frequented dining-clubs, thus forming a wide circle of acquaintance among the Cambridge residents and encountering a steady procession of visitors. In 1913 and again in 1914 he dined at Jesus College as Cockerell's guest, Thomas Hardy being a fellow-guest on both occasions. In the latter year he also met two American ladies who were spending a few days in Cambridge, Gertrude Stein and Alice B. Toklas: Miss Toklas sat next to Housman and talked to him ('but all the time I was more interested in watching Doctor Whitehead'). She has left on record a memory of their conversation: 'he said to me, Since you are from California, tell me about your great ichthyologist, Dr David Starr Jordan'. Not many maiden ladies could have risen to such a conversational gambit, and one is inclined to suspect Housman of being mischievous; however, 'the great ichthyologist' happened to be a friend of her grandfather, and Miss Toklas was able to oblige.* In 1918 came a meeting with André Gide, who was spending the summer in Cambridge.

Private dining-clubs flourished during this period, among them The Family,* with which Housman was associated for seventeen years. This long-established club (it claimed Jacobite origins) met on alternate Fridays during the Cambridge term and was restricted to twelve members, who took turns to give a dinner. Housman joined in 1919, presumably as soon as a vacancy occurred, and was regular in his attendance. J. J. Thomson recalled that 'he was very seldom absent from their dinners . . . he usually . . . talked freely and, as might be expected, incisively . . . I always found him excellent company, and was very glad when I could sit next to him'.* (Benson, another member of The Family, was less appreciative of Housman's conversation: after a dinner in 1923 he confided to his diary, 'Housman . . . told me two of the most obscene French stories I have ever heard in my life – not funny, only abominable'*.) S. C. Roberts remembered the great care with which Housman always prepared his menus; a surviving specimen is of a lavishness nowadays almost unknown. Something of the atmosphere of The Family's dinners is conveyed by M. R. James's recollections* of a slightly earlier period: one of the members was a clergyman-scholar of the old school who made his way to Cambridge from his rural parish every other Friday

and, when it was his turn to provide the dinner, invariably
produced a swan. He sent invitations to R. C. Jebb in Greek verse,
and when they played whist after dinner would groan, 'Crazy!
Crazy! Seventy years have I played, and never a trump in my
hand!'

Three of the members of the club came to be numbered among
Housman's closer friends – though even his closer friends, in these
later years, were not very close. Andrew Gow, a classical scholar,
had become a Fellow of Trinity in 1911 and, after a period
teaching at Eton, returned there in 1925. Arthur Benson, already
referred to, was a member of a prominent and gifted family; he too
had taught at Eton, became a Fellow of Magdalene in 1904, and
became Master in 1915. Benson was the author of most of *The
Times*'s obituary of Housman, although he predeceased his subject
by eleven years – a joke Housman would have enjoyed. He was a
prolific and popular author; and, as if his daily stint of words for a
public eager to read his smoothly-phrased ruminations were not
enough, he was also a compulsive diarist – to the tune of nearly
five million words. The third was R. V. Laurence, another Fellow
of Trinity and tutor to the undergraduate princes (later George
VI and the Duke of Gloucester) when they were at the College in
1919–20. When Laurence died in 1934 Housman described him as
'one of my best boon-companions'.*

All of these relationships were long-lived, but none was very
profound. The most fully-documented is that with Benson, whose
diary has recently become available for consultation. Benson was
an unstable personality and his accounts of meetings with
Housman between 1911 and 1925 lack objectivity to a remarkable
degree: his judgments swing violently between approval and
hostility, and ought not to be taken too seriously. There are
occasional bursts of cordiality:

> Housman came to dine and was very pleasant . . . very friendly
> and companionable. People are afraid of him and his sharp
> tongue and he enjoys much respect – but he is really cordial and
> deprecatory. [May 1913]

> He is really both genial and goodhumoured when one knows
> him, and *quite* simple . . . [October 1913]

and there were rare moments of intimacy:

I had curiously intimate talk with Housman, about books and people. [November 1912]

But the majority of Benson's entries are severely critical. Like others, he is struck by the incongruity between the man and his reputation:

> Housman is very curious. His two public characters are passionate and rather macabre verse (Shropshire Lad) and very incisive criticism – in ordinary life he is a prim, old-maidish, rather second-rate, rather tired, rather querulous person. [November 1912]

One detects in Benson's attitude a touch, or more than a touch, of envy: his own career as the author of about sixty books brought him fame and wealth, but he knew very well that he had written nothing that enjoyed, as *A Shropshire Lad* did, the status of a modern classic; what is more, Housman was a scholar of the front rank, he himself no more than a belletrist. He obviously also resented the extent to which Housman was sought after as a guest:

> Why or how Housman is regarded as a social treat here I can never divine . . . Housman fairly genial. But *why* is he regarded as a desirable guest? Pure snobbishness. He can occasionally be persuaded to talk, but he sits prim and grim, and casts a chill over the table – no *ease*, nor is his wit very good.

The charge of snobbishness levelled against those who invited Housman rather than Benson to their dinner-tables is amusing, for Benson's trump card in the spacious privacy of his diary is to accuse Housman of low breeding:

> Housman showed himself inclined to correct everyone as to the details of their stories. He inspires a sort of terror, and I have no doubt would not be displeased to hear it . . . Housman does not mean to be offensive, but he's a common fellow, after all. [June 1912]

> Housman is a common little soul, who thinks that the don-epicure is a gentlemanly thing – it is not; it's the worst development of snobbish greediness. [late 1914]

Housman was so conscious of being in high company with Bishops and M.P.'s, that he was extremely amiable and tolerant. I felt that he was able both to gratify his sense of ambition and also to preserve an attitude of superior unworldliness. [April 1915]

this precise, formal, cautious little man . . . resentful, with the terror of deficiency in social equipment. [1923]

Some of these observations tell us more about Benson than about Housman, but the longest of the entries, a summing-up of Housman's character written towards the end of 1912, is worth quoting:

Housman was shy and quiet at first, but warmed up; and I did not form at all a favourable opinion of him. He looks rather attractive and he is shy and formal in manner – but as he got easier he got *vulgar*, I thought. He was censorious and seemed to delight in saying little bitter icy things about people. He was going off alone to Sicily and it seemed to me that he was proud of this, proud of saying that he could find no one really congenial enough to accompany him. I suspect him of being vain and fastidious, despising other people. I don't think he is quite a gentleman. He seems suspicious and acid. He pulled up O [liffe] R [ichmond] rather sharply for mixing up Stafford-shire and Shropshire – I think he meant to be agreeable and that made it rather pathetic, because he appeared to me to be sharp and unkind . . . Perhaps if one knew him better still, one might like him better; but I think he is petulant, small-minded, and vaguely disappointed with life. Perhaps it is that he can't write poetry any more, and that there is something pent-up in him which can't get out and turns sour. He interested me, because his cold trim and demure manner seems to conceal something pretentious and even disagreeable.

There are some shrewd touches here; and, when all due allowances have been made for Benson's hostility, his diary offers some vignettes of Housman's social life during this period that have the ring of truth. But the overall picture of Housman that emerges from his fluent pages – a very unattractive picture – may well be questioned, for it is unconfirmed by other witnesses during the same years. And without trivializing the notion of friendship it is scarcely possible to accept R. P. Graves's claim that the two men were close friends. There is no record of Housman's reactions to Benson, but they are not difficult to guess. His reference, after Benson's death, to 'our lamentable loss' has something perfunctory about it; the ·collective form of the phrase suggests that he thought of the Master of Magdalene as a member of a social group rather than an individual in his own right. If Housman had a friend at Cambridge, as distinct from a colleague or a fellow-diner (and it is doubtful whether he did), that man was not Benson.

The entertaining and exasperating figure of Arthur Benson has taken us into the twenties, and we need to return to Housman's first days in Cambridge. Soon after he took up the Professorship of Latin a change was made in its title. Benjamin Hall Kennedy had contributed five hundred pounds to the fund for its establishment 'on condition that his name should not be attached to the proposed Professorship'; but since he was now long dead the cause of modesty was deemed to have been sufficiently served, and the Senate agreed on 15 June to change the name to 'the Kennedy Professorship of Latin'. As holder of this office Housman's public duties were not onerous. He was mindful, however, that his first obligation was to pursue his studies, and he did so unremittingly to the end of his days. During the short Cambridge terms he lectured twice a week and, when necessary, attended meetings of the Faculty Board of Classics as an *ex officio* member. His other responsibilities seem to have been minimal. In a quarter of a century he examined for the tripos only twice, and only once did he supervise a research student.

He seems to have taken very readily to the change in the pattern of his working life after quitting University College, and as early as 1913 we find him complaining of examining duties as a tedious interruption of his proper business ('if you ever have to examine for University Scholarships you will find as I do that all one's leisure is fully occupied by wishing that one was dead'*). Having once taken on a task, however, he performed it with his customary punctiliousness. A revealing document now in Cambridge University Library refers to an application by a candidate for the degree of Doctor of Letters on the basis on an edition of the letters of Fronto. The veteran scholar Sir John Sandys had already reported favourably though rather perfunctorily: Housman's report, dated 17 January 1921, is anything but perfunctory: long and detailed, it shows that he had examined the edition very thoroughly. There is nothing half-hearted about his criticism: 'in style and diction', he observes, 'the translation does not often fall below mediocrity nor often rise above it: if it did, it would rise above Fronto',* and one feels that his severity is based on standards that he would apply unhesitatingly to anyone's work, including his own. His recommendation is that the degree should not be awarded.

Whenever possible, however, he kept clear of such time-consuming duties. In 1920 he refused the Public Oratorship, vacated by Sandys after more than forty years; it was an office that he would have discharged superbly, but it must inevitably have stolen time from his textual studies. Between those studies and his lectures, on the other hand, there was a direct link, for he lectured on textual criticism to those who had selected the literature option in Part II of the Classical Tripos – in other words, to advanced students with literary and linguistic rather than historical or philosophical interests. He dealt with such authors (mainly poets) as were prescribed for special study each year, and his method, like his manner, was austere: 'he simply dictated arguments for and against various readings'.* Put like that, the lectures could hardly sound duller to the layman; but to those with ears to hear they were a memorable intellectual experience – indeed, inspiring is not too strong a word. Apart from the material presented (and their composition involved an enormous amount of labour), Housman's standards of scholarly excellence could excite his listeners with an invigorating sense of what true learning is like and send them away with a model for their own efforts. Gow said that 'he had commonly a devoted if not very numerous class',* and some of those who attended have left on record their impressions of his teaching. He looked, wrote one, 'exactly like a coiled spring . . . the only person I have known who habitually – and so ominously – "looked down his nose"'.* D. S. Macnutt, who later (as 'Ximenes') turned his textual ingenuity to good account as a famous composer of crossword puzzles, describes Housman's treatment of latecomers:

> I attended every possible lecture of Housman's when I was up at Jesus: I remember especially his lectures on Martial VIII and IX . . . My only regret about that course is the fact that I

could not help arriving five minutes late from a lecture elsewhere, and his practice of stopping in the middle of a sentence, and continuing without repeating the beginning of the sentence after one had sat down, was a little daunting. Still, it was worth it.*

Not every listener became an admirer, however. F. L. Lucas, a man temperamentally very unlike Housman (though a great admirer of his poetry), detected a resemblance to Calvin preaching on predestination and was filled with 'rebellious repugnance':

> immaculate in his starched linen and icy in his impassive aloofness as the Pole Star, he seemed the awesome embodiment of a steely, mathematical precision; but his faith that *all* knowledge was precious, whether or not it served the slightest human use, revolted me then, as it revolts me still . . . I sensed something morbid and unhealthy in this formidable ascetic pressing into his own skin the harsh folds of his intellectual hair shirt.*

But J. Enoch Powell's testimony shows that Housman's teaching could provide for some an unforgettable intellectual and moral experience:

> The severity of Housman's presentation was the severity not of passionlessness but of suppressed passion, passion for true poetry and passion for truthfulness. For Housman textual criticism was the exercise of moral self-discipline. . . . Under the radiation of this display of a great critical mind in action, one's own powers, such as they might be, developed – above all, the spirit of bold but temperate self-reliance without which no criticism is possible.

Powell recalls a particular occasion:

> No one, I believe, ever heard Housman on Horace, *Epistles* 1.7.29, the passage where Bentley by conjecture restored *nitedula* (fieldmouse) in place of the nonsensical *volpecula* (little fox) of the manuscripts, without receiving the moral enlargement of a great sermon.*

Such recollections expose as ignorant or wilfully false Auden's dismissive line, 'Deliberately he chose the dryasdust'; there was nothing dryasdust about textual scholarship for Housman, and no-one with the faintest imaginative grasp of its excitements and rewards could suppose for one moment that there was.

Andrew Gow said that 'certainly nobody with tastes at all akin to his own could witness that easy command of the relevant learning, that lucid exposition and dispassionate judgment, without setting before himself a new standard of scholarship'. The standards Housman set himself did not relax with advancing years: rather than simply blowing the dust off old lectures, he worked at new ones to the very end, and only weeks before his death he wrote with pardonable pride, 'I hear that I am lecturing better than ever.'* The notes of some of his lecture-courses survive* and suggest that his style did not rule out wit. On a very few memorable occasions he would intrude an uncharacteristically personal note. The most famous of these is his reading, at the end of a lecture on Horace in May 1914, of the ode beginning 'Diffugere nives' and of his own translation (*MP* V): '"That," he said hurriedly, almost like a man betraying a secret, "I regard as the most beautiful poem in ancient literature" and walked quickly out of the room.'*

Neither Housman nor his audience can have realised that his reading of Horace's ode was a farewell to a civilisation that was about to vanish, or at any rate to be changed utterly; for that lecture must have been one of the last he gave before the outbreak of war during the long vacation of 1914. When, in 1935, Housman undertook to compose on behalf of 'the Chanceller, Masters, and Scholars of the University of Cambridge' an address of congratulation to George V on his quarter-century on the throne, he also found himself looking back on his own life at Cambridge during almost exactly the same period. He remarks, safely enough, in that address that 'the events of that reign, for greatness and moment, are such as have rarely been comprised within twenty-five years of human history';* yet momentous events in the public sphere had singularly little impact on his own life. This becomes strikingly, and somewhat disturbingly, evident when we consider his attitude to the Great War. The long epilogue to the Victorian age itself came to an end in August 1914, and very quickly Cambridge was 'completely transformed' and* 'normal undergraduate life almost came to an end'* except (in the phrase of the time) for 'infants, Indians and invalids'. In 1913–14 there had been 3676 undergraduates; within a short time only a handful remained, and, as S. C. Roberts said,

> the colleges were put to strange uses: they became barracks, hospitals, staff colleges, headquarters of cadet battalions; khaki was recognised as academic dress and war service as part qualification for a university degree; elderly professors became recruiting officers, special constables, postal censors.*

But not Housman, even though at fifty-five he was not so elderly. The general upheaval could not fail to impinge on his daily experience, both professional and domestic. In 1914, 113 students were successful in Part I of the Classical Tripos; by 1916 the number had dropped to seventeen, of whom ten were women. At the outbreak of hostilities the War Office asked for Nevile's Court at Trinity to be used as a temporary hospital, and the wounded soon began to arrive from the front: by 17 September it was 'a Hospital for more than two hundred beds, [with] nurses everywhere'.* New Court was occupied by officer cadets. As Housman wrote in the 1935 address, 'Our courts and cloisters welcomed the invasion of soldiers undergoing instruction in the necessary arts of war', and the stilted phrases – as if the war were being waged against Carthage rather than Germany – seem to betray an unbridgeable distance between the actuality and Housman's personal response to it. H. M. Butler, Master of Trinity, was an old man, old enough to be Housman's father; but he did what he could to raise the spirits of the wounded and each day took four privates out for a drive. There is nothing to suggest that Housman, famous as a poet of young men called away from their homes to suffer and die, ever went so far as to speak to one of these soldiers who had moved into his own home. In his references to the war there is what looks like an unattractive mixture of hardness and flippancy – attitudes that seem woefully ill-judged and insensitive when one remembers what was happening on the other side of the Channel. Consider the tone of the following in conjunction with their dates:

> The thirst for blood is raging among the youth of England. More than half the undergraduates are away, but mostly not at the front, because they all want to be officers. I am going out when they make me a Field Marshal.* [24 November 1914]

Of a planned trip to France:

> Hitherto I have always refused to go to the Riviera, but now is
> my chance, when the worst classes who infest it are away.*
> [7 March 1915]

He is so well pleased with the joke, such as it is, that he repeats it to
another correspondent on the same day:

> Providence, for my benefit, has cleared [the Riviera] of
> Germans. In its normal state I always refused to visit it.*

(It is startling to learn that he did indeed go, with Grant Richards,
on an Easter pleasure-jaunt to Nice via Dieppe and Paris.) At
such moments Housman seems uncomfortably to resemble the
civilians, safe in their beds, who are scarified in Siegfried
Sassoon's poems, were it not that something worse than witless
complacency seems involved – a heartless facetiousness.
'Whewell's Court is now a barracks', he wrote, 'and soldiers above
my ceiling practise step-dancing with a vigour which ought to be
prophylactic against frost-bite.'* Did he never stop to consider
that those young men might shortly be facing something worse
than frost-bite – or was the thought too painful for words and only
to be kept at bay by a feigned indifference?

On one occasion he dreamed the following couplet:

> Above the soldier's grave there twine
> The Woodbine and the Concubine*

and, whilst none of us is responsible for his dreams, none of us is
under an obligation to retail them as witticisms when they exhibit
such heartlessness – or appear to. And yet of course Housman was
not a heartless man, nor was he hard and flippant in the face of
suffering. It may be that a mechanism is operating analogous to
that which produced the ruthless rhymes circulated among his
family. The unfeeling manner conceals feelings to which he was
unwilling to give direct, naked expression. At its outset the war
moved him sufficiently to impel him to make the odd symbolic
gesture of sending his savings to the Chancellor of the Exchequer;
and when the time came for him to respond to personal rather
than general tragedy, he could do so very touchingly, as in the

letter of 5 October 1915, written to his sister after her son had been killed in action. (He also copied out for her his poem 'Illic Jacet' and sent it with the comment that the business of poetry is 'to harmonise the sadness of the universe'.*)

Most startling of all, and yet enlightening on the question of Housman's response to the Great War, is his observation much later that it 'cannot have made much change in the opinions of any man of imagination'.* This flies in the face of, for instance, Paul Fussell's persuasive thesis in *The Great War and Modern Memory* that fundamental perceptions and associations were radically and permanently altered by the unprecedented experience of mass conscription, trench warfare, poison gas and other now-familiar horrors. But the remark makes sense in relation to Housman's own longstanding convictions. Those with a belief in progress were shocked, dismayed and depressed by the war; for one who 'expected trouble' and believed that life contained 'much less good than ill', the European cataclysm could come as no surprise. What it did do was to present a challenge to a man's personal conduct: he who has long ago come to terms with the worst life can do will not flinch or panic, for that would be to admit a kind of defeat. To persist with one's plans to holiday in France whilst its soil is being drenched with young men's blood may be less a sign of stark insensibility than a stoic refusal to be intimidated by the well-known horrors of the world. When in 1916 Housman cancelled his French holiday – the Dieppe route he had used in the previous year was now closed, and the Southampton-Le Havre crossing threatened to be tedious – it was for purely practical reasons and 'not on account of mines or torpedoes, which I despise as much as ever'.*

In the same year the internal affairs of Trinity College were thrown into turmoil by a *cause célèbre* involving one of its members. Bertrand Russell had been appointed a college lecturer in 1910 with the prospect of election to a fellowship after five years. His involvement in pacifist activities led to a conviction under the Defence of the Realm Act and a fine of a hundred pounds; the College Council thereupon decreed (11 July) that 'he be removed from his lectureship'. Butler, the Master, wrote that 'I never discharged a more painful public duty than in taking action against B. Russell, and I was never more clear as to the necessity in the interests of the College'.* Some of the Fellows were less sure, and twenty-one of them remonstrated against this decision, including Adrian, Broad, Cornford, Eddington, Gow, Hardy and Whitehead; the decision was not, however, revoked. After the war, twenty-seven Fellows signed a letter urging the College Council to reinstate Russell. Housman did not sign it, but his decision was not lightly taken:

> Russell is a great loss to the College, not merely for his eminence and celebrity, but as an agreeable and even charming person to meet; on the question of conscription I agreed with him at the time, though I now see I was wrong, and I did not feel sure that the action of the Council was wise, though his behaviour was that of a bad citizen. So far therefore I am nearly neutral: what prevents me from signing your letter is Russell's taking his name off the books of the College. After that piece of petulance he ought not even to want to come back. I cannot imagine myself doing so; and my standard of conduct is so very low that I feel I have a right to condemn those who do not come up to it . . . I am afraid . . . that if Russell did return he would meet with rudeness from some Fellows of the College, as I know he did before he left. This ought not to be, but the world is as God made it.*

With the end of the war Cambridge ceased to be a barracks and a military hospital and reverted to its pre-war function – but not, in all respects, to its pre-war nature. The Edwardian Cambridge of schoolboy-undergraduates, caught in Forster's *The Longest Journey*, gave way to a student body which included many demobilised servicemen; and the pressure of demands for change was quickly felt. The history of the post-war years is a record of shattered traditions, constitutional and academic. A Royal Commission set up in 1919 reported in 1922 and recommended State support for the ancient universities; the effect was to diminish the power of the colleges and to increase that of the University. The demand for full membership of the University for women, which had been rejected in 1897, was revived and led in 1921 to a compromise whereby they could be granted the titles of degrees. The Ph.D. degree was instituted in 1919, largely in order to attract American students who in an earlier generation would have betaken themselves to Germany; and a new Cambridge species, the research student, came into existence. 1919 also saw the first examination for the English Tripos under the new regulations, English having hitherto been merely an option in the Modern and Medieval Languages Tripos. As a result Classics found itself competing for students with English and with other 'new' subjects such as History. Compulsory Greek for 'Little-Go' (the Previous or matriculation examination) was abolished in the same year of change, 1919. At Trinity College new statutes were introduced in the twenties which made the life tenure of fellowships no longer automatic and set a retiring age for the Mastership.

Among the founding fathers of the English Tripos were brilliant young classicists such as F. L. Lucas and E. M. W. Tillyard, and it seems possible that the approach to classical studies which Housman so impressively and influentially embodied was responsible for some of the desertions. Tillyard, who had gone up to Jesus College before Housman arrived on the Cambridge scene, had found the Classical Tripos 'a mainly disillusioning experience'.* Recalling his pre-war classes, he wrote:

> 'Literature' in the Classical Tripos of those days was overshadowed by the superstition that textual criticism was the noblest kind of scholarship and altogether superior to the acts of literary assessment to which the settling of textual questions was supposed to lead.

He cannot have found much comfort in Housman's declaration in the 1911 inaugural that 'of the duties of a Latin Chair, literary criticism forms no part'. But the times were changing, and even among those who remained faithful to classics there was some discontent with the 'minute and pedantic studies'* which Housman unashamedly so described and unrepentantly practised. At least one of those who attended his inaugural lecture had 'disapproval writ large on his face':* this was T. R. Glover, whose disapproval was not solely due to the fact that he was a disappointed applicant for the Latin Chair. Glover's view of classical studies was entirely different from Housman's: he believed that the study and teaching of literature were important because of its value as an Arnoldian 'criticism of life', and that the teacher's role was to communicate literary appreciation. His biographer tells us that after the lecture he 'noted in his diary the worst of Housman's heresies', and he can have had no shortage of material. Glover was not alone, for a generation was emerging

1(b)   Alfred Housman at the age of eighteen

1(a)   Alfred, aged 7, with his brother Robert, aged 5

2 Family chart (incomplete) drawn up by Housman in 1908

3 The crew of St John's College, Oxford, 1880 (Moses Jackson is on the extreme right)

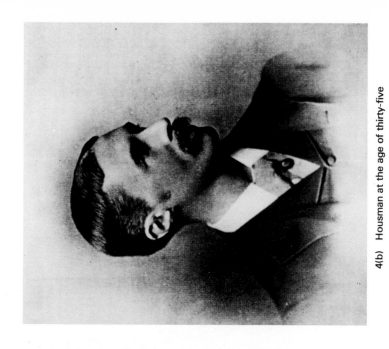

4(b) Housman at the age of thirty-five

4(a) Moses Jackson in later life

5   Caricature of Housman at University College by Mortimer (later Sir Mortimer) Wheeler

THURSDAY 21 [141—224]

FRIDAY 22 [142—223]
Ember Day

[Sunday 1876, 10.45 p.m., said good bye]

SATURDAY 23 [143—222] 21st Week
Ember Day

45

THURSDAY 18 [169—196]

FRIDAY 19 [170—195]

Wrote to him by today's mail.

SATURDAY 20 [171—194] 25th Week

53

7(b) Housman at seventy (his passport photograph)

7(a) Housman in about 1911

8 Housman's last correspondence: a postcard to his sister (Katharine Symons) written five days before his death (the date and day have been added in another hand)

that would conceive of classical studies, and literary studies of all kinds, in very different terms from Housman's.

Between the wars two classical chairs were founded: that they were in Ancient Philosophy and Classical Archaeology indicates in what directions the tide had turned. Preoccupation with the establishing of sound texts was giving place to a more comprehensive conception of classical learning, involving a broader range of aspects of ancient civilisation. *The Golden Bough* was becoming more central to the student's thinking than the editions of Bentley and Porson; Aeschylus was becoming recognised not merely as the author of tragedies whose text presents difficult and fascinating problems, but as a starting-point for the investigation of the origins of Greek religion and its place in Greek culture. Nor was this simply a change of fashion or the chafing of young men against orthodoxy. There was a not unreasonable feeling that satisfactory texts now existed for the major classical authors – that, in a word, textual criticism had had its day. What had still been a legitimate enterprise for a young scholar when Housman was at Oxford had, forty or fifty years later, lost its centrality; and he has been blamed for diverting able students into the field of textual criticism (by the power of his example, that is; never by personal exhortation) when their talents might have been more profitably employed in other areas of classical study. (He has also been blamed for the opposite offence of intimidating students by his severity so that they fled Latin for Greek.)

Notwithstanding all this, he continued to work and publish as he had done from the start, and to lecture on those authors who lent themselves to the textual critic's labours. But if he had to some extent been left behind by events, it must be stressed that he continued to possess for a few students, an Arnoldian remnant, the inspiring power of a model. He sought no converts and shunned disciples; as Gow said, 'he held no Seminar and established no school of Latin scholars in Cambridge, and those who sat at his feet came away rather with new ideals and new standards of scholarship than with specific impulses to undertake this or that piece of research'.* Not only what he said about Martial or Juvenal, but what he unassertively but unforgettably *was*: this is what his students remembered for the rest of their lives.

The routine inescapably attaching to academic life – the year regularly parcelled into terms and vacations, the small climaxes

as a lecture-course reaches its planned conclusion or another
generation of students sit their final examinations – hardly makes
for lively biographical narrative. But a scholar needs routine, and
in Housman's case the academic rhythms were supplemented by
the routines he established and maintained in his personal life. A
man dedicated to study needs a constant framework for his day
and his year, lest attention be distracted from weightier matters
by petty decisions: if, for instance, he always dresses in the same
style, in defiance of changing fashions, he will be spared from
wasting precious minutes in wondering what to wear. Housman's
habits came to seem mildly eccentric only because, like many, he
clung in old age to the habits of youth, continuing to wear suits
and boots of a style which had become antiquated, and to use a
hip-bath (his sister had to see that one was provided when they
stayed together at a hotel).

As a celibate whose domestic arrangements were in the expert
hands of college officers and servants, he was liberated from the
petty concerns that trouble or console most of us; he could hardly
otherwise have accomplished so much. But he clearly needed the
reassurance of a fixed timetable for his life in order to keep at bay
the menace of a social and emotional vacuum: where other men's
lives are punctuated by family anxieties and celebrations, measles
and birthdays, the bachelor don tended to accumulate self-
defensively certain rituals and ceremonies which, no matter how
slight in themselves, gave stability and order to his existence.
Thus (a trivial but suggestive example) Housman and Stephen
Gaselee, the scholar and bibliographer, met once a year to eat a
stew of tripe and oysters washed down with stout; and indeed it
was better than not meeting at all, though some will find such
customs oddly formal and unspontaneous. Among the members
of his own family Alfred had been, at least since Oxford days, the
loner: Laurence and Clemence lived together for a lifetime in a
very close relationship, Basil and Kate had both married.
Although he kept in touch with the others, the bond does not seem
to have been very close.

There was no lack of conviviality in Housman's life; even
during vacations there was no day that he was obliged to spend
entirely alone; but among all his acquaintances there was none
who could be called a friend in the deeper sense of the word. In any
case that was a word reserved for one man. There is something
sadly significant in the name of the dining-club frequented by

Housman, 'The Family'; at the same time a club is tolerant and undemanding as a real family is not, and its regular meetings and guaranteed companionship clearly meant a good deal to him. His last social act was to attend one of its dinners, though he was past eating; in his will he left his wine to the members.

Housman's arrangement of his days in Cambridge allowed for the interruption of work by the sociable evening gatherings at Trinity high table and by an afternoon walk of several miles. This latter custom – his milder version of the donnish tradition of closing one's books in order to climb mountains – was made famous by his account in the 1933 Leslie Stephen Lecture of his experiences of poetic composition. He also speaks there of 'looking at things around me and following the progress of the seasons', and his letters contain many precise references to the appearance of leaf and blossom and the eccentricities of the Cambridge climate. (Birds and animals, it seems, held no appeal for him: like people, but unlike flowers and trees, they are apt to make demands as well as suffering attention.) He kept scrupulous records and enjoyed making comparisons across the years: in the fine spring of 1933 he was able to observe that 'I have known certainly two better springs, 1893 and 1894.'* Cambridge is not the best place in the world for walking, but he contrived to vary his routine to the extent of setting off on different days in different directions. One walk took him along King's Parade, 'looking neither to right nor to left'* (as an observer recalls), towards Trumpington, past the nursing home where he would die; another favourite walk took him to the Coton footpath, whence he would return through the splendid grounds of St John's College. On one occasion this habit led him to snub T. R. Glover, a Fellow of St John's between whom and Housman no love was lost:

> They were joint examiners for some prize essay and Glover, meaning to be helpful, said to Housman, 'Don't bother to put it in the post when you have read it: just drop it in my rooms as you pass through John's on your afternoon walk'. Housman – so Glover told me – was furious. 'How dare you make such a suggestion', he said; 'you have been spying on me. My private life is my own affair'. And he sent the essay through the post!*

Housman's irritation, gleefully recounted by Glover, will of course have lost nothing in the telling. His appearance on these walks is described by Dr Woods:

> His favourite afternoon walk took him past the Botanic Gardens where he could be seen, clutching a walking stick and attired in a nondescript grey suit, elastic-sided boots, high stiff single collar and close-fitting cap with a button top, like a schoolboy's.*

Any acquaintances he encountered were passed by ungreeted, for he was out for exercise, not conversation.

As with the day, so with the year. The continental visits which, from the turn of the century, had become a regular feature of the revolving year for Housman were continued after the move to Cambridge. Between 1911 and 1935 he travelled abroad at least once each year except in 1916–18. France was still his favourite destination and in later years the only one, but there were also a number of visits to Venice (the last in 1926) and one in the Easter vacation of 1912 to Sicily. (A winter visit to Egypt in 1934 was planned but cancelled; apart from the trip to Constantinople in 1904 he never ventured outside Europe.) His habit was to break up the Long Vacation by absences from Cambridge at both ends of the summer. In 1913, for instance, he was in Paris and Normandy in June and back in Normandy at the end of August; in 1919 he spent a fortnight in the Cotswolds in June, in July was back in Cambridge and had 'settled down to work',* but set off for France at the beginning of September, having completed a major project and dispatched it to the publisher. Sometimes he went abroad during the Easter vacation. In France he would customarily spend a few days in Paris and then tour some provincial region with the aid of a hired car and driver. From 1920 he usually crossed to Paris by air; he showed an unexpected schoolboyish delight in the new game of flying, and his letters contain some vivid glimpses of the days when going up in an aeroplane was still an adventure:

> on the return journey we were two hours late in starting because the machine required repairs, having been damaged on the previous day by a passenger who butted his head through the window to be sick. My chief trouble is that what I now want is no longer a motor and a chauffeur but an aeroplane and a tame pilot, which I suppose are more expensive.*

And he was vain, this elderly don, of his own adventurousness: legend has it, not improbably, that he would on occasion astonish his colleagues at Trinity by casually remarking at dinner that the food was inferior to the lunch he had eaten that day at Maxim's in Paris.*

Housman's most recent biographer suggests that he travelled abroad 'in search of illicit pleasures';* and, predictably, the titbit was gratefully seized by reviewers (becoming, in the hands of one of them, 'the annual holiday for sex in Paris'*), to be shared by readers who will never trouble to look at the evidence for themselves. Of such stuff are legends made. If Housman's French holidays were no more than sexual escapades, it seems odd that he should have spent much of his time pottering around small cathedral towns, where this variety of pleasure must have been hard if not impossible to come by. In any case there is evidence that he formed in France less casual and less sordid associations than have been suggested.

A week before he left for Paris at the end of July 1923 he wrote to Grant Richards, whom he was planning to meet there, that 'I probably should not be free in the evenings but should be during the day'.* This seems to me to suggest not so much an anticipated debauch (for if so, why 'probably'?) as the expectation of regular meetings with someone not free during the day. Richards says of another occasion when they were in Paris together that 'Housman after dinner went off to keep some engagement'.* In 1932 Housman is more explicit: he is to be in Paris but, he tells Richards, he 'cannot offer you anything of an invitation, for I shall have a friend with me who would not mix with you nor you with him'.* 'Friend' was not a word Housman used lightly or often, and the implication is of a relationship of some standing.

What is in question is no mere pick-up but a companion with whom he corresponded and whom he arranged to meet in advance, for in June 1933 we find him writing of being 'disappointed of a companion for France in August';* happily the disappointment does not last, for in August he is touring that country with 'a French companion'.* In these last years there is a notable access of frankness, for the young Frenchman's existence is no longer a secret confided only to the easy-going Grant Richards: to Withers he is described as 'a French companion, though not one of much education . . . though amiable, he may be bored';* to his sister Katharine he is referred to as 'a nice young

man, not much educated, who regards me as a benefactor'.*
Whether it was the same helpful companion who took such good
care of him when he met with a slight accident in Lyons in 1935* –
and the same who wrote to Laurence a few weeks after Housman's
death to ask for money, saying that he had been told he would be
remembered in Housman's will – matters little. It is clear enough
that the relationships Housman formed in France were not
exclusively (if at all) nasty, brutish and short – though this is not
to say, of course, that they did not include a sexual element.

I had better say quickly that my concern is not to suggest, for
whatever reason, that Housman's sexual longings were never
satisfied. They may well have been; but the question cannot be
settled with such crude certainty as some have supposed.
E. M. Forster expressed the hope that Housman tasted of the
stolen waters he recommended so ardently to others;* but our
business is not to hope but to determine what is likely to have
happened or not to have happened, to distinguish as dispassion-
ately as possible what is or may be true from what may be or must
be untrue. This is the place to raise also the question of Andrea,
the Venetian gondolier. Mr Graves argues – at least he does not
argue, for there is no evidence on which to base an argument, but
he chooses to believe – that Housman had a 'love-affair'* with
Andrea which lasted for several years, but that by 1908 he was
'falling out of love with him'.* Perhaps; on the other hand,
perhaps not. The known facts are few and simple. Housman first
visited Venice in 1900, arriving there 'on a romantic evening after
sunset',* as he recalled a quarter of a century later. Soon afterwards he must have engaged Andrea's services as gondolier, for he
is mentioned in a letter to Lucy Housman – a context which seems
to suggest either a remarkable degree of coolness or a total absence
of feelings of guilt and shame. Andrea was employed on
subsequent visits to Venice and became 'my gondolier'.*

The only other references to Andrea are in two letters to
Katharine Symons written in 1926, and in the posthumously
published poem beginning 'Far known to sea and shore' (*MP* 44).
In June 1926 Housman made a brief visit to Venice 'where my
poor gondolier says he is dying, and wants to see me again'.* It
was not, after all, a death-bed reunion, for Andrea survived to
enjoy Housman's generosity for another four years. It needs a
good deal of determination to detect a romantic motivation in
Housman's last visit to this old retainer, a sick man now nearly

fifty years old; but even in his prime Andrea cannot have been a figure of high romance, for one of his eyes had been kicked out by a horse. There seems to me to be a touch of the *grand seigneur* in Housman's prose references to Andrea, but nothing at all of the lover or ex-lover; the failure to visit Venice after 1908 makes sense as the disinclination of an aging man to undertake a long and tiring journey, without the need to invoke a waning love-affair; and the brief last visit (actually a side-trip from a visit to Paris) can plausibly be seen as an act of *noblesse oblige*. On the flight back from Paris Housman met E. V. Lucas, the essayist, and told him – with, one suspects, a mildly snobbish pride – that he had been sitting at the bedside of a gondolier who had asked for him; he added, also with pride, that it was his seventeenth flight.*

As for the poem, it can be read as 'a poem about his gondolier'* only by distortion. It is not even superficially a poem about Andrea, who is mentioned only near the end of the poem: exactly four words are devoted to him. Superficially, it is a poem about Venice; more profoundly, it is Housman's farewell to his own past, with a prose counterpart in a moving but quite unsentimental passage in the second letter to Kate. In that letter, after a cool dismissal of Andrea ('I suppose he will go steadily down hill'*), the tone suddenly grows warmer as Housman's feelings become more than merely conventional:

> I was surprised to find what pleasure it gave me to be in Venice again. It was like coming home, when sounds and smells which one had forgotten stole upon one's senses; and certainly there is no place like it in the world: everything there is better in reality than in memory. I first saw it on a romantic evening after sunset in 1900, and I left it on a sunshiny morning, and I shall not go there again.

Nor did he; and he was understandably annoyed when Andrea's relatives tried to sponge on him. Mr Graves sees the Campanile as a phallic symbol;* but Housman did not invent it, and there are times when a tower is just a tower.

Naturally none of this *proves* that Housman did not join Andrea in bed as well as in his gondola; and if I have seemed unduly sceptical or dismissive it is in necessary reaction against the fantasies of Mr Graves, who has been tempted into making biographical bricks without straw. (His method is neatly illustrated by one of his illustrations, 'A Venetian Canal' – did Housman once look at it, or fall into it? we are not told – and by his speculation, in the absence of any record of Housman's feelings as he explored Venice, that 'perhaps' he felt the same as Theodore Dreiser did when *he* explored Venice.) We cannot be sure either that Andrea was Housman's lover or that he was not; and even if we regard Housman's 'illicit pleasures' as more likely than unlikely (which I do), we cannot give them a local habitation and a name without crossing the ill-guarded frontier separating biography from romantic fiction. But a quiet agnosticism holds no attractions for some, who make it their business to propagate a colourful legend which, at second and third hand, soon passes for established fact.

It is true enough that Venice was a favourite resort for English homosexuals: sexual relations between men had been legalized in Italy in 1891, and John Addington Symonds and 'Baron Corvo', among others, made full use of the Venetian homosexual underworld. Symonds (who boldly brought *his* gondolier, Angelo Fusato, to England) was described by Swinburne soon after his death as 'the Platonic amorist of blue-breeched gondoliers who is now in Aretino's bosom'.* Housman had an interest in Corvo's writings, and was acquainted with Horatio Brown, Symonds' friend and biographer. But there were and are other reasons for visiting Venice, and the other reasons may have been Housman's reasons. We know that he was acquainted with the Parisian *bains de vapeur*, which were meeting-places for homosexuals (but not, of course, only that); and one wonders whether it was just guesswork on his part that masochism is 'cheaper to indulge'* than sadism (the phrase occurs in an interesting letter to Edmund Gosse mainly concerned with Swinburne). But wondering is about all we *can* do unless we see fit to indulge a taste for fiction; and in that case the only limits are those of the imagination. Housman *might* have been Jack the Ripper: the dates at least fit: at any rate, we cannot prove that he was not; and for some this seems to be sufficient.

What is certain is that Housman took advantage of his sojourns in the more permissive atmosphere of Paris to stock up on pornographic literature, of which he came to possess a choice collection in several languages. A reference to Swinburne's *Whippingham Papers* as 'sold in Paris to Anglo-Saxons'* speaks for itself. This flagellatory classic, his copy of which Housman lent on one occasion to Gosse, exemplifies the bias of Housman's private library of *curiosa*. When he died, Housman's library was sold by Blackwell's on Laurence's instructions; but two groups of material were for different reasons excluded, and were presented by Laurence to Cambridge University Library. One was a collection of classical pamphlets, presumably of negligible value; the other about fifty titles on sexual perversion.* Some examples are: Colman's poem *The Rodiad* in a private reprint (1898) of the 1820 edition; A. Eulenberg's *Sadismus und Masochismus* (1902); Aretino's *Capricciosi* (1660); Cleland's *Fanny Hill* (Paris edition of 1900); Pierre Guénolé's *L'étrange passion: la flagellation dans les moeurs d'aujourd'hui* (1904); H. Rau's *Der Sadismus in der Armee* (1904); and *Dialogus* (1926), one of seventy-five copies privately printed 'for subscribers only' of a homosexual idyll in Latin by P. G. Bainbrigge, minor poet and former scholar of Trinity. The Library did not catalogue the books as a collection, and apart from the occasional neat correction of a misprint there is nothing in them to indicate that they ever belonged to Housman.

His taste in pornography, as in other matters, was discriminating: although *Lady Chatterley's Lover* 'did not inflame my passions to any great extent', he found it 'much more wholesome than Frank Harris or James Joyce'.* (Had he, one wonders, glimpsed Lawrence across the table at Trinity when Bertrand Russell took the latter to dine there is 1915?) Of Baron Corvo's homosexual letters from Venice, on the other hand, he commented that 'I have been more amused with things written in urinals.'* A curious wedding of his scholarly and salacious tastes was the learned article 'Praefanda', written in Latin, which investigates the use made by Roman poets of indecent words; already in proof, it was turned down by the *Classical Quarterly* when the Board of Management raised objections, and published in 1931 in a German journal. Housman, who might justifiably have been annoyed, found the episode amusing; and although the article represents a perfectly legitimate scholarly enterprise, one suspects also an element of impishness – a desire to *épater les savants*. The same motive prompted him to write to Sir Henry Stuart-Jones, who was at work revising Liddell and Scott's Greek lexicon, pointing out that the Greek term for a sexual perversion had been wrongly defined in earlier editions of the lexicon and by other scholars, and explaining what it really meant.* To his letter he added the postscript, 'To-day, by the way, is the feast of the

Holy Innocents.' Truth, however, did not prevail, and the revised dictionary took no account of Housman's comments.

Apart from continental holidays and family visits, Housman's social life sometimes took him outside Cambridge. He frequently spent weekends at the homes of friends such as Grant Richards, Percy Withers and William Rothenstein. In 1911 he visited the poet Wilfrid Blunt at his Sussex home, Newbuildings Place, for the weekend. Blunt found him 'a typical Cambridge don', though he had only just arrived in Cambridge, 'prim in his manner, silent and rather shy, conventional in dress and manner, learned, accurate, and well-informed'.* He 'had a "disconcerting way of refusing to smile" when anything funny was said, even when he saw the joke – "I suppose dons are like that", remarked Blunt'.* He was willing to discuss his poems but 'refused absolutely' to read them aloud. Blunt liked him, and they sat up until midnight telling ghost stories. Francis Meynell, another guest, also recalled the occasion: 'very pleasant talk with A. E. Housman and our host and Desmond MacCarthy'.* On his single visit to Scotland in 1931, however, Housman fitted less happily into the assembled company, and the painter Henry Tonks found him 'very precisely dressed, and looking shy and restrained in a group of sporting men and women who had not yet changed'. Housman and Tonks took long walks together over the moors, 'Housman as usual in dark clothes and elastic-sided boots'.*

It was an age when a little eccentricity was thought appropriate to a don, and Housman may at times have deliberately played up to what was expected of him. Certainly in his *obiter dicta* he was not innocent of a wish to scandalize: he would no doubt have been delighted to learn that those with a sense of humour less well developed than his own have sometimes taken at face value remarks made in a spirit of fun or teasing. Hence, for example, a reputation for misogyny has been constructed on the basis of some of his observations but is difficult to reconcile with his long list of feminine friendships from Sophie Becker onwards. As usual, friendship for Housman did not imply an unstinted giving of oneself, a sharing of confidences; and some might think his version of it a poor thing at best. But there are plenty of signs that the man who once spoke of 'the deplorable sex'* enjoyed the company of women and could win their affection as well as their respect. Many a relationship begun in awe and trepidation grew into an appreciation of the human qualities not far beneath the austere surface: the 'keep off' signs, once challenged by love rather than mere curiosity, were soon thrown away.

Joan Thomson, daughter of the Master of Trinity, in her sensitive and perceptive little memoir found Housman capable of 'emotion terrifying in its strength'; she observed that though he was impatient of conventional tokens of friendship and would cut his acquaintances dead when he passed them in the street, 'if genuine affection and sympathy were offered him . . . Housman responded in full and gave unexpected proofs of deep feeling'.* Another acquaintance, the American actress Mary Anderson (Mrs de Navarro), wrote: 'I never heard Housman say an unkind word – even about people who had the reputation for being tiresome',* a tribute that his professional colleagues might have found it hard to believe, but which may have been true for all that. He got on well with his brother Basil's wife Jeannie and with the wives of his male friends such as Platt, Richards, Rothenstein and Withers. R. W. Chambers noted the 'reserved, chivalrous friendliness which marked his relation with the womenkind of the men he really loved'.* Most of the time, it seems, Housman inhabited unreluctantly the masculine world of work and controversy, food and wine, donnish scandal and bawdy stories; but he welcomed, especially in his later years, the relaxation afforded by occasional excursions into the feminine world of attentive and affectionate sympathy. Behind it, perhaps, was the need to inhabit, however briefly, a home – something that, in the usual sense, he had not enjoyed since his youth. It makes for a bolder portrait to call him, as Withers does, 'an avowed misogynist';* but it hardly fits the evidence

6   Cambridge II

The great popularity of *A Shropshire Lad* led to frequent enquiries about a successor and frequent rumours of its impending appearance. One persistent enquirer was the young American Witter Bynner, whose long-distance enthusiasm Housman permitted himself to find beguiling. His first letter to Bynner, in 1903, parries the question with good-tempered irony:

> I wrote the book when I was thirty-five, and I expect to write another when I am seventy, by which time your enthusiasm will have had time to cool.*

Seven years later he tells Bynner:

> The other day I had the curiosity to reckon up the complete pieces, printed and unprinted, which I have written since 1896, and they only come to 300 lines, so the next volume appears to be some way off. In barrenness, at any rate, I hold a high place among English poets, excelling even Gray.*

Yet, as this remark makes clear, he was writing poems from time to time, though not in any quantity; something comparable to the 'continuous excitement' of 1895 would be needed to stimulate the flow. Three hundred lines in fourteen years is not a much higher average than twenty lines – one or two poems – a year; and this may have been no mere modest understatement, for in 1912 he refused Edward Marsh a contribution to *Georgian Poetry* with the remark that 'none even of my few unpublished poems have been written within the last two years',* and at the beginning of 1920 he tells Withers, 'Last year I think I wrote two poems, which is more than the average, but not much towards a new volume.'* It was admittedly 'not much'; but at least a 'new volume' was in his mind, if only as a fairly remote possibility. Later in the year comes the bombshell, in the final sentence of a letter to Grant Richards mainly concerned with the publication of his edition of the fourth book of Manilius:

> Suppose I produced a new volume of poetry, in what part of the year ought it to be published, and how long would it take after the MS left my hands?*

Housman must have been aware of his publisher's eagerness to bring out another volume of verse under his name, and have enjoyed anticipating his astonishment at the casual-artful afterthought. But four months later Richards' hopes were dashed:

> 'My new book' does not exist, and possibly never may. Neither your traveller nor anybody else must be told that it is even contemplated. What I asked you was a question inspired by an unusually bright and sanguine mood, which has not at present been justified.*

That last sentence seems a little evasive: it was not like Housman to act impetuously on a passing mood. And not much more than another year passed before he told Richards

> It is now practically certain that I shall have a volume of poems ready for the autumn . . .*

The above record contains some curious features. One of them is the concern with timing: 'How long would it take . . . ?' Housman was not as a rule in any haste to see his work in print, and it seems out of character for him to enquire about the publishing schedule of a book he has not yet written 'and possibly never may'. An explanation would be that he had, or believed he might soon have, some strong reason for wanting to bring out a book at that stage of his life, and that in such a case time would be of the essence. It seems certain, too, that 1921 and the early part of 1922 saw a dramatic increase in his rate of poetic production; for the book that is not even on the horizon at the beginning of 1921 is 'practically certain' to be ready (which for Housman means that it is virtually finished) by the spring of 1922. (Of the poems included in the 1922 volume for which dates have been proposed, a good handful belong to the early part of 1922 and a number of others were old poems revised or completed at about this time.)

How can we account for the sudden increase in Housman's output that enabled *Last Poems* to appear when it did, and for the quite uncharacteristic hurry to get it into print? He had continued to exchange letters with Moses Jackson, not frequently, one must assume, but often enough for the correspondence to be described as regular. Since he had become godfather to Moses' youngest son Gerald, his role in the Jackson family may have modulated from that of old college chum to adopted uncle. Although the godfatherly function is not one for which Housman might have been expected to feel much enthusiasm, he must have valued this link; he certainly took his responsibilities seriously, helping in due course to pay Gerald's way through medical school. Towards the end of 1920 (and here the biographer permits speculation to edge its way along a limb that may not bear its weight), he may have learned that his friend was ill. Whether or not he knew any details, he was well enough aware that they were both men in their sixties – old men by the measure of their generation – and that for at least one of them the end might well be near. This would account for the otherwise inexplicable flash of interest in 'a new volume of poetry'; reassuring news in a later letter might explain the frigid withdrawal ('does not exist, and possibly never may'). But by the spring of 1922 Housman was not only writing poems hard but virtually promising the volume 'for the autumn' – and rapid publication was indeed essential, for he must have known by now that Moses was seriously ill. He was in fact suffering from stomach cancer.

The manuscript was sent to Richards on 19 June, but the poems were still to be arranged in their final order. The affair was to be kept very quiet; however, two or three friends (Ker, Mackail, and perhaps also Pollard) were asked to read the collection. Housman held himself ready to take their judgment into account if they found any poem unworthy, but in a letter to Mackail he was candid about the use he would make of advice:

> I want you to note anything which strikes you as falling below my average, or as open to exception for any other reason ... You need not be afraid of stifling a masterpiece through a temporary aberration of judgment, as I am consulting one or two other people, and shall not give effect to a single opinion unless it coincides with my own private suspicions.*

Proofs were read in August; the book was published on 19 October; and on the morning of publication, forty-five years almost to the day from their first meeting, he wrote his last letter to Mo, to accompany a presentation copy of the new volume. The letter survives in private hands but (alas for the reader of this book!) may not be reproduced, quoted or paraphrased; there can be no harm, though, in saying that it is a very moving document and contains the most self-revealing sentence in all Housman's correspondence. He was properly proud of his own eminence: *The Times* had not only reviewed the book but devoted a leader to it (how many slim volumes of verse have received a similar accolade?), and the cuttings were enclosed for Jackson to peruse on his sick-bed. There is an unexpressed contrast between the fame of one and the other's obscurity that might have made for awkwardness; but between the lines runs a clear message: what has been done is, first and foremost, an offering to their friendship. Since one of them is dying it is, inevitably, *Last Poems*.

D. H. Lawrence had at least been able to press *The White Peacock* into the hands of his dying mother. For Housman there was only the bleak last duty of addressing the little packet to British Columbia and dropping it into the letter-box. Book, letter and cuttlings cannot have reached Vancouver much before the end of the year; and Moses died on 14 January 1923. Housman's anxiety during the winter months as he waited for the slow-travelling news must have been considerable; perhaps that is partly why the success of *Last Poems* gave him, as he wrote to Withers just before Christmas, only 'a faint pleasure'.* By March he must have known of Mo's death, and he had himself fallen ill, 'as ill as I have ever been in the course of a fairly healthy life'.* The carbuncles that plagued him may have originated at least partly in his emotional state. The trouble dragged on for months; he took a seaside holiday during the Easter vacation, but in July he was still undergoing treatment and in August was 'better, but not well'.*

Even though thoughts of Moses' suffering and death marred whatever gratification Housman might have derived from the success of *Last Poems* (as his mother's death had marred his twelfth birthday and Adalbert's the first term at University College), that success was beyond question. False modesty not being a form of hypocrisy he practised, Housman had suggested a first printing of 10,000 copies; Richards, who was footing the bill, had intended 5000 but had been discouraged by the booksellers and settled for

4000. It was Housman who was proved right by the event, for all 4000 were ordered before publication and a second printing was at once put in hand. By mid-morning on the day of publication, as Housman sat writing to Moses, the Cambridge bookshops were sold out. Four further printings followed in November, and by the end of the year 21,000 copies had been printed. Apart from *The Times*'s fifth leader, Housman received the tribute of that other British institution, *Punch*:* Bert Thomas's cartoon (for which Housman had declined to supply a photograph) appeared on 25 October and a parody by E. V. Knox on 24 January. Sydney Cockerell lost no time in obtaining the manuscript for the Fitzwilliam Museum. Meanwhile, *A Shropshire Lad* was selling an average of more than 3000 copies a year; the War had given fresh point to Housman's proleptic preoccupation with the soldier's lot, and at the same time his red-coats belonged to an age not indeed historically very distant but lending itself much more readily to idealism and sentimental regret than the age of khaki and Flanders mud.

Although *Last Poems* had been produced with some urgency, Housman was not dissatisfied with it. This much is evident from the long list of presentation copies* he caused to be sent. Many of the recipients – Clemence and Laurence and Kate, Pollard, Frazer, Benson, Rothenstein, Withers, Bynner, Mackail, Ker – are predictable enough, but they are worth mentioning as a reminder that Housman was by no means a man without friends, and that many of his friends were of long standing. The extent of his contacts with the literary world is also evident: copies went to Gosse, Masefield, Bridges, Hardy, Drinkwater, William Watson, Festing Jones, Herbert Trench, Horatio Brown. And there are some mild surprises, ghosts from the past: his old headmaster Herbert Millington was remembered; as were Snow, his tutor at St John's; Mrs Maycock of Putney, the widow of his Patent Office colleague; and Fräulein Sophie Becker of Wiesbaden (she had returned to Germany 'very badly off',* and Housman had lost touch with her during the war; but with the return of peace, contact had been re-established). He did not forget those he had cared for and who cared for him; but then the volume that had come into existence in order to be held in the hands of the dying Mo was a suitable one to commemorate affeections that had stood the test of time.

Last Poems brought an increase of fame and substantial

royalties; Housman could also have enjoyed, had he wished, the distinctions traditionally conferred on men of letters, but these he consistently declined. As early as 1905 he had refused an honorary degree from Glasgow ('I long ago resolved to decline all such honours, if they should ever be offered me');* St Andrews received a similar refusal in 1922, Oxford in 1928 and 1934, Liverpool and Wales on other occasions. In 1929 he turned down the Order of Merit – the refusal being a distinction of which Housman was a little proud and which he seems to have shared with Bernard Shaw. A contempt for worldly honours of a formal nature; a sense that his fame must rest on his published work, his 'monument', rather than on dignities conferred at the whim of those enjoying a little brief authority; an arrogance that led him to derive more satisfaction from refusing an honour than from accepting it; a conviction of his own secret unworthiness (moral, not intellectual or literary) – each of these explanations of Housman's consistent attitude towards honours makes sense; some combination of them, in unguessable proportions, is probably the true explanation. But it is difficult to believe that the profound and permanent impression made by the verdict of the Oxford examiners in 1881 was not also involved: 'they' had refused him what he needed when he desperately needed it, and he would reject their blandishments now that he could well afford to do so. For a parallel one remembers the bitter pride of Johnson's letter to Lord Chesterfield. It is surely significant that the only exception Housman made to his lifelong rule was to accept an honorary fellowship from St John's College, Oxford – a distinction he was prepared to mention in his generally reticent *Who's Who* entry, and one which must have had for him an irresistible irony.

Another honour was declined in 1925, when he refused an invitation to deliver the Clark Lectures at Cambridge. This refusal to assume the critic's role was consistent with his argument in the Cambridge inaugural that literary criticism could be only a handicap to one who was studying a text scientifically with a view to establishing its accuracy. But in 1933 he yielded to persuasion and consented to deliver the Leslie Stephen Lecture – a decision that was quickly and keenly regretted, for the honour turned out to be onerous. In the previous year he had declined to contribute an essay on Coventry Patmore to a volume called *The Great Victorians*, saying that it would give me more trouble than you can imagine, whereas I want peace in my declining years; and the result would not be good enough to yield me pride or even satisfaction.*

It was in the event to be a shrewd forecast of his struggles with the 1933 lecture, which gave him much trouble to compose; he took no pride in it when it was printed, and refused to send presentation copies. When Grant Richards asked him to inscribe his copy, Housman replied, "'I'm damned if I will . . . I wrote every line against my will. I shall inscribe no copy to any one".'* He told Witter Bynner:

> I do not think highly of my lecture, which I wrote against the grain and almost under compulsion*

– against the grain, no doubt, because it involved breaking two of his rules: not to set up as a literary critic, and not to allow the man who wrote the poems to be seen to inhabit the same skin as the Professor of Latin. For all that, the lecture was a brilliant success and in printed form was widely read: 10,000 copies were printed within a few weeks of its delivery. For better or worse, it has been easily the most widely influential of all his prose writings.

During the Easter vacation Housman worked at the lecture with a disagreeable sense of the deadline, for it was to be delivered early in May and he wished to read it from a printed text. At the end of March he declined an invitation from Richards: 'until I have broken the back of that infernal lecture I have no time for anything else'.* There is not much doubt that the labour so little delighted in made him ill and depressed: it fell at a time when, as a man well into his seventies still actively pursuing his profession and indeed carrying out precisely the same duties as twenty years earlier, he should have been relaxing instead of undertaking an arduous and unwelcome task; and its effects were far-reaching. It cannot be entirely accidental that, soon after it was delivered, he was unwell enough to have to spend a week in a nursing home 'for alleged weakness of the heart'* (as he put it), and that in July he was still 'in a very low nervous condition'* and missing his usual exercise. His holiday that year ('my disagreeable tour in France'*) was, quite unusually if not uniquely, a failure, being marred by 'a form of influenza';* he was probably ill-advised to set off, for a letter written on the day before his departure shows a

startling deterioration in his handwriting and a highly uncharacteristic slip of the pen ('siezed'). Later he was more than
once to express the wish that his life had come to an end in the
summer of 1933.

The Leslie Stephen lecture, then, was written by a very tired
and depressed old man whose physical health was failing rapidly.
But when all due disagreements with its arguments have been
registered, it must be recognised as an accomplished performance,
elegant in construction and poised in tone, and admirably devised
for the occasion it served. Its delivery on 9 May was a great
success; the Senate House was packed, and when Housman rose
to speak (one of the audience told me) 'you could have heard a pin
drop'.* He spoke very quietly, but every word was audible; as he
paused before the peroration describing his experience of poetic
composition, there was (Sir Sydney Roberts recalled) 'a slight stir,
followed by the complete hush which betokens a wholly attentive
audience'.*

Housman began by linking the occasion with that other
occasion, twenty-two years earlier to the day, when in the same
building he had delivered his inaugural lecture. He had declared
then that literary criticism was a supremely difficult undertaking,
and that good literary critics were rarer than 'returns of Halley's
comet'; and he now quoted this passage from the earlier lecture by
way of disclaiming any pretensions to special fitness for the task he
had embarked on. Nor was this simply a conventional and
personal modesty. Before he reached the end of his first paragraph
the warning signs began to appear that the lecture would be
provocative, and that one of its provocations would be to attack
those, not far away, whose pretensions were less modest than his
own. His audience must not expect

> to be addressed in that tone of authority which is appropriate to
> those who are, and is assumed by some of those who conceive
> themselves to be, literary critics. In order to hear Jehovah
> thundering out of Zion, or Little Bethel, you must go elsewhere.

And elsewhere, it was surely understood by his audience, would
not take them beyond the boundaries of Cambridge, where I. A.
Richards, F. R. Leavis and others had establisahed a new and
vigorously iconoclastic school of criticism, which was attracting
converts in large numbers. (*Scrutiny* had been founded in the

previous year.) That school, Housman continued (without explicit reference to it), claimed to offer 'truths to be imparted as such with sureness of superior insight and knowledge'; but truth and knowledge, he implies, must be sought elsewhere – in, for example, the practice of *textual* criticism. The literary critic's stock-in-trade, however much refined and mellowed, could consist in nothing more than 'personal opinions'. That first minute or two of the lecture must have raised expectations, and hackles, among the audience: after a long absence Housman had returned to the vein of the literary papers read at University College.

After this provocative exordium he went on to say that he would endeavour to treat 'with some degree of precision' a subject not inherently precise. His first task must be to clarify terminology in order to avoid 'wresting the term ['poetry'] to licentious use and affixing it either to dissimilar things already provided with names of their own, or to new things for which new names should be invented'. He proposes a hierarchy in which verse, thanks to the 'superior comeliness of that form', stands higher than prose; poetry ('pure language and liquid versification') higher than verse; and a particular species of poetry 'which moves and touches in a special and recognisable way' highest of all. This leads to a description of 'the peculiar function of poetry': 'not to transmit thought but to set up in the reader's sense a vibration corresponding to what was felt by the writer'. The antithesis of thought and emotion is taken up again later; but first Housman makes a historical excursion to demonstrate which of his categories of verse/poetry have at different periods been dominant. His field of enquiry is restricted to English literature from the seventeenth to the nineteenth centuries, with a side-glance at Chaucer by way of Dryden's translation. Seventeenth-century wit cannot be called poetry, nor can the 'sham poetry' produced between *Samson Agonistes* and *Lyrical Ballads*. The explanation is that during this period the intelligence was dominant; and the intelligence produces good prose but is an enemy to poetry.

It seems clear that this argument was, even in 1933, stubbornly unfashionable. The rediscovery of Metaphysical poetry, the rehabilitation of the eighteenth century, Eliot's insistence that in the best poetry (in Donne, say, as opposed to Tennyson) thought and emotion are inseparable – Housman will have none of this.

For him, poetry is non-intellectual; poetry and ideas can be separated; religious poetry can be enjoyed by the undevout and Wordsworth by those 'who care nothing for his opinions and beliefs'. He is moved not by ideas but by language, rhythm and sound: this much he regards as proved by his differing reponses to different translations of the same Biblical passage. 'Poetry is not the thing said but a way of saying it'; and one logical extreme of this claim is that poetry can say nothing at all and still be poetry (he finds the best examples of 'pure poetry' in English in Blake and in some of Shakespeare's songs); another is that the sense of a poem and its emotional effect can work in opposite directions.

Such assertions flew in the face of the most advanced and influential Cambridge criticism of the day, and were no doubt intended to. The rejection of meaning ('Poetry indeed seems to me more physical than intellectual') looks like an attack on Richards (*The Meaning of Meaning* had appeared in the previous decade), Empson (*Seven Types of Ambiguity* was published in 1930), and Leavis. This much might have been predicted; but no-one could have anticipated what Housman was to do in the last couple of minutes of his lecture. To reinforce his claim that poetry – not poems, or verse, but that highest kind of poetry which may be found in a single line – has nothing to do with the intellect, he offered a brief but memorable account of his own experience of poetic composition. For him a poem was 'a morbid secretion, like the pearl in the oyster', and he has 'seldom written poetry unless I was rather out of health'. His view of it as a 'passive and involuntary process' is orthodoxly romantic, recalling the Wordsworthian 'spontaneous overflow of powerful feelings'. The lecture ends with a teasing reference to the last poem in the 1896 volume, and there has been argument ever since (as Housman of course intended there should be) over the solution to his conundrum, insoluble because he carefully, and no doubt gleefully, destroyed the manuscript evidence.

Another half-century of intense critical activity has shot much of the lecture full of holes; such notions as 'pure poetry' and the antithesis of thought and emotion beg exceedingly complex questions; a conception of poetry which sees Dryden and Pope as classics of our prose rather than of our poetry seems impossibly narrow and exclusive; and some crucial passages are simplistic and facile in the manner of a style of criticism already outmoded when they were written. But this may be to approach the question too solemnly, for there are good grounds for believing that the lecture was, in part at least, a *jeu d'esprit*. Max Beerbohm was amused by it, and Housman was 'glad you were amused'.* He told Laurence that 'its success here has taken me aback. The leader of our doctrinaire teachers of youth is reported to say that it will take more than twelve years to undo the harm I have done in an hour',* and this remark (if, indeed, it was not invented) obviously gave him satisfaction.

Some, indeed, were ready to see the joke: *The Times* not only summarised the lecture with long quotations but devoted to it a fourth leader ('What is Poetry?') in which the leader-writer describes the famous test of poetic merit – does it produce a physical reaction? – as 'surprisingly, almost naughtily, simple, like a "long nose" made at pedantic solemnity'.* And Housman's linking of poetic composition with ill health, though consistent with his repeated declaration that *A Shropshire Lad* had been generated by a sore throat, could well be a snook cocked at the eminent Victorian critic commemorated by the lectureship; for it was Leslie Stephen who had insisted that 'the greatest poetry, like the highest morality, is the product of a thoroughly healthy mind'.* Housman had described the 1892 Introductory Lecture as 'rhetorical and not wholly sincere'; I suspect that something of the same quality – the taking up of an extreme position partly for the delight of startling an audience, and partly for the intellectual exercise of defending it – seasons the 1933 lecture.

A few weeks after its delivery G. H. Hardy sat next to Housman in hall and asked him, ' "Did he really mean what he had said to be taken very seriously?" ' They argued all through dinner, and (Hardy wrote) 'I think that finally he agreed with me', his reply to the question being ' "Perhaps not entirely". '* The latter portion of the lecture has become the most familiar and makes the liveliest reading; the earlier, historical section is little more than a musuem-piece, though it serves to show the narrowness of Housman's poetic tastes: he has little time for poetry radically different in kind from his own. But a good word must be put in for his comparison of Chaucer and Dryden – ironically enough, an accomplished piece of practical criticism. Although Housman was an unwilling critic he was not an inept one, and even in his letters there are suggestive observations – as, for example, in his comments to J. G. Frazer on Addison:

He is a terribly industrious humourist, like Charles Lamb, and Fielding in the introductory chapters to the various books of *Tom Jones*; and his admired English has nothing like the vernacular raciness of the best of Cowper's earlier letters, for instance. Indeed I really think the vogue of the *Spectator* impoverished the language of prose . . .*

Some unexpected praise for the lecture came from T. S. Eliot in *The Criterion* – to the amusement of Housman, who noted with satisfaction that Eliot was 'worshipped as a god by the writers in the paper [*Scrutiny*] which had the only hostile review'.* Eliot began his review by saying that 'It has long been known to the majority of those who really care about such matters, that Mr. A. E. Housman is one of the few living masters of English prose; and that on those subjects on which he chooses to exercise his talents, there is no one living who can write better.'* This is high and unorthodox praise, but it is a little odd that it should have been prompted by the 1933 lecture, which, though elegant and polished – Housman never wrote, let alone published, a sloppy sentence – is not one of his most sparkling performances. The passionate intensity of his finest prose is missing from it; but this ought to be attributed to the generalized nature of the subject rather than to any late-autumnal mellowing or any waning of his powers. Housman is at his best when he grapples with specific issues or personalities, and especially when he attacks vanity and incompetence posing as scholarship.

In the attempt to define the distinctive quality of Housman's prose style, various names have been invoked as 'influences' or parallels: Pope, Bentley, Gibbon, Macaulay and Shaw among them. Without rejecting any of these, I should want to put my own money on Dr Johnson and Oscar Wilde, but to insist at the same time that Housman's remains an essentially personal style, deriving its tone from his particular attitude towards his subject-matter. In much of his best prose the passion for truth and certainty, and the corresponding scorn for intellectual laziness, complacency and dishonesty (the intellectual shading necessarily into the moral exposure and censure), inform a highly specialized activity: he is wrestling with the problems of editing classical texts, and is seeking to form a just assessment of the endeavours of those who have already laboured in the same field. That passion and that scorn create a balance of forces which gives the prose its distinctive quality – urgent yet tightly controlled, intolerant yet judicious, witty and even farcical yet deeply serious, emotional yet bearing the stamp of a sharp and powerful intelligence. Confident, epigrammatic, by turns slyly ironic and openly abusive, with a masterly discipline of syntax and a diction ranging from the homely and colloquial to the pedantic and biblical, Housman's style is at once original and direct in its expression of his ideas; and the reader has a keen sense of a mind delighting in the activity in which it is engaged. Nothing could be simpler than to say of an editor of Manilius that

> The commentary is plain and concise, but meagre, and a student without other resource would starve on it*

and nothing could be more damning: the sudden vividness of 'starve' startles us, as Housman intended it should, for this is no mere academic response to an academic issue but a matter of intellectual life and death. Compare his dismissal of another bad edition: 'Works of this sort are little better than interruptions to our studies . . .'*. The manner is Johnsonian: a man might produce such works of 'scholarship' for ever it he would abandon his mind to it. Housman, like Johnson, is a master of the one-line verdict that leaves nothing more to be said ('Mr. Merrill has special disqualifications for editing a poet'*); and he is fond of the Johnsonian trick of ridicule by reductive metaphor or analogy: of the notes in the hapless Merrill's edition of Catullus, he declares that 'half the ship's cargo has been thrown overboard to save the bilge-water'.* But he can also handle with great skill the architectonics of the long sentence which works cumulatively towards its destined end without any loss of lucidity. In the following central statement of faith, the words fall with un-ignorable weight, and the final abrupt transition from Latinistic polysyllables to Saxon alliterative plainness is highly effective:

> To read attentively, think correctly, omit no relevant consideration, and repress self-will, are not ordinary accomplishments; yet an emendator needs much besides: just literary perception, congenial intimacy with the author, experience which must have been won by study, and mother wit which he must have brought from his mother's womb.*

Or consider the brilliant modulation of tone in the following, from the exalted (but, as it turns out, mock-heroic) opening, through the seemingly judicious imparting of information, to the calculated afterthought in the last phrase in which the reviewer tosses aside his kid gloves in delighted contempt:

> If a man will comprehend the richness and variety of the universe, and inspire his mind with a due measure of wonder and awe, he must contemplate the human intellect not only on its heights of genius but in its abysses of ineptitude; and it might be fruitlessly debated to the end of time whether Richard Bentley or Elias Stoeber was the more marvellous work of the Creator: Elias Stoeber, whose reprint of Bentley's text, with a commentary intended to confute it, saw the light in 1767 at Strasburg, a city still famous for its geese.*

Enough of the decencies of debate and the language of scholars and gentlemen, that final monosyllable seems to hiss: let us call a fool a fool and be done with it. The sensibility behind such a sentence seems worlds removed from that which produced *A Shropshire Lad*; yet Housman's best prose has in common with his best poems an irresistible rightness – to tamper with a single word, even a comma, would mar its combination of strength and delicacy. Those geese exemplify, too, a favourite gambit: the precisely controlled admission of the language of the market-place into scholarly discourse. Again: 'A textual critic engaged upon his business is not at all like Newton investigating the motions of the planets: he is much more like a dog hunting for fleas.'*

Housman's prose is the instrument of a ruthless logic and an inflexible refusal to be seduced by the smooth-tongued evasions and conventional self-disparagements of inferior scholars. In some of his most effective demolitions he brings to a reading of their words an intelligence and seriousness considerably greater than went to their writing. Of an edition of Lucretius, he remarks:

> Mr. Bailey says in his preface that he has been sparing of original conjectures because he does not wish to inflict new wounds upon the text. This estimate of his own talent in that department is certainly modest and seemingly correct.*

He himself refuses to affect such modesty whilst making pretensions to scholarly authority: 'I had rather be arrogant than impudent.' Of a bad translation of Propertius he writes, with relentless and self-delighting logic:

> 'Scholars will pardon an attempt, however bald, to render into English these exquisite love-poems.' Why? Those who have no Latin may pardon such an attempt, if they like bad verses better than silence; but I do not know why bald renderings of exquisite love-poems should be pardoned by those who want no renderings at all.*

Hypocrisy, like incompetence, excites his contempt on moral as well as intellectual grounds: of another bad edition, he writes that 'hardly a page . . . can be read without anger and disgust'.*

But the expression of his disapproval often takes comic or mock-heroic form, and the explanation of this may be that Housman, in whom scholarship (good and bad) is capable of arousing strong emotion, nevertheless distrusts emotion as a pitfall in the quest for truth, and finds it necessary to convert the intensity of his feelings into the different intensities of wit and satire. An Italian scholar who rashly allowed a confession of his feelings to break the surface of a scholarly context is the victim of Housman's irony:

> It was a fine August morning which placed in Monsignore Ratti's hand the envelope containing this fragment, and he gives us leave to imagine the trepidation with which he opened it and the joy with which he discovered that the parchment was in two pieces instead of one. When a scholar is so literary as all this, it would be strange if he were quite accurate . . .*

But Housman, who can admit elsewhere to finding an emendation 'beautiful', is not above breaking his own rule.

Wit, irony, invective, ridicule, the comic and the mock-heroic: Housman is a master of all these, but our relish of them must not be allowed to obscure the fact that, for him, textual criticism was a moral as well as a technical enterprise, a quest for truth which involved wrestling with the enemies of truth. Emendation, as he said, requires 'moral integrity and intellectual vigilance';* and the order in which he placed these qualities is surely significant.

Hence the characteristic and often rapid advance, even within a single sentence, from the specific to the universal, and the habit of moral generalization in the context of a specialized discussion:

> the average man . . . believes that the text of ancient authors is generally sound . . . just as he believes . . . that he will rise again from the dead.*
> How the world is managed, and why it was created, I cannot tell; but it is no feather-bed for the repose of sluggards.*
> . . . that habit of treading in ruts and trooping in companies which men share with sheep.*
> . . . the sloth and distaste for thinking which are the common inheritence of humanity.*
> The faintest of all human passions is the love of truth.*

As some of these remarks indicate, his view of scholarship was unashamedly élitist: 'emendators should thank their stars that they have the multitude against them and must address the judicious few'.* In his important paper 'The Application of Thought to Textual Criticism' (1922), he describes the textual critic's work as 'an aristocratic affair, not communicable to all men, nor to most men';* he placed on the title-page of his Juvenal the phrase 'Editorum in usum edidit' ('edited for the use of editors'), and in his preface to the last book of Manilius defined his ideal readership at the ultimate pitch of exclusiveness: 'the reader whose good opinion I desire and have done my utmost to secure is the next Bentley or Scaliger who may chance to occupy himself with Manilus'.* He must have known that the world was hardly likely to see such a reader.

Much has been made of Housman's venomous and vitriolic manner as a controversialist; but this is more striking in brief quotations than when the prose is read in quantity. I find in Housman's prose an excited and exciting sense of great intellectual energy applying itself to a congenial task – an exuberance more in evidence than the negative qualities that have usually been stressed. It is true that he is unafraid on occasion to resort to direct attack:

> The names of Nicaeus and Paulus make an ugly smear across the scholarship of half a century, and posterity should titter a

good deal at the solemn coxcombries of the age which I have had to live through.*

The readers of Robinson Ellis, a scholar long dead when this unenviable epitaph was bestowed, 'were in perpetual contact with the intellect of an idiot child'.* But Housman by no means stands alone in his taste for invective: it is important to remember that there was a long tradition of what H. W. Garrod nicely calls 'the inhumanity of humanism'.* Poggio and Valla conducted a war of pamphlets 'scurrilous and obscene beyond belief' on grounds of hostility which were 'inconceivably trivial'; Scaliger, Milton, Bentley and others are famous for their asperities; and Housman, who consciously sought to place himself in the company of these great scholars, is the last representative of a tradition which, as Garrod says, 'harks back to the beginnings of scholarship'. More often, though, he employs the relatively genteel weapons of wit and irony; and it is only fair to add that he could praise handsomely when he deemed praise to be due. Although he had, for instance, the reputation of being a Germanophobe, he had enormous admiration for Wilamowitz, regarding him 'in verbal scholarship and textual criticism' as 'the greatest now living and comparable with the greatest of the dead'.* It is pleasant to know that his high regard was reciprocated.

The formality of the classical papers and prefaces (which did not exclude a vigorously colloquial element only too rare in such contexts) is naturally somewhat relaxed in the private letters; but here too the wit and irony, economy of means and brilliance of effect, are often to be found, and there is never a sentence carelessly shaped, never a word ambiguous or ill-chosen. A few examples will illustrate the continuity of style between the letters and the writings intended for publication:

Sciatica is one of the few ailments I sympathise with, as I used to have it myself, no doubt in a mild form, twenty years ago . . . Cancer is worse, they say, and being shot through the palm of the hand makes one scream louder.*

Death and marriage are raging through this College [Trinity] with such fury that I ought to be grateful for having escaped both.*

[Mark] Pattison . . . was a spectator of all time and all existence, and the contemplation of that repulsive scene is fatal to accurate learning.*

(Postcard) I suppose the Braille people may do *Last Poems* as they did the other book. The blind want cheering up.

(Referring to A. J. A. Symons, who had requested permission – which Housman refused – to include some of his poems in an anthology of nineties verse) He may be consoled, and also amused, if you tell him that to include me in an anthology of the nineties would be just as technically correct, and just as essentially inappropriate, as to include Lot in a book on Sodomites; in saying which I am not saying a word against sodomy, nor implying that intoxication and incest are in any way preferable.*

The notorious 'stored ammunition'* of the notebooks (the phrase is Laurence Housman's) shows Housman practising the epigrammatist's art. It has been supposed that Housman set down these sentences, some 160 of which were transcribed by Laurence, against the day when he might use them in scholarly polemic; and many, taking it on trust (perhaps a little too eagerly) that they are uniformly splenetic, have been repelled by what they supposed to be the malice aforethought that prompted them. And indeed, if the collection were nothing more than a reservoir of invective filled in the hope that occasions when it might be drawn on would present themselves, there would be something saddening as well as unattractive in so much emotional energy finding so inadequate an outlet. It is true that some of the entries are crushingly censorious caps to be worn by whoever they may fit; but it is equally true that others are light-hearted general observations: 'If an Irish baby cries when teething it is quoted as an instance of the Celtic melancholy'; 'Any fool can write a sonnet, and most fools do.' Some are moral reflections in the manner of La Rochefoucauld: 'Think for yourself and feel for others.' If they were shafts intended for delivery, it is odd that very few of them found their way into Housman's published writings (one group has the air of being discarded fragments from the Leslie Stephen Lecture). To me they have the flavour of stylistic exercises or the kind of *bons mots* a man might set down for his own pleasure with no thought of use. It may be that some found their way into Housman's conversation. A few include names:

Meredith has never been treated justly. He once wrote admirable books which were not admired. He now writes ridiculous books which are not ridiculed.

Swinburne reading Shakespeare was like a bear rifling a bee's nest. He eats and enjoys the honey; and the bees cannot sting him through his hide.

Jowett's Plato: the best translation of a Greek philosopher which has ever been executed by a person who understood neither philosophy nor Greek.

Kipling's *Jungle Book* is described as 'a tract in wolf's clothing'. (Elsewhere he described the poet T. Sturge Moore as 'a sheep in sheep's clothing'.) A good many leave blanks (if we assume that they were not left by Laurence):

If Mr. — were a postage-stamp, he would be a very good postage-stamp; but adhesiveness is not the virtue of a critic. A critic is free and detached.

Conjectural emendation as practised by — is not a game, an exercise requiring skill and heed, like marbles or skittles or cat's-cradle, but a pastime, like leaning against a wall and spitting.

— , whose self-love is a great passion squandered on an unworthy object.

But a great many make no reference to personalities:

Heaven lies about us in our infancy, and we lie about heaven when we grow up.

Nothing that could call the blush of shame to the cheek of a medical student.

My favourite work of fiction, the Latin dictionary.

As some of these suggest, the influence of Wilde is at work; but occasionally Wilde's wit has turned a little sour:

Parricide is returning good for evil.

Bentley's biographer, Monk, speaks of his prose as 'epigrammatic and witty', 'manly, bold and uncompromising'; 'every sentence has its weight, and impresses itself deeply upon the mind and memory of the reader'; but as well as 'pointed wit and sarcasm' there is an 'occasional playfulness' to be found in Bentley's writings.* All of this can be applied to Housman, though what is in question is less a matter of influence or imitation than a similarity of results when two wonderfully powerful and agile minds work at similar tasks. Although, like Bentley, Housman has come to be remembered as a controversialist who gave no quarter, the element of wit, humour and 'playfulness' in his writings needs also to be remembered. It has already become evident from some of the passages quoted, and it was a particular manifestation of a sense of humour that was generally strong. The fun and games of the Housman children, in which Alfred was the leader, and the stock of anecdotes and jokes of the elderly don show that delight in various manifestations of the comic extended throughout his life. Propagators of the Housman legend say nothing of his laughter: a curmudgeon provides better copy; but Laurence remembered that 'he had about the happiest *laugh* I have ever heard – ringing and bell-like. It came from his saving grace – his keen sense of humour . . .'.*

Another product of that keen sense of humour was the comic verse and parodies which he frequently composed, not for publication but for private amusement, and usually for a member of his family or a friend. Quoting thirteen examples, Laurence suggests that they were written over a period of almost fifty years (1880–1927); and there are others extant which Laurence does not give. Some are *vers d'occasion*: the entertaining 'Fragment of an English Opera', for instance, was sent to Laurence when he was at work on a libretto; the 'Fragment of a Didactic Poem on Latin Grammar', its artfully lumpish heroic couplets in the style of Erasmus Darwin, was written for the students at University College; and 'The Elephant, or the Force of Habit' for one of Rothenstein's children.

Some, though not all, of these poems share with the nonsense world of Carroll and Lear an element of sudden irrational violence disrupting the sedate conventional world. Housman had read both Victorian masters of nonsense in childhood, and had something in common with them. Both remained unmarried and became obsessive precisians. Housman did not go as far as Lear, whose 'every action [was] timed, not only by the day but by the hour';* but, as Grant Richards said, 'his plans were never elastic',* and the pattern of his life, with its little rituals, had a certain inflexibility. Carroll was a 'stickler for exactitude'* over printers' punctuation, insisting (for example) on *ca'n't* and *wo'n't*; Housman's letters to Richards inveigh against the iniquities and imbecilities of printers. Like Carroll, Housman was a brilliantly funny parodist (of, for example, the Salvation Army's style of hymnody). In his comic verse the outrageous and the bizarre coexist with the severely decorous; and an anecdote recounted by R. W. Chambers suggests that in real life Housman's customary stiffness could on occasion yield to the absurd:

> Did Sir Stanley Leathes ever tell you about his encounter with Housman? He had come to Trinity for a celebration, and was given rooms next to (or opposite) Housman's, and he was told that if he wanted anything he could knock up Housman. 'That is the very last thing I should think of doing', said Leathes, but he found, when he started to dress very much against time, that he had neglected to pack any trousers. There was nothing to do but to knock up Housman. But a rapid survey of Housman's figure when he answered the door convinced Leathes that the fit would not be satisfactory, and he coupled his request for the loan of a pair of trousers with a request to be allowed, for this occasion only, to split them down the back. Housman consented to both requests with a good grace. As Leathes said, if he had merely wanted to borrow a collar stud Housman would probably have been annoyed: it was the outrageous nature of the request that saved the situation. It bears out my feeling that you could often get under Housman's guard if you could be sufficiently surprising and extravagant in your demands on his patience.*

Chambers was right: it was not the only occasion on which someone succeeded in penetrating Housman's reserve by the simple device of taking him by surprise.

> Arthur Benson told me of a little incident which threw a faint but perhaps appreciable light on Housman's shy reserve. Arthur was spending the copious gains of his pen on a new Hall at Magdalene, which was the pride of his life. He delighted to

stand in the street and watch the masons at their work, and one day, catching sight of Housman, he did on an impulse what as a rule he would never have dreamt of — seized him by the arm and dragged him into the building, 'for to admire and for to see'. Something seemd to melt under his touch, a barrier fell, and for the first time Housman became entirely human. It was borne in upon Arthur that if people could only take to slapping him, so to speak, on the back, he would become a different person; but I never heard of anyone carrying the experiment farther.*

When Wittgenstein, on the other hand, stricken with diarrhoea, asked permission to use Housman's lavatory, he was refused: the intrusion was, one presumes, insufficiently outrageous to take his sense of privacy by storm. A calculated outrageousness could also characterise Housman's behaviour on carefully selected occasions. At his brother Basil's wedding, he gave a speech as best man and 'commended the custom of a certain African tribe which . . . made a religious practice of eating the mother-in-law at the wedding-feast'.* one of the mothers-in-law being among his listeners.

Anecdotes of Housman abound, especially from the Cambridge years; and the reader will by now have noted, gratefully or disapprovingly, that it is not difficult to string them together. In a stable, enclosed community such as academic Cambridge, where leisure bred gossip (more generously known as the art of conversation) and gossip turned on personalities as the sparks fly upward, it was not surprising that a Housman legend should flourish – as, indeed, it still flourishes. A delight in donnish eccentricity is the homage paid to the learned by the ignorant, who, failing to comprehend the true grounds of distinction, seize on (or invent) something they can both understand and feel indulgent towards. Housman was only one of many who gratified this taste in an age before dons, their thoughts running on mortgages and American lecture-tours, sank to a tame normality. (Robinson Ellis, already mentioned more than once in these pages, was eccentric to a degree that makes Housman seem commonplace.) Now that dons, genial and ambitious, can often be mistaken for civil servants or salesmen, it is easy to forget that the Victorian don (a species that survived well into our century) was a very different article. Housman's taste for solitude and silence was not at all unusual and must be sensibly seen as a condition of his vast learning and the extraordinary amount of work he got through. Jowett's silences were famous, and Ker, Mayor and Sandys (to restrict the list to those already referred to) were all reserved, withdrawn men.

The Housman legend, which began during his lifetime, may have been a form of flattery, but its subject had little reason to be grateful for it: by exaggerating his unapproachability and aloof disdain for ordinary amiability or bonhomie, it must often have discouraged those who wished to offer their friendship, even though that friendship might sometimes have been gratefully accepted. For the biographer, the legend presents the problem of distinguishing the genuine Housman anecdote or epigram from the spurious article that has become attached to his name. Apart from simple invention, the sayings and doings of others, if sufficiently 'characteristic', were apt to be attributed to him. Thus he was confidently reported as observing at table that the lamb he had been served was harder to swallow than the Lamb of God, though the remark was probably made by Nathanial Wedd. Whether, as legend holds, Housman actually kept a record of the dogs he kicked on his afternoon walks we shall probably never know, but it seems unlikely. One would like to believe, though, that it was he who composed the dialogue attributed to him by oral tradition:

> *First don.*   O cuckoo, shall I call thee bird,
>   Or but a wandering voice?
> *Second don.* State the alternative preferred,
>   With reasons for your choice.*

And there seems no reason to disbelieve John Fothergill's account of showing Housman round his garden:

> I proceeded to point out all the plants with vile names. . . . 'Over there I have a *Phallus amorphus*, but it hasn't come up yet.' — 'Perhaps modesty forbids?' he conjectured in his attractive thin mandarin voice.*

Sometimes his sayings are quoted out of context and their intention is misunderstood. His well-known quip that he had found Cambridge an asylum in every sense of the word sounds ungrateful until one learns the occasion of its utterence: it was first heard, probably in 1922, at a dinner of Oxford men resident in Cambridge, and hence can be taken, like so many of his *obiter dicta*, as 'rhetorical and not wholly sincere'. H. J. Chaytor was present and later recalled the speech:

> There was only one toast, Oxford, and . . . this was proposed by Housman. He made the best speech that these dinners ever produced. Addressing the company as 'fellow exiles', he referred to the beneficial effects of exile upon people from the Israelites onwards, the suitability of Cambridge for exile – it contained a large number of willow trees upon which harps could be hung, if we happened to possess any, and went on to say that, exiled from Oxford, he had found Cambridge an asylum in every sense of the term. I am sure that he would not have said this, if Cambridge men had been present, and that it was not meant for repetition abroad.*

But it was not only in the hope of hearing this prim elderly don say something atrociously rude that Housman was sought after at Cambridge dining-tables. One of the most potent ingredients of the Housman legend was the knowledge that he inhabited, but kept quite distinct, two worlds: the man whose unashamedly romatic poems enjoyed a wide popularity was also a scholar devoted to arcane research and savage controversy unintelligible to all but a handful of specialists. Housman took pains to keep the two roles asunder. He was visibly annoyed when attempts were made, *viva voce* and on academic territory, to persuade him to talk about his poetry; one enquirer over the port at Trinity was snubbed with the remark that 'the kindest action the Dons have ever done me has been never to mention my poems'.* His suggestions to Grant Richards for the announcements of *Last Poems* refer to 'Mr. A. E. Housman':* the professorial title belonged to his other self, not to the writer of the poems. Conversely, in the advertisement for his edition of Juvenal he wanted 'no nonsense about Shropshire lads'.* (One is reminded again of Lewis Carroll, a more extreme case of academic-creative dualism.) Perhaps Housman's refusal to accommodate in his public personality the part of his nature that wrote poetry helps to explain his disinclination to accept royalties for his poems or academic honours: the author of *A Shropshire Lad* was not quite the man who owned a cheque-book; the honours, prompted at least in part by his fame as a poet, would amount to a public admission that Professor Housman was a maker as well as an emendator of verses.

The dualism is also evident in the consistent inconsistencies of his behaviour towards others. The testimonies are numerous and so contradictory that it would be wrong to try to explain them away as merely reflecting a greater or lesser sympathy on the part of the witnesses. They suggest, rather, that his personality incorporated two sets of characteristics between which he would fluctuate rather disconcertingly. Anecdotes stress the sourly misanthropic element, not because it necessarily predominated but because kindliness and good humour lend themselves less readily to the raconteur's art than bad temper and rudeness. On the other hand, allowance must be made for the charitableness of memory as well as the natural tendency to overcorrect a picture felt to be misleading. After all the caveats have been dutifully entered, however, enough remains to suggest that Housman could strike different people in very different lights, and even lead a single witness who knew him well to qualify his statements by acknowledging that the opposite was also true.

Laurence's description of his brother's laughter has already been quoted; but it was also Laurence who suggested that the adjectives to describe Housman were 'shy, proud, reserved, reticent, taciturn, staid, sardonic, secretive, undemonstrative, and *glum*'* (his italics). *The Times* obituarist, presumably Benson, testified that he had 'a laugh which betokened a great capacity for enjoyment', described him as 'a good raconteur, of the pithy and caustic order . . . by no means averse to gossip', but could not forbear adding that 'he walked alone, and, either intentionally or unintentionally, seldom recognised a passer-by'.*

Some saw only one side of Housman. William Plomer described him as 'unsociable and decidedly sour';* Richard Middleton compared him to 'an undertaker's mute';* Max Beerbohm said 'he was like an absconding cashier';* and a famous guest at a Family dinner, Stanley Baldwin, found him a 'most unclubbable man'.* But it is significant that all of these were very slight acquaintances. From those who knew him better, the accounts can be very different. Rothenstein said that 'underneath the dry asperity lay an odd affectionateness';* J. D. Duff found it 'strange that he should be so fierce with others editors. He is quite gentle and kindly in ordinary intercourse';* Oliffe Richmond declared that 'at all times he was kindness itself to me';* Platt's son, recalling Housman's visits to the family home, remembered him as 'a genial person without any trace of malice'.*

As we have already seen, in spite of his reputation as a misogynist he could be charming to women: Mrs Lily Thicknesse wrote that 'of long talks I had with him, I chiefly remember the delicious humour of his descriptions of things and poeple'.* Pollard, a friend of almost sixty years' standing, said that 'not even Moses Jackson could make Alfred *babble*, but he was never stiff or reticent with me'.* Housman had a well-deserved reputation as a wit and raconteur; and not all his sallies were scathing or all his stories obscene, though he was fond of an element of the unconventional. A. C. Benson noted in his diary Housman's recounting of an anecdote about Wilkie Collins' funeral:

> There was a pause when the body was laid in the grave, when a woman and two boys in deep mourning came forwards and knelt down. In the silence the rich and bell-like voice of Holman Hunt was heard saying 'There are the bastards!'.*

But any hint that he was being lionized put Housman on his guard: the sense that he was being watched would cause the shutters to fall, the mask to be donned. Alan Ker found him on a social occasion 'extremely witty, and perfectly charming to us', but added perceptively that it was 'perhaps because it had been kept from him that we were all devoted admirers'.* The crushing retorts, the conversation-stopping snubs, followed the attempt to take him by surprise conversationally. Only in his letters, where the sense of being watched was absent, could he relax sufficiently to speak of his feelings and his poetry.

To bear the deaths of many of one's contemporaries is part of the normal lot of any man who lives to grow old, and Housman was no exception. The death of Moses Jackson in 1923 was the first of a series of severances, as friends, colleagues, companions, and one loved member of his immediate family predeceased him. Later in 1923 W. P. Ker died in his late sixties and as he would have chosen – on a mountaineering holiday; and soon afterwards, in 1925, the third member of the old University College triumvirate, Arthur Platt, also died. Housman had kept in touch with both men, and he might have had Platt's company in

Cambridge for a few years if his friend had succeeded in obtaining the Greek chair, for which he was a candidate in 1921. Ker had visited Housman at Trinity and had given his advice on *Last Poems*. Soon after Platt's death, Housman broke one of his rules and agreed to write an introduction for a posthumous collection of his papers; and the volume took up a good deal of his time during 1926. He also wrote a short but touching obituary for the *Classical Review*, in which he praised the width of Platt's reading in many languages ('in Platt's company one felt that one was not an educated man') and also paid a tribute that gives the lie to those who suppose that Housman never gave expression to his feelings:

> We have lost as genuine and straightforward a mind and character as can ever have been born into the world, and a delightful creature whom it is a precious treasure to have known.*

A. C. Benson also died in 1925; J. P. Postgate in 1926; and Thomas Hardy in 1928. Housman had known Hardy since 1899 and had both visited him at Max Gate and met him in London at the home of Edmund Gosse. When it was decided to give Hardy (or most of him) a Westminster Abbey funeral, Housman was invited to be one of the pall-bearers – a distinguished group which included Barrie, Galsworthy, Kipling and Shaw as well as a couple of prime ministers. At first Housman refused: he is reported to have remarked that, if he found himself standing behind Galsworthy, he would not be able to restrain himself from kicking him on the bottom, and that would never do in the Abbey. He finally agreed, but was unenthusiastic about a painting of the group of pall-bearers that Rothenstein wanted to execute. (Barrie refused outright, and the project was dropped.) Of these losses, the deaths of Platt and Hardy may have been felt most keenly. For Platt, a friend of thirty years, Housman felt both intellectual respect and something warmer: he was both a man who 'knows everything'* and 'a dear and wonderful creature'.* 'For Hardy', he wrote to Maurice Pollet, 'I felt affection, and high admiration for some of his novels and a few of his poems.'*

Robert Bridges, another old friend, died in 1930, leaving the Laureateship vacant – a post to which Housman had no aspirations. He had known Bridges since 1913, and in 1924 wrote to his sister Kate a vivid letter recounting a weekend spent with

Bridges, 'an amazing old man',* at his home near Oxford. His letter of condolence to Mrs Bridges blends the formal with the personal tribute impressively and with complete sincerity; it is worth quoting as an instance of the masterly tact and sensitivity with which Housman, celebrated for his rebarbative manners, could carry out a difficult task:

> I write to offer you my sympathy in your loss, which indeed we all share in a measure; but of your husband's departure it may be said, if of anyone's, that nothing is here for tears, nothing to wail or knock the breast. A fortunate and honoured existence is ended in the fulness of time; life did not long outstay strength; and his poetry, though the vulgar could never admire it rightly, did at last win him fame even among the vulgar. For myself, I do not suppose that there is anything which I have read oftener than the first four books of *Shorter Poems*.*

Sophie Becker, in every sense the oldest of all his friends, died in 1931; and in the following year another link with boyhood was broken with the death, after much suffering, of his brother Basil, 'my favourite among my brothers and sisters'.* Housman himself was now well past seventy, though – 'an almost ascetically slight figure'* – he looked younger. The record of the last ten years of his life reads to a large extent like that of a man in his prime. The energetic annual tours in France continued, often in very hot weather, and Grant Richards, who accompanied him in the summer of 1927, said that 'he knew not fatigue: each day had to be full'. It goes without saying that his scholarly work and his academic duties were pursued unflaggingly: the last book of Manilius, published at the end of 1930, completed a task begun some thirty years earlier, and the Cambridge lectures saw no interruption – Housman never retired, and in his entire career had only one term's leave (in the Lent Term of 1934). By the end of 1932, however, there were signs of physical decline, and 1933 was a bad year for him. When he turned seventy he had asked his doctor to 'overhaul' him; the outcome, characteristically expressed, was that

> my heart is not as stout as it was and ought to be, and I found this out when climbing the Puy de Parioux [during an extensive tour of France], about the height of Snowdon, on a hot afternoon.

In May 1933, the month of the Leslie Stephen Lecture, he writes simply that 'I have grown older in the last twelvemonth.'* A few months earlier, he had reported to Kate a diminution in his walking powers: 'after five or six miles, though I do not get tired, my legs tend to act sluggishly'.* These bulletins on his health are brief, without self-pity, and often intended to allay the concern of his correspondent. But writing to Percy Withers, himself a physician, near the end of 1934, he complained more fully of physical fatigue and added: 'My life is bearable, but I do not want it to continue, and I wish it had ended a year and a half ago.'* The period referred to is the summer of 1933, which had seen the beginning of a period of illness lasting several months (according to his doctor's records, he was 'illish'* from 30 June to 13 November). From the nursing home where he spent a week in June of that year he wrote to Withers of his 'nervous depression',* and to Laurence at the same time that 'the real bother is what I have often had before in the course of my life, depression and causeless anxiety'.* He persevered with his French tour, but the heat was exceptionally trying and he picked up an infection which spoilt his holiday. It was not all gloom, however: he was touched by the solicitude of the young Frenchman who accompanied him ('My companion has been as kind and helpful as can possibly be imagined'; 'my companion takes all trouble on his shoulders, and really does not seem to be bored'*), and by 1 September had rallied sufficiently to enjoy the first oysters of the season.

1934 was a better year, and his doctor saw him only twice, though – perhaps exhausted by the rigours of the Cambridge winter – he complained in March of being 'neither strong nor comfortable'.* Later in the year R. V. Laurence died; Housman had come closer to friendship with him than with any other of the Fellows of Trinity, and he was sorely missed. Housman wrote of Laurence that 'he was ill for nearly two years, but so brave that he had arranged and intended to lecture on the day he died'.* It was an example that he himself was even then in the process of imitating; but the sentence that follows quickly neutralizes any impulse to sentimentality or self-pity: 'he talked so much about me to his nurse that she has written to bespeak me for her next death-bed'; and Housman liked the jest so much that he repeated it a week later in a letter to his sister-in-law, and doubtless also in conversation.

Early in 1935, Housman's doctor noted that his heart 'showed

signs of definite failure in its task',* and with the end of the
academic year in June he was back in the Evelyn Nursing Home in
Trumpington Road for a rest. From there he wrote to Percy
Withers: 'You probably know all about Cheyne-Stokes breath-
ing . . .: sleepness nights spent in recurrent paroxysms of failure of
breath, which can be combated if one is broad awake, but which
overwhelm one if one dozes'.* He was not, it was clear, to enjoy
the 'sudden and painless end'* which he told Withers was the
greatest blessing of life. In September he wrote to Lady Frazer:

> My life ought to have come to an end more than two years ago:
> age and weakness of heart in combination cause me to spend my
> days in fatigue and somnolence, except for periods after meals,
> and I often feel as if I had no marrow in my bones.*

But if he could not conquer old age, he could at any rate struggle
with it; and none of this had prevented him from touring Savoy
and Dauphiné, again 'with a helpful companion'. After the
passage quoted above, he goes on to treat Lady Frazer to a lively
description of how he had injured his head getting into a taxi, had
had stitches, and was forced to wear a cap indoors, which made
his companion say 'that I might be taken for a great scholar'. This
was his last trip abroad, and his slight frame had managed to
summon up a burst of energy for his farewell to France and the
pleasures it had for so long stood for. One is glad to know that he
had not lost his capacity for enjoyment; and there is something
very touching about the repeated references to his companion, as
if he felt a kind of surprised pride that he was not making the tour
in solitude.

But the new academic year was only a couple of weeks old when
he was back in the nursing home again for almost a month;
according to his own account he had been 'going downhill at a
great pace'* since his return from France. His duties were not
neglected, however, for twice a week a taxi took him from the
nursing home into the College, where he delivered his lectures as
announced. After nearly a quarter of a century the gloomy rooms
in Whewell's Court had been quitted: he had gone on climbing
those forty-four stairs two at a time (hoping, as he said, that he
would drop dead at the top); but now, by the kindness of friends
which moved him greatly, his belongings were transferred to a
ground-floor set in Trinity Great Court, where the splendid

bathroom was his pride and joy.

A letter written on 20 December shows a very shaky hand – a poignant contrast with the bold and elegant script he had always written; and on Christmas Eve he went back into the Nursing Home, to remain there until the end of the vacation. When the new year opened he was 'unable to write a cheque without advice and assistance',* and a letter written on 10 January is in a very feeble hand and, pathetically, misdated. A young Fellow of King's, L. P. Wilkinson, had been alerted to take over his lecture-course on Horace's Satires if the need arose; but Housman was not to be kept out of the lecture-room. 'I am now [in College] and lecturing', he wrote on 20 January, 'but my strength is barely sufficient for necessary work',* and he was concerned at having got behind with the preparation of his lectures, a task to which he normally devoted time during the vacation. Mr Wilkinson, who attended the lectures, has said that there was a marked change in Housman's attitude to his audience at this time:

> The material was as austere as ever, but the barrier of impersonality had gone. He gave us biographical sidelights on the scholars whose names cropped up, and paused from time to time to ask us if we had understood him, appealing for encouragement.*

This was one of several manifestations of an unwonted gentleness towards the end, an eleventh-hour opening up of himself, as if he wanted to retract a lifetime's habit of aloofness. To Mrs de Navarro he talked of the plays he and his brothers and sisters had got up as children, and on his last visit to Withers' home his host noted that whereas

> All his many previous visits were flavoured, faintly or otherwise, with, shall we say, unchristian spicery; this last one was as benignant and mellow as the sunset of a still autumn evening.*

He was overwhelmed by the kindness of those who showed concern for his state, and told Withers that 'the extreme and undeserved kindness and generosity of your letters move me almost to tears'.* To speak of 'undeserved kindness' was no mere conventionality or affection: Housman really believed himself to be unworthy, and was deeply touched by signs that others could feel differently. Moses Jackson's inability to accept his love and to return it in kind had a lot to answer for. At about the same time Housman uses almost the same phrase in a more formal context: he has declined 'a considerable number of honours, even when offered me by my own two Universities and by the King of England with the same excess of kindness and over-estimate of desert'.* He must have known quite well that he was the equal at least of most recipients of honorary degrees; and if this is not false modesty (a quality not much in evidence elsewhere) it seems to show a profound sense of his own unworthiness, not as a poet or a scholar but as a man: a sense generated both by unrequited love and by a lifetime's consciousness of secret guilt underlying public respectability.

Few letters survive from the Lent Term of 1936, and presumably few were written; but he kept on lecturing until term ended, when he returned promptly to the nursing home, whence he wrote on 22 March a long letter to Houston Martin, a young American admirer whom he had never met. He told him that

> In philosophy I am a Cyrenaic or egoistic hedonist, and regard the pleasure of the moment as the only possible motive of action.*

The moment can by this time have brought him few pleasures, but he made the most of them. In the nursing home he had 'reading to fill my hours',* and he welcomed many visitors. One of them was his godson Gerald Jackson, and their conversation must inevitably have turned to memories of Moses. On 2 April he wrote to Kate that he had taken a 'great turn for the better'* on his birthday, 26 March. This letter shows a marked improvement in spirits from one written to Kate nine days earlier, when he had said 'I fear I shall live to be seventy-seven';* but his condition was evidently still very weak: he wrote Kate's address incorrectly on the envelope, and the letter was returned to him by the post office. His passion for accuracy was part of the ground he found himself forced to abandon as his last illness pressed hard upon him.

The Easter Term began on 22 April, and, amazingly, Housman once again began a course of lectures, this time on Catullus 64. But he gave only the first two lectures; J. J. Thomson saw him on the day he gave his last lecture and later wrote that

He was terribly ill and must have had invincible determination to lecture in such a state.*

On the evening of the 24th he attended his last meeting of The Family, but could eat and drink practically nothing; the next day he went into the nursing home, and from there wrote a postcard to Kate: 'Back to Evelyn nursing home to-day. A.E.H. Ugh'.* That the last word from his pen should have been a cry of protest, and that its last letter, at first shakily formed, should have been meticulously amended, were both entirely appropriate. He grew steadily weaker; Dr Woods visited him for the last time on the evening of the 29th, and was touched by his expressions of gratitude. To change the subject he told his patient a mildly indecent story, and it was relished. Housman had a good night and woke cheerful; later in the day he lapsed into unconsciousness and died quietly. None of his family or friends was present; but some of them saw his body as it lay in the nursing-home chapel, and Laurence said that the look on the face was Roman.

A lifetime's vigilance in the never-ending struggle against error was over: no living printer or long-dead copyist could disturb his rest, 'ensured release', with their blunders. Swift's phrase comes irresistibly to mind: savage indignation could tear his breast no longer. But indignation was not the only emotion of which Housman was capable, and his sense of humour would have been wryly gratified by some aspects of the aftermath of his passing. For, as if to dance on his grave, the forces of error set quickly to work. The announcement of his death in *The Times* gave his age incorrectly; there was a gross inaccuracy in the sheet printed for use at the funeral service in Trinity Chapel, and the occasion was otherwise bungled (according to Sydney Cockerell 'no public announcement had been made, and . . . it was poorly attended'*). His ashes were buried at Ludlow, a site with less relevance to his experience than to the fantasy-world of his poems. Laurence thought the rector made the service 'rather too Christian';* his brother might have retorted that any service was too Christian for him.

Today his poems are misquoted even by those who should know better; there is a long tradition of error over the title of his best-known book; his very name is not infrequently misspelt (as it at first was, for instance, when the Housman Room was opened at University College). Every biography has had its larger or smaller quota of errors, and it would be folly to suppose that this one is an exception to the sad human rule: folly worthy of the scorn of Housman, who was driven by a 'passion for perfection'* in a world known to be irredeemably imperfect. Near the end of his own very long life, Laurence Housman gently ridiculed the sentimentality of an American biographer who had spoken of his brother's 'survival in a better world'. 'I have to admit', he wrote, 'that I cannot conceive of A.E.H. hovering over us benevolently – unless he becomes a totally different character'; and he added that his brother would be 'tolerantly critical' of the next world.* It is an epitaph that Housman might well have found acceptable.

7   The Scholar

It has been urged that only a classical scholar can adequately write the life of Housman – which is perhaps like saying that only a Jesuit ought to undertake a biography of Hopkins, only a thief one of Genet. Probably it is true that only a classical scholar can properly evaluate Housman's distinctive achievement in that field; and certainly it is salutary to be reminded that, however posterity may see Housman, he saw himself as a professional scholar who occasionally strayed into writing English verse, and that for every hour he spent writing poems in English, he spent hundreds of hours studying poems in Latin. However, whilst textual criticism may be caviare to the general and much of Housman's work may fail to tempt the palate of even classical specialists, it is possible to exaggerate the arcane nature of his scholarly pursuits. Like theology, and perhaps thieving, classical scholarship can be a highly technical affair; but the nature of textual criticism is more easily grasped by the non-specialist than that of, say, nuclear physics, and one does not have to be a practitioner in order to have some faint appreciation of the qualifications it calls for, the discipline it imposes, or the satisfactions it offers. Housman himself insisted that it was 'not a sacred mystery' but 'purely a matter of reason and of common sense'* – to which the only objection that can be made is that the kind of sense required in a good, let alone a great, textual critic is evidently most uncommon.

To find Housman's equal within his own field, at any rate within the English tradition, one has to go back to a much earlier generation. Among his contemporaries, his closest rival was Ulrich von Wilamowitz-Moellendorf (1848–1931), who was reported as saying that 'although we Germans know Housman to be a rabid Germanophobe, we, nevertheless, unanimously pronounce him to be the greatest living authority on both Latin and Greek in the English-speaking world'.* Since Housman worked mainly in Latin and Wilamowitz was pre-eminently a Greek scholar, the rivalry was not intense; and, Germanophobia notwithstanding, his high regard for Housman was reciprocated and even bettered (see p. 144 above). There is no evidence that they met or even corresponded, though the German visited England at least twice. Housman could pay a handsome tribute as well as deliver a devastating attack; but he also had a proper sense of his own merits, and though he could laugh at, he did not undervalue, himself.

In his preface to *Manilius V*, he speaks of 'my notorious arrogance', and adds that 'I had rather be arrogant than impudent':* that is to say, the more heinous offence in his eyes was to make unfounded pretensions to scholarship. It was not fools, but fools who published, that he was unable to suffer gladly. His self-esteem, though, was not boundless; and to the genius of Bentley he deferred with obstinate modesty. One informant recalled that 'he was very sensitive about being compared with Bentley. I remember my talking with him a few days after the publication of Manilius V: he said "I wish my friends would not compare me with Bentley: Bentley would cut up into four of me."'* When Percy Withers 'guilelessly' repeated to Housman the remark of a Cambridge don that Housman was 'our greatest classical scholar since Bentley', he was disconcerted to find that it produced not gratification but agitation and anger: '"I will not tolerate comparison with Bentley", he said. "Bentley is alone and supreme. They may compare me with Porson if they will – the comparison is not preposterous – he surpassed me in some qualities as I claim to surpass him in others."'* Professor Shackleton Bailey has ventured on the comparison with Bentley in his discussion of Bentley's edition of Horace:

I have read one comparable book, Housman's Manilius, and that was certainly much influenced by Bentley, whom of all successors Housman may be thought to have approached most nearly, however forcefully he himself deprecated comparison. Both wrote Latin with unfailing lucidity . . . and arresting vitality. Compared with Housman's pointed, economical style Bentley's sometimes seems coarse and diffuse . . . In his author Bentley will generally be held to have the advantage . . . To many readers Bentley's gusto and geniality commend him; and he repels none by that quasi-emotional dedication to truth which makes some scholars fidget when Housman's name is mentioned.*

The other side of Housman's respect for Bentley was a disregard, not always tactfully concealed, for the talents and efforts of lesser men. I have quoted earlier his declaration in *Manilius V* that the reader whom he has felt to be looking over his shoulder was 'the next Bentley or Scaliger who may chance to occupy himself with Manilius'. In a letter to one of his reviewers, he wrote

> If the next Bentley or Scaliger came along and told me that *uincunt* in 114 is no improvement on *uictum*, I should be discomposed and begin to examine myself; but when one of you gentlemen says it I only think of him what you think of me, that he ought to be more modest.*

The reader must decide for himself whether such remarks indicate overweening and insufferable arrogance or the admirable forthrightness of one resolved, in Johnsonian phrase, on clearing his mind of cant. It is not difficult to see how Housman acquired a reputation for haughty pride; as he saw the situation, however, he was simply stating the matter as it existed, and to pretend otherwise would have been mere conventional insincerity. Nor must we leave out of account the extent to which he was deliberately trailing his coat, and those who are disturbed by his more outrageously provocative remarks may be doing no more than fall into the trap he has set for them. Acrimonious scholarly controversy was once a flourishing if minor literary genre; and its decline may not be an unmixed blessing. (Professor Shackleton Bailey has recently and nicely said that 'no critic will get far without a touch of the critical temper, a questing malcontent turn, inimical to the gladness of fools and the mendacities of sleeping dogs'.*) In any case, it is Housman's wit and intellectual energy that are usually more striking than his acrimony. He enjoyed polemic, and his enjoyment is obvious and, in his best passages, infectious. Failure to recognize the wit and the huge enjoyment have led to some extraordinary lapses of judgment. How odd, for example, that the brilliant and funny passage in which Housman castigates the German lexicographers who forgot to mention Juvenal in their article on the use by Latin authors of the Greek word for a cat should be seen as 'morose' and 'sombre' by a critic as intelligent and eclectic as Edmund Wilson, or that the mock-heroic use of biblical language should strike Wilson as 'almost Isaiah'.

One ought to remember, too, that by the time he wrote the words quoted above from *Manilius V* Housman had devoted more than half a century to the strenuous study and practice of textual criticism, a length of experience which gave him, if not infallibility, at least an impressive authority. As we have seen, he settled on his special field exceptionally early, in his under-graduate years; and he stuck to it, and at it, for a lifetime. Textual criticism has both a technical and a moral aspect. By Housman's time the study and collation of manuscripts had become established on a scientific footing; and if he lacked the full intensity of Bentley's divinatory genius, he had the advantage of a knowledge of the most highly developed editorial methods. The intellectual challenge, the fascination of what's difficult, and the practice of a discipline calling for the vigilant exercise of exceptional powers of observation, memory and reasoning: this constituted part of the excitement that textual criticism held for Housman. But it was also – or, more accurately, first and foremost – a moral enterprise. For the textual critic is engaged in the pursuit of truth and the banishment of error; textual criticism derives its existence from the human capacity for error, since if scribes had never made mistakes textual scholars would have nothing to do. The perpetuation and multiplying of errors as texts are transmitted over a long period is not a bad image or paradigm for human delusion and deterioration in general: we say of texts, as of men and ideas, that they become corrupt.

To determine what an ancient author actually wrote is, in a small but significant way, to repossess a lost certainty, to be enabled once again to see things as they really are. It is not an activity that the majority of mankind, even educated mankind, are ever likely to be stirred by: compared with the achievements of such Trinity contemporaries as J. J. Thomson or Bertrand Russell, Housman's work as a textual critic is bound to seem trivial to the man on the omnibus or in the public library. As E. J. Kenny has said, 'The very notion of textual exactness – let alone the possibility of achieving it – is for many people a difficult one, and respect for the precise form of a text even in a literate and cultured society cannot be taken for granted';* and in our time the point might be made in stronger terms without much risk of exaggeration. To give oneself endless trouble about the precise form of a single word – *uincunt* or *uictum?* – in a long poem that almost the entire human race, including most students of Latin, will pass through life without reading or wishing to read: put thus, textual criticism seems a bizarre activity, fit for the madhouse, or at least a sad or reprehensible waste of human and other resources.

But Housman suffered no delusions about the nature of his life's work; he knew that for very few, living or dead, would it have any significance, and was perfectly content to labour for the few, or if necessary for no-one. The pursuit of truth needed no further justification in his eyes; if it had no practical effects, it was so much the purer and less likely to be corrupted by considerations of expediency. The ideal material for a textual critic (to push this argument to its extreme) is a bad poem that no-one will ever wish to read. Housman did not go quite so far as to defend that position, though he adjured his friends (with perhaps more than a touch of affectation) not to waste their time reading Manilius. Not many bosoms, even scholarly bosoms, are likely in these days to return an echo to Housman's sentiments; but at least his position was consistent, and it may not be a bad thing, in an age that has made 'relevance' a shibboleth, to be reminded of the case for the opposition.

As a textual critic, Housman was largely self-trained. Gow remarked that his scholarship 'was founded less on the teaching he received at Bromsgrove and Oxford than upon long and profound study of the great scholars of the past',* above all of Bentley. His training-ground was the edition of Propertius begun, with astonishing confidence and precocity, in his undergraduate years, submitted to Macmillan without success, and never published. But in his twenties, as we have seen, he was receiving acceptances from the classical journals; from 1887 he published something every year, and he averaged three or four papers a year over a period of half a century. His collected classical papers, published in 1927, fill three substantial volumes; the editors make no apology for disregarding his express wish that no such collection should ever appear, arguing plausibly that 'posterity cannot be bound for ever'.* His name began to be known at a time of considerable activity in the area he was to make his own; a historian of classical scholarship has said that the years 1890–1910 were 'peculiarly rich in contributions to our knowledge and understanding of Silver Latin poetry',* with British scholars making a major contribution. At first he worked on both Latin and Greek authors, and R. W. Chambers later expressed regret that Housman had not obtained the Greek chair at University College and thus spent his time on Aeschylus and Sophocles rather than Manilius and Lucan. But his acceptance of the Chair of Latin in 1892 committed him almost exclusively to Latin studies, and changing fashions in learning over the next forty years had little effect upon him. As Professor Shackleton Bailey has said, over a period of more than fifty years 'Housman's philological *persona* changed little'.*

Apart from a mass of papers ranging from short notes to substantial articles, Housman produced three major editions of Latin poets: of the satires of Juvenal (1905; second edition 1931); of Lucan (1926; second edition 1927); and of Manilius (five books published separately, 1903–30). It is natural to ask why he should have seen fit to devote his great abilities and enormous labours to these authors rather than to, say, Virgil, Horace, or Catullus; but Housman would have found the question childishly naive. The textual critic is a solver of problems, and the material he selects to work upon must not only contain problems that await solution but must contain problems susceptible of solution. Since Housman made a firm distinction between textual and literary criticism, the literary merits of the textual critic's subject-matter were not a prime consideration. On the other hand, it would be wrong to exaggerate the inferiority of the authors he chose to work with. Juvenal and Lucan have an assured place in world literature; if Manilius is a harder case, it is not entirely baffling.

When Auden wrote of Housman that 'Deliberately he chose the dryasdust', he missed the point about Housman's scholarship in his anxiety to make a point about his masochism; and Edmund Wilson was tempted into the same blunder by the seductions of a vivid journalistic paradox when he said that Housman 'deliberately and grimly chose Manilius when his real interest was in Propertius', and deduced from this 'an element of perversity, of self-mortification, in Housman's career all along'.* Wilson failed to grasp the situation. In 1888, Housman wrote that he saw 'no hope of completing a presentable commentary on Propertius within the next ten years', but was publishing some of his conjectures without further delay, 'as I am for ever seeing them forestalled by other students'.* This suggests the frustration of working in an overcrowded field: the editor of Manilius was certain to suffer less competition, and less anxiety during a long-term undertaking that he might be beaten to the post. In any case, he had long put Propertius behind him before he settled on Manilius. Moreover, there was nothing dryasdust about Manilius *for the textual critic*: after all, both Scaliger and Bentley had deemed him worthy of attention. Whether the interest of the text makes it an object worthy of the labours of thirty years is unanswerable except from the depth of one's own convictions. But it is plain that for Housman, who had declared before he ever turned to Manilius that all knowledge is worth having because its pursuit satisfies one of man's highest appetites, there could be no doubt on this point.

The astrologer-poet Manilius is not one of those authors whom a well-read man, or even a professional classical scholar, is ashamed not to have read. Both his subject-matter and his Latin are technical and difficult. Housman told Bridges that 'he writes on astronomy and astrology without knowing either. My interest in him is purely technical';* and to Arthur Platt he made what was essentially the same point with characteristic irony: 'If you prefer Aeschylus to Manilius you are no true scholar; you must be deeply tainted with literature . . .*'. His position is perfectly consistent: a strong literary interest can be a positive handicap for a textual critic, and a 'purely technical' interest can still be completely and intensely engaged. But one suspects also some deliberate playing down of his own enthusiasm, a certain posturing as the single-minded scholar working away at a task of no earthly interest to anyone – a pose which has been mistaken for the real thing.

It is as well to remember that Scaliger praised Manilius as 'a most ingenious poet and a most elegant writer', that Professor Shackleton Bailey has called him 'perhaps the most ingenious, though certainly not the most generally enjoyable, of Latin poets',* and that Professor Lloyd Jones has recently said that 'by the canons of his own kind of art, he is a poet of considerable merit'.* That ingenuity attracted a notable line of editors from Scaliger onwards, and Housman must have been moved by the excitement as well as the intellectual challenge of competing for an honoured place in the great tradition. Even in the late twentieth century, Manilius finds readers: Shackleton Bailey has said of Housman's edition that 'to read it closely, intelligently, and completely is more than a unique intellectual experience',* and the most recent edition, heavily indebted to Housman, appeared in 1977.

Housman seems to have read Manilius's long poem through for the first time in about 1894;* he published his first conjectures in

1898 and 1901, and his edition of the first of the five books appeared in 1903, and included both a dedicatory Latin poem to Moses Jackson ('sodali meo . . . Harum litterarum contemptori') and a long, provocative and brilliant preface. The other books followed in 1912, 1916, 1920 and 1930. Probably Housman had not originally conceived it as a thirty-year task: at any rate, when Andrew Gow asked him why emendations relevant to the later books had been included in his edition of the first, he was told that there had been no initial intention to commit himself to editing the entire poem. But when Cambridge bestowed upon him the leisure he had lacked in London, he may have resolved to make the edition his monument.

Predictably, it was far from being a best-seller: as he noted at the end of his labours, all of the volumes had been 'produced at my own expense and offered to the public at much less than cost price; but this unscrupulous artifice did not overcome the natural disrelish of mankind for the combination of a tedious author with an odious editor'.* Four hundred copies of each had been printed; only the first had been sold out, and that had taken twenty-three years – and then only because, as Housman speculated, 'the unlearned' had 'hoped to extract . . . a low enjoyment' from the 'scurrilous preface'. The tone, mocking his own efforts as well as the world's indifference, is entirely typical of his public and private utterances in connection with the Manilius: it is as though he is fearful of betraying the serious, dedicated, even passionate application that had kept him going from middle life into old age.

As work on the final volume reached its later stages, he was genuinely concerned that he might not live to finish it. In the summer of 1929 he broke with his custom of flying to France as, statistically, too risky: 'I am taking great care of my life till the book I am now engaged on is finished.'* Sixteen months later, he was able to write that 'the last volume of my great work is now published, and now perhaps I shall have leisure to improve my mind and prepare to meet my God'.* The ironic, self-mocking tone does not really disguise the fact that he sincerely believed it to be a 'great work'.

It is a commonplace to call the Manilius Housman's monument, but the smooth phrase has not altogether allayed nagging doubts, cogently expressed by L. P. Wilkinson, who suggests that 'the desire to build such a monument . . . is not rational for one who disbelieves in any "perfect witness of all-judging Jove"'' and, moreover, that

> an edition of Manilius was a fast-diminishing monument in the
> modern world. Even between its beginning, some time before
> 1900, and its completion in 1930 it probably suffered some
> devaluation as a potential source of fame. In the Natural
> Sciences the establishment of any fact, and the acquisition of
> any knowledge, is worthwhile because it may prove to be the
> missing piece in some important puzzle, whereas in the
> Humanities omniscience in a limited sphere is only for would-
> be monument builders. For the rest of us the price . . . is too
> heavy to pay.*

Housman would not have objected to the implication that, in
judging the game to be worth the candle, he differed from most of
mankind; and one answer might be that his conception of a
worthy monument was long-sighted enough to make
'devaluation' in a mere forty years a matter of little concern. To
quote yet again his aristocratic boast, 'the reader whose good
opinion I desire and have done my utmost to secure is the next
Bentley or Scaliger who may chance to occupy himself with
Manilius'. One whose working life is spent with authors dead for a
couple of thousand years will have absorbed the lesson that the
opinions of the passing generations are in the long run of little
moment.

Still, on its completion the work was hailed by most of those
competent to judge as a magnificent achievement. It has been
called 'the supreme glory of Manilian – one might almost say of
Latin – scholarship in the present century . . . striking evidence
that the spirit of Scaliger and Bentley has survived into our
present age'* – a verdict that, had he lived to read it, would surely
have warmed Housman's heart. Soon after his death, one
reviewer described it as 'a monument of scholarship which admits
its author to the company of Scaliger and Bentley';* another said
that it was 'equalled by no other achievement of recent years in the
field of classical studies in its display of great learning, clever
interpretation, brilliant emendation, keen criticism, and violent
invective'.* It is true that the voice of scepticism was not silent,
and a reviewer in the *Classical Journal* observed tartly: 'that a man
of a taste too nice to endure even his colleagues should bear for
more than thirty-five years with a fifth-rate poet windily

discoursing on a tenth-rate subject is a performance little short of heroic'.* But the majority vote was overwhelmingly in Housman's favour.

The edition of Juvenal was completed in 1904 and published by Grant Richards; it thus stands between the first two books of Manilius and attests to Housman's tirelesss industry even during the University College years, with their heavy burden of teaching. On its title-page Housman used for the first time the formula 'Editorum in usum edidit', which he later translated as 'for the behoof of editors'. In the judgment of Gilbert Highet, the edition 'is based on an inadequate number of manuscripts but is intelligently, if acrimoniously, edited'.*

Work on the Lucan occupied Housman between the fourth and fifth books of Manilius, and his edition was published in 1926. To a correspondent he wrote that 'Lucan would do you no good. He has rhetoric and epigram but no true poetry. My edition . . . is for advanced scholars and is scientific – not literary.'* Again, Housman's policy is clear: poetry belonged to another part of his life; editing was a matter of science in which literary considerations could only be a hindrance and a distraction. It is significant that Housman should have chosen to work on authors whose poetry was as different as possible from his own. That he should, on the evidence of the Leslie Stephen Lecture, have found eighteenth-century English poetry unappealing suggests that he may have been unprepared to concede the literary merits of didactic verse; but in any case, as so often, a certain affectation, disarming or provocative, but in any case self-defensive, is evident in his dismissive comments on Manilius and Lucan as poets. The preface to the Lucan goes even further than usual in its proud consciousness of appealing only to a tiny minority:

> Emendators should thank their stars that they have the multitude against them and must address the judicious few, and that moral integrity and intellectual vigilance are for them not merely duties but necessities.*

'Moral integrity and intellectual vigilance': again, the order is significant. The scholarly excellence of his edition was widely recognized, and it 'justly elicited superlatives from the reviewers'.* One of them called it 'the event of the year, both for what it does for its author and as a model of sincere investigation

and masterly condensation'; another went further and described
it as 'one of the greatest events of the present century for the Latin
scholar'. The most recent study of Lucan (by Frederick M. Ahl,
1976) uses Housman's text.

During the Patent Office years, Housman had toiled as a part-
time scholar; at University College, he had carried a burden of
teaching and administration; but with the move to Cambridge in
1911 he was for the first time able to devote his energies mainly to
his studies. L. P. Wilkinson has written:

> The statutes of Cambridge, by not prescribing that a Professor,
> or even a Reader, must give lectures, allow for the existence of
> scholars who would be best occupied exclusively in scholarship,
> though F. L. Lucas compared Housman editing Manilius with
> Apollo picking the oakum of Admetus, 'divinely, but oakum'.*

The same writer has speculated on Housman's influence:

> Housman may have done some harm to classical education by
> his attitudes. It may be that textual criticism at its highest
> demands a combination of talents and knowledge beyond any
> other classical activity, since they must include literary
> perception; but that does not mean that it should attract all the
> most gifted young scholars. The number of worthwhile texts
> that still need its attention will gradually diminish: Housman
> himself removed Juvenal, Lucan, and Manilius from the list.
> We shall always need textual critics, but theirs must become
> increasingly a minority activity.

The case against Housman's influence has been stated most
strongly by J. P. Sullivan:

> It has been perhaps our great misfortune that in a critical
> period for classical studies, in a time of educational change and
> reform, Housman with his considerable talents and equally
> considerable influence should have added his weight to an
> already powerful tendency. He thus created within our literary
> studies a strange rarefied atmosphere of intellectual snobbery
> and so prevented the development within classics of a literary
> discipline which would produce not simply more scholars and
> textual critics but educated men.*

Others have spoken in very different terms of Housman's inspirational and exemplary power, and some of them have been quoted earlier in this study. Housman would no doubt have demanded of Professor Sullivan what it is that he would have had him do. He decided early in life in which field his particular talents could most successfully be employed, and he pursued those 'minute and pedantic studies' for a lifetime: the narrowness of the elderly scholar was the narrowness of the young candidate for Finals. Being a professor of Latin was, he declared, his 'trade': no-one could say that he did not execute his duties conscientiously, and the universities he served got value for their money. We can count the committees on which a man serves, but it is impossible to quantify influence; still, there must have been hundreds to whom Housman gave an ideal of scholarship and many who transmitted his influence to others over many years and in many places. At the very least, his energy and perseverance must be admired; not every life sets itself a goal and works unflinchingly to its attainment. Housman's ambition was exceptionally, almost audaciously, high; but he lived to fulfil it. Nor, though they go without saying, should we leave unmentioned his powerful intellect, immense learning, prodigious memory and tireless industry.

More eloquently than anyone else in our generation, Professor Shackleton Bailey has championed Housman's scholarly achievement in vigorous language that surely (and I intend the observation as high praise) owes much to Housman's influence; and I cannot do better than to quote at length from the appreciation he wrote for the centenary of Housman's birth, in which he set out 'to isolate the thing which makes it possible to revere him beyond any other classical scholar, even beyond those who were by and large incontestably greater':

It is not that he started or represented a trend, though that in a sense he did. In the latter half of the last century a foolish practice had established itself among the editors of ancient authors, especially in Germany – the practice of adhering through thick and thin to the readings of a chosen manuscript. You decided, not always on adequate grounds, that one manuscript preserved the author's original text more faithfully than the rest, and you stuck to its readings whenever they could by any stretch be defended, and sometimes when they could not. I am simplifying a little, but that was the tendency, one which made life easy for editors and hard for readers. It was a fashion none the less foolish because it reversed an earlier fashion of violent and irresponsible conjecture. Housman attacked it by precept and example; and, so far as battles against stupidity are ever won, he triumphed. Here are his words, from the preface to his final volume of Manilius which was published only six years before his death:

> My first reception was not worse than I expected. I provoked less enmity and insolence than Scaliger or Bentley in proportion as my merits were less eminent and unbearable than theirs. But my disregard of established opinions and my disrespect for contemporary fashions in scholarship made the ignorant feel sure that I was greatly and presumptuously in error and could be put down without much difficulty; and critiques were accordingly published which I do not suppose that their authors would now wish to rescue from oblivion. Not by paying any attention to any of them, not by swerving an inch from my original principles and practice, but by the mere act of living on and continuing to be the same, I have changed that state of things; and the deaf adder, though I can hardly say that she has unstopped her own ears, has begun to stifle her hisses for fear that they should reach the ears of posterity.

The tone may not be to everybody's liking, but the words are true. It is largely thanks to Housman that we do not find so many editors nowadays eager to construe, as the phrase goes, through a brick wall.

All the same, his refusal to subscribe to a false method was not the exaltation of a rival method: he did not much believe in methods. Housman believed in treating philological problems on their individual merits: you could lay down hard-and-fast rules, he said, but if you did, they would be false rules. To do as he did successfully needs a rare combination of gifts and acquirements: learning, for one. Housman's was enormous: he took no pains either to parade or to conceal it. Since the Romans are not here to be asked what is or is not good Latin, their usage has to be deduced from the writings that survive, so that to edit a Latin author effectively one must go through a large quantity of literature in search of parallel passages which may throw light on this or that difficulty. Housman's notes are storehouses of these; he deployed them, never superfluously indeed or irrelevantly, but with gusto. And I have always suspected that the animus which he sometimes seemed to show against the great German dictionary, the *Thesaurus Linguae Latinae*, had partly to do with a feeling that such compilations help lazy scholars to conceal their lack of reading.

Housman's acuteness in diagnosing a textual fault and his resourcefulness in emendation were as remarkable as his erudition. Sometimes they led him astray, particularly in his earlier work in which, like Ovid, he was often too much in love with his own genius: it takes a good many years under modern conditions to mature a textual critic. Even to the end he could be too reluctant to admit defeat when victory was impossible, or over-much inclined to credit his authors with as sharp a sense of logic as his own. But in the poets among whom he felt most at home, Ovid and the post-Augustans, his literary tact saved him from the lapses of less sensitive emendators. And however complex or recondite his matter, his style in Latin or English remained clear as light – an agile, provocative, intensely personal style, partly deriving from Bentley's but with a closer affinity, I sometimes think, to Bernard Shaw's.

Greatly as I admire these things, I do not venerate them. When I ask myself what it is that has made my readings of the *Manilius* the most memorable intellectual experience of my life, I look to another quality, which I find in no other comparable scholar to anything like the same degree. I mean Housman's unremitting, passionate zeal to see each one of the innumerable problems in his text not as others had presented it or as he might have preferred it to appear but exactly as it was. Is that so unusual? Unfortunately it is. Dull critics solve difficulties only by accident, clever ones are continually being deflected, as Bentley and Housman himself in his early period so often were, by excitement at their own ingenuities, or perhaps by some half-conscious prejudice – the desire, for instance, to support manuscripts against conjectures or one manuscript against another. The result is plausibility rather than truth.

Housman calls two eminent contemporary Latinists (who were largely responsible for the manuscript worship to which I have referred), Bücheler and Vahlen, 'men of wide learning and no mean acuteness, but without simplicity of judgment'; and of an earlier editor of Manilius he writes that he was 'no marvel of learning or brilliancy or penetration; but the prime virtue of a critic, worth all the rest, he had: simplicity and rectitude of judgment'. Housman *was* a marvel of learning and brilliancy and penetration: and he had, or came to have, the prime virtue; which is to say that he clung to reality, abhorring from the bottom of his soul all efforts to fit it upon frames or smother it in cotton wool. Reality, in philology as elsewhere, is often inconvenient. So much the worse: 'They say my verse is sad'.

The devil's advocate must have his word: 'Didn't Housman tend to put things too dogmatically, wasn't his presentation of a case often rhetorical and one-sided?' This is true, and it is the heaviest count against him – though one must not forget that he followed a rhetorical tradition and that editors who set out all that can be said for every point of view may lack publishers (or readers) for their interminable notes. But the distinction is this: he would always – or nearly always, being human – make up his mind without bias. Of the conclusion once formed he became sometimes too exclusive, even egotistical, a champion.

Other criticisms are less valid. W. M. Lindsay used to gird at him incessantly for his disregard of *Überlieferungsgeschichte* – the history of particular texts – and other palaeographical matters. In fact Housman kept palaeography in its proper place as the servant of critical judgment, while Lindsay would have put it in control. An eminent American Latinist, Professor Hendrickson, has expressed surprise that Housman so often took his reports of manuscript readings from others instead of collating the manuscripts himself. Collation is a job for clerks or electronic machines, and a scholar who happens to possess a brain capable of more delicate operations is right to let others do it for him whenever he fairly can.

Another line of attack is that Housman spent his efforts on authors of inferior calibre. That is partly untrue and it is partly irrelevant. Hardly anything in the remnants of ancient literature is without some value for those who value such things at all. And a born textual critic is like a physician; he does not go too anxiously into the merit of what he heals: he gives his aid where it is most needed and most effectual. That Housman lacked aptitude for broad generalization or for the arrangement of masses of unco-ordinated material, everyone must admit; this was the corollary of his intensely clear vision of detail But he knew his limits, and kept well within them.

His ferocity towards other scholars – in print, never in person – is a fundamental matter, and if one does not understand and to a great extent sympathize with that, one cannot understand Housman. I have seen it stated again and again that he denounced inaccuracy. Sometimes he did, when it was flagrant and habitual, but it is a gross mistake to imagine him as lying in wait to pounce upon the occasional factual error, to which the best of scholars is liable. His *saeva indignatio* was nearly always reserved for pretentious incompetence, intellectual fraud, meanness of spirit, and that compound of the three which makes men band together, with cries of mutual encouragement, round a fashionable totem. Against these things Housman waged war, without respect of persons or enmity towards them (the myth of his anti-Germanism was long ago exploded by Mr. Gow). That notorious notebook of his in which he entered verbal shafts, not pointed against anybody in particular but for use as occasion might arise, is evidence of a hatred of certain human tendencies (not men) which left him no rest. He could not – and it is the emotional mainspring of his poetry – just 'see injustice done'. Let it be added that Housman, while his praise was occasionally partial, was hardly ever wrong when he denounced. Robinson Ellis *had*, among scholars, the intellect of an idiot child, Francken *was* a born blunderer, marked cross from the womb and perverse, van Wageningen's commentary *does* most resemble a magpie's nest.

Housman might have agreed with Napoleon that the worst form of immorality is to engage in a calling of which one is not a master. But such anger and disgust in connexion with classical learning may seem ludicrous to people who do not reflect that a bad reading in Manilius and a world war can spring from the same moral and intellectual roots. It is easy to put down his life work as a squandering of intellect upon laborious trifles. The question 'was it worth while?' plunges into metaphysics. I suppose it cannot be answered, and yet, in the retrospect of such a career, it will not be put aside. Housman, who was no philosopher, answered it himself in an inaugural lecture at London, but not to his own lasting satisfaction. Shall we say that one man edits Manilius, as another climbs Everest, because it is there? But the pebbles on the shore are there, and only children count them. I am no philosopher either, but I will risk two not specially original suggestions. First, a pursuit which engages the interest of a considerable number of intelligent people can empirically be reckoned 'worth while'. Second, a society which cares only for work that is somehow aimed at the situation of its lust for power or its physical appetites (and, by the way, Housman did not neglect his appetites, at least so far as eating and drinking were concerned) should be in a fair way towards an inglorious end, of bombs or boredom.*

8   The Poet

Declining an invitation to a reception at his publisher's, Charles Lutwidge Dodgson wrote that 'the fewer there are who are able to connect my face with the name "Lewis Carroll" the happier for me'; and in 1890 he took the extraordinary step of having a circular printed at Oxford stating that 'he neither claims nor acknowledges any connection with any pseudonym, or with any book that is not published under his own name'.* Housman's impulse towards the dissociation of his literary personalities never carried him to these lengths; but he maintained a barrier between Professor Housman, whose 'trade' was to study and teach Latin and to edit classical texts, and Mr Housman, who, very occasionally, wrote and published poems; and conversational attempts to flatten the barrier could irritate or perhaps scare him into a much-publicized but rather uncharacteristic rudeness. On the other hand, and after all, he chose to publish the poems under his own name and was certainly gratified by the fame they brought him, which he compared to a cushion interposed between himself and the cold ground. So that it will not do to exaggerate the scholar's reluctance to be recognized as a poet.

Long before his death, he must have realized that, having set out to build himself a monument, he had succeeded in building two; and he probably appreciated without bitterness the irony that for every reader of his Manilius (the product of thirty years' labour) there were thousands of readers of *A Shropshire Lad* (the alleged result of a sore throat). His sister Kate, noting that he often broke his rule of refusing permission for his poems to be anthologized, commented that he was 'very amenable to importunity and was flattered by it. In my view, what he cared for most was as wide a circulation as possible of his poems, and that they should help to perpetuate his name.'* This sounds shrewd and convincing, and it is consistent with Housman's anxiety, evident right from the start, to keep the price of his volumes of verse as low as possible, and with his wish, only semi-jocular, to learn that a bullet had been stopped by a copy of *A Shropshire Lad* in a soldier's breast-pocket – a function traditionally performed, of course, by the Bible.

A Shropshire Lad was not an instant best-seller, but its reputation climbed steadily, and by 1918 it was possible for an academic survey of contemporary literature to declare that 'the genius of Mr. A. E. Housman places him with the first of living English poets [that is, Hardy]'.* Within the next twenty years, the impact of the modernists was to make Housman's poems seem to belong to a vanished age, as indeed many of them did: *Last Poems*, though published in the same year as *The Waste Land*, is in no real sense a postwar collection, and some of the poems included in it were written, or at least started, before Victoria died. Still, for the generation that came of age in the second and third decades of this century, Housman exercised a potent and perhaps a unique influence. Writing soon after Housman's death, George Orwell charted the rise and decline of his reputation:

> At the beginning of the period I am speaking of, the years during and immediately after the war, the writer who had the deepest hold upon the thinking young was almost certainly Housman. Among people who were adolescent in the years 1910–25, Housman had an influence which was enormous and is now not at all easy to understand. In 1920, when I was about seventeen, I probably knew the whole of the *Shropshire Lad* by heart. I wonder how much impression the *Shropshire Lad* makes at this moment [1940] on a boy of the same age and more or less the same cast of mind?*

Orwell does not add, as he might have done, that some of his age-group remained faithful to Housman as they grew older: a whole generation of schoolmasters were still exposing the young to their enthusiasm when he wrote, and indeed much later. Orwell himself seems to have been anxious to explain away the sources of Housman's appeal in order to cast him aside with other embarrassing relics of his middle-class youth. But he is honest enough to conclude that 'there is no need to underrate him now because he was overrated a few years ago', though his comment that 'there are a number of poems . . . that are not likely to remain long out of favour' is qualified by the revealing clause, 'although one gets into trouble nowadays for saying so'.

In the same year that Orwell wrote, Stephen Spender judged Housman's to be a poetry of negation and of missed opportunities: 'he might have thrown aside the role of repression altogether and written a poetry which explored his own personality'* – a judgment that seems to betray either lack of understanding of that 'personality' or an unawareness of the social realities of the age. Spender makes an interesting comparison between Housman and Donne as love poets, and fails to discover in Housman's work the 'honesty and audacity' of Hopkins; his touchstones reflect, of course, the critical fashions of a new generation. Thirty years later, a third member of that generation, W. H. Auden, echoes Orwell's tribute while also echoing his limiting reference to adolescence:

> I don't know how it is with the young today, but to my generation no other English poet seemed so perfectly to express the sensibility of a male adolescent.*

Forty years or so after Housman's death and the pronouncements of Orwell and Spender would seem to be about par for the revival of interest in a writer whose neglect for a generation or two may have been no more than a normal reaction against his great popularity. Alternatively, it gives enough time for a poet worthy of oblivion to receive his just deserts: the academic survey already cited couples Housman's name in 1918 with that of Herbert Trench, and who now reads Trench? Literary reputations are hard to measure, but anthologies, though subject to the personal whims of their compilers, provide a crude yardstick as both indicating and helping to create popular taste. In the year of Housman's death, Yeats's *Oxford Book of Modern Verse* included five of his poems, and soon afterwards (1939) the new edition of the *Oxford Book of English Verse* only three; but the latest successors to these volumes (1972 and 1973 respectively) each raise the number to eight. The most recent edition (1979) of the *Oxford Book of Quotations* includes almost twice as many passages from Housman as the previous edition; and one anthology put into the hands of large numbers of the American thinking young, the *Norton Anthology of Modern Poetry* (1973), includes no fewer than seventeen poems. It is too early to start cheering, but it looks as though a return to favour may be taking place. A comparable case is that of Kipling: enormously popular in his lifetime, dramatically eclipsed since his death (in the same year as Housman), he has lately become the subject of renewed attention.

Housman has not lacked readers during this interim: anthologies, syllabuses and dissertations are not infallible guides to the obstinate vitality of an author; the general reader is not merely an invention of optimistic publishers; and there are some whose work remains defiantly alive long after it has been pronounced dead by academic authority. Like Hardy and the Brontës, Housman is one of those writers who exercise a continuing attraction for many whose enthusiasm for literature is blended with other enthusiasms: for landscape, topography, genealogy, 'folkways', nostalgia for a vanished England, and strenuous physical exercise. But for a long time, and for fairly evident reasons, Housman has received only a limited amount of attention from critics (though, as we shall see, the *quality* of that attention has often been very high). Probably we ought to be grateful for this, but the cause is suggestive. The apparent simplicity, even naivety, of his poems has been seen as offering little scope for exegetical ingenuity: in a critical tradition in which poetic recalcitrance is highly valued, who will think it worth struggling to say something original about 'Is my team ploughing?'. Still, some have long ago recognized that Housman's simplicity *is* only apparent. In the same year as Orwell's essay, John Peale Bishop wrote:

> Despite an apparent clarity such that almost any poem seems ready to deliver its meaning at once, there is always something that is not clear, something not brought into the open, something that is left in doubt.*

'Always' is perhaps drawing the generalization a bit strong, but the caveat is a necessary one; and the sense that the reader of Housman is not confronted merely with a poetry of surface has been shared by some of the outstanding critics of our time. Not many minor poets have impelled critics of the calibre of (among others) Edmund Wilson, Randall Jarrell, Cleanth Brooks, F. W. Bateson, William Empson and Christopher Ricks to feel that there was something that needed to be said about them. Small-scale though they be, their contributions constitute a collective recognition that Housman's poetry does not lack subtlety and nuance.

I call Housman a minor poet not dismissively but descriptively – some of the poets one returns to most eagerly are minor poets – and with the assumption that the matter calls for no debate. His output was small (about 175 published poems all told, excluding translations and comic verse), and his range narrow. The strength of that narrowness is well conveyed by Bishop, when he says that 'the limits within which Housman was able to feel at all were strict, but within them he felt intensely, and both strictness and intensity are in his verse'.* This small body of work is the product of the intermittent poetic activity of thirty years or more: not a high output, but then Housman's pride in his 'barrenness' was not affected, and he genuinely deplored the productivity of such contemporaries as Hardy and Bridges. But to speak of barrenness is in any case misleading.

Housman's rate of production was by no means steady: as we have seen, a major burst of creative activity produced the 1896 volume, a less intense but still exceptional period of activity the 1922 volume, and in many years he must have written practically nothing. He wrote only fitfully because he did not go in search of poems (or so he would have had us believe, and we probably ought to believe him) but waited for them to find him out. There is little point, therefore, in comparing him with more prolific poets (Hardy, say, or Auden) who made a profession of poetry and would sit down at their desks of a morning to write poems as a clerk might sit down to his files. After all, Housman's profession lay elsewhere, and he sat down at *his* desk, morning and night, to write lectures or reviews or to edit Manilius. On the other hand, it won't do to imply that Housman wrote poems as a genteel pastime, like a maiden aunt executing needlework.

The emotional intensity that Bishop detected in his best work distinguishes it from the great mass of minor poetry of the period 1890–1930, most of it now virtually unreadable. Housman wrote from an urgent personal need to find expression for the inexpressible. They are not for the most part 'biographical,' these poems, at least not in any straightforward sense; and disaster awaits (and has already overtaken) those who search them, as others search Shakespeare's sonnets, for the story of a hidden life. But they have a personal element that cannot be ignored, since it is both the reason for their existence and their true as distinct from their apparent subject. Between the life and the poem a transformation has usually taken place, though different poems show different degrees of transformation, rather as if we were confronted with a chemical or perhaps an evolutionary process arrested at different stages in different specimens.

Sometimes, though much less frequently than some have supposed, experience seems to be presented in direct and literal terms without the intervention of a symbol-making or mythologizing process:

> He would not stay for me; and who can wonder?
> He would not stay for me to stand and gaze.
> I shook his hand and tore my heart in sunder
> And went with half my life about my ways.
>
> (*AP* VII)

This has the immediacy of a diary entry; we recall that Housman's vestigial diary also uses the pronoun 'he' without an explicit referent. It is, in content and form, both fragmentary (part of a life; a stanza from an otherwise unwritten poem) and complete (a moment that, summing up a relationship once and for all, is preserved in the memory like an old photograph; a perfectly shaped monument to that moment). It combines a striking emotional intensity with a curious flatness of style – all but three words in the poem are monosyllables: is that a record? – and this seems to mirror the peculiar nature of the remembered or imagined situation, in which powerful feelings are constrained by a formality of behaviour demanded by a relationship as well as by time and place. The tension between social surface and inner emotion that belongs to the occasion is mimed in the structure of the lines that make up this poem or epigram, each line being pulled in different directions by implicit contrasts: movement is set against stasis, an impatient awareness of time against unawareness, formal outward contact ('hand') against real private desolation ('heart'), social decorum against inner chaos. Stylistically, the tension produces a contrast between prim cliché ('shook his hand', 'went . . . about my ways') and the language of feeling ('tore my heart', 'half my life'): a contrast that, again, energizes the line-unit. I spoke above, evasively, of the remembered or imagined situation; and if we are eager to ascribe the experience recorded in the poem (assuming that 'recorded' is the word) to a particular instant of clock and calendar, 10.45 p.m. on Sunday, 22 May 1898 will do better than any other (see p. 86

above). In that case (but it remains a supposition, of course), this would seem to be a rare instance of a poem in which experience in a pure form has been turned by Housman into a poem.

This does not happen very often, and it is not surprising that this poem was not published during his lifetime. But even here there might be a case – though not, I think, a very powerful one – for arguing that the poem distils or dramatizes a relationship rather than depicting a historical moment, and that the leave-taking is a metaphor for estrangement or unrequited love. I suggest this possibility because it serves to introduce a second category of poem, in which the circumstantial world has undergone a dreamlike transformation. Now and again we can actually catch the fantasy-making in process, and in such instances the code is not hard to decipher:

> Oh were he and I together,
> 　　Shipmates on the fleeted main,
> Sailing through the summer weather
> 　　To the spoil of France or Spain.
>
> Oh were he and I together,
> 　　Locking hands and taking leave,
> Low upon the trampled heather
> 　　In the battle lost at eve.
>
> Now are he and I asunder
> 　　And asunder to remain;
> Kingdoms are for others' plunder,
> 　　And content for other slain.
>
> 　　　　　　　　　　　(*AP* II)

This, too, remained unpublished until after Housman's death, and the fact causes no surprise: it is evidently a very personal poem, embodying both an attempt to translate raw experience into myth and an acute self-consciousness concerning the process. In the first two stanzas the mood is, as Housman might have said, the optative: sexual fantasy settles on images drawn from the romantic fiction of boyhood (with perhaps some contribution from Victorian genre painting), and hence capable of being entertained without guilt-feelings. But the wish is after all – or not so much after all as from the very start – *only* a wish; and the third stanza bluntly states the bleak contemporary fact. The sundering is a matter not of high romance but of prosaic reality; the 'fleeted main' is really the salt estranging sea (the epithets are Matthew Arnold's: cf. *MP* VII); the locking of hands, unexaggerated, is no more than the brief formal handshake of farewell in *AP* VII. (Housman was much preoccupied by hand-contact: see the striking lines on the subject in *ASL* XXXVII.) In the present poem, Housman is both converting personal anguish into distanced myth and recognizing that such efforts are, in the long run, ineluctably fruitless. The explicit recognition of the final stanza recalls that of *In Memoriam* VII: there too the illusion of a clasped hand is never unqualified by the awareness that an illusion is all it can ever be. Housman's poem, one might add, contains ingredients that are encountered repeatedly in his verse: the fascination with a life of action and with early death, especially death in battle, as the not unwelcome culmination of such a life. As the work of Stevenson and Kipling strikingly testifies, it was a fascination curiously pervasive in the generation that produced *A Shropshire Lad*.

The message is not always so readily decoded, however: occasionally, the poetic situation substituted for the original experience or emotion seems so puzzling or incomplete that the situation for which it stands as a kind of metaphor cannot be reconstructed with any confidence. This is not to say, of course, that the poetic quality is necessarily impaired. Consider these haunting though baffling lines:

> He, standing hushed, a pace or two apart,
>   Among the bluebells of the listless plain,
> Thinks, and remembers how he cleansed his heart
>   And washed his hands in innocence in vain.
>
> (MP XXVIII)

The circumstantiality, conventional though it was, of the previous poem quoted is here absent. 'Listless plain' is a striking phrase, but more striking than clear and more like Auden than Housman; bluebells are flowers of woodland and hedgerow, not of plains; from whom or what is he, whoever he may be, 'a pace or two apart,' and why is he 'hushed'? The suggested allusion to Psalm 73, verses 13–14, hardly resolves these enigmas. And yet, intelligible or not, the poem or fragment has a good deal of power, the power of a vivid and incomprehensible dream. It is as if

Housman had tried to communicate a mood of desolation and regret without passing through the normally obligatory stage of creating a situation fully adequate to embodying that mood.

These small-scale and posthumously published examples have exhibited Housman apparently working with very personal material – moods and yearnings and perhaps actual historical occasions – and transposing them with different degrees of completeness into imagined poetic and dramatic situations. In the volumes published during his lifetime, and notably in *A Shropshire Lad*, he does this with greater completeness and consistency; and it is time to look at the ways in which he objectifies certain preoccupations in order to be able in his poems to work out problems and attitudes (giving expression to them being one way of working them out) that he was unable or unwilling to communicate to anyone in direct and literal terms. Two contemporary parallels come to mind. Hardy* repeatedly insisted that his poems were 'dramatic and personative' when they were often quite clearly nothing of the sort (see, for example, the prefaces to his first two collections of verse). It is not surprising that he and Housman should independently have hit on a similar gambit, for both were intensely reserved men in search of acceptable modes for the expression of intimate feelings. Housman, however, creates a more elaborate system of substitutions than Hardy and clings to it more tenaciously.

A very different but still suggestive parallel is provided by the plays of Oscar Wilde, which (like Hardy's first collection of verse) belong to the same decade as *A Shropshire Lad* and, like that work, undertake a kind of truthtelling in art that was at that time impossible for their author in life. Richard Ellmann has shown how Wilde was preoccupied by the idea of exposure: 'exposure or usually near-exposure is always the focal point in Wilde's plays . . . It is easy to guess what effort to free himself lay behind this recurrent and dominating interest on the part of Wilde's characters in giving themselves away'.* Housman too was driven to allegorize a personal predicament in the hope of freeing himself; but his mode is not comedy and for him there can be no 'pardon and transfiguration' (in Professor Ellmann's phrase) at the end, cancelling the 'nightmare of being found out' – perhaps partly because he is writing after, not before, the Wilde *débâcle*.

Discussions of Housman's poetic themes seem to me to have sometimes put the emphasis in the wrong place. He has been

regarded as a poet of nature and landscape, even a regional poet;
but he insisted that he was 'not a descriptive writer and do not
know Shropshire well',* he is manifestly indifferent to local
accuracy, and he writes relatively little about the natural world
except in so far as it prompts or confirms a human mood. His real
landscapes are of the heart. R. P. Blackmur said that Housman
writes 'almost entirely of death',* but this too is to exaggerate.
Exile and love as well as nature are also among his themes, though
it is true that any of these can be associated with the idea of death:
death is the final exile, hopeless love leads to the grave, nature can
be a *memento mori*. How does Housman present these themes, as
Hardy would say, dramatically and 'personatively' (that is, by
impersonation)? He does so by creating certain recurring figures
or roles of which the most prominent are the soldier, the lover, the
rustic, the exile and the criminal.

Jean Genet has written of his 'desire for all the manly types: the
soldier, the sailor, the adventurer, the thief, the criminal',* and
the confession might have been silently echoed by Housman, a
more reticent man in a more reticent age. Of these types it was the
first that for Housman exercised the most potent spell. His
boyhood soldier-games and the impression made on him by 'the
Guards' on his first visit to London suggest a familiar pattern: the
bookish, physically underdeveloped boy's fascination with a life of
action he is unlikely to share. Later, the implicit sexuality of the
strong, colourful and confident soldier-figure became consciously
apprehended. W. H. Auden has reminded us that the Guards
regiments had a long tradition of part-time prostitution for beer-
money, and John Addington Symonds' autobiography shows very
strikingly that the cruising soldiery in late-Victorian London
could be objects of disturbing excitement to the respectable
middle-class homosexual.

The nature of his calling also made the soldier a perfect
embodiment of Housman's preoccupation with two other themes,
exile and death. In these respects the criminal's fate is not so very
different, if we read prison for service in foreign lands and the
gallows for the battlefield. The figure of the criminal, moreover,
was attractive for other reasons. It allowed Housman to explore
his own feelings of guilt without adopting an obviously
autobiographical stance; and it rendered legitimate and
unsuspicious the expression of strong feelings for a young man.
Here a suggestive parallel can be found in the case of Walter

Pater, of whom Michael Levey has written that 'over a beautiful, youthful but dead body [in the Paris Morgue] he could linger looking freely and unashamed; it prompted a pity which was, as he probably understood, really a suppressed lust'.* Pater, like Housman, linked youth and love and beauty with death and corruption: the beautiful heroes to whom he is addicted die young, like the soldiers and peasants of Housman's world. A dead young man does not constitute – and even more importantly does not appear to constitute – a temptation, except to a sentimental regret that camouflages the sexual attraction.

Early in *A Shropshire Lad* (III: 'The Recruit'), the soldier is presented as a special instance of a common fate: in this poem of farewell and separation, the soldier leaving his home is caught up in a situation of which, as Housman well knew, soldiers have no monopoly. The speaker is not the soldier, however, but the one left behind. It would be foolish to propose any close biographical parallels, since from different points of view Housman occupied both roles: he was the one who had gone away into permanent exile from 'home,' the world of his childhood (less the geographical world of Worcestershire or Shropshire than the irrecoverable world of the past); but he was also the one who had had forced upon him the harder role of staying behind when Moses Jackson left England to sail, by the route that so many soldiers travelled, to India. The important point is that these themes are very close to Housman's deepest emotional experiences, and they recur persistently. *ASL* IV ('Reveille') takes a more positive view of departure; XXII ('The street sounds to the soldiers' tread') repeats the situation of II but goes further in allowing a revealing moment of personal involvement (the eye-contact by the 'single redcoat' surely has a strong sexual suggestion); XXXV ('On the idle hill of summer') again shows the departure of soldiers destined to die overseas, but now stresses the shattering of a pastoral idyll by the noise and colour of the military life, rather as in Hardy's *Far from the Madding Crowd* the aggressive masculinity of Sergeant Troy impinges on the rural scene.

The soldier going overseas (often, like Herbert Housman, to India) is only one kind of exile. *ASL* XXXVII-XLI forms a group of five poems on exile. The best-known and best of them is XL ('Into my heart an air that kills'), but the situation it presents is characteristic of the group. The 'land of lost content' and the 'blue remembered hills' are seen from a distance, for the speaker now inhabits 'London streets' (the Blakean phrase – and Blake too, one recalls, has a 'hapless soldier' sighing – occurs in both XXXVII and XLI). XXXVII ('As through the wild green hills of Wyre') is a poem of departure in which the city is seen, as in Wordsworth's 'Michael', as a place of temptation; by XLI ('In my own shire if I was sad'), the misery of the city-dweller and the ill-will of his fellows have become familiar. (It is a little odd to find in Raymond Williams' comprehensive study *The Country and the City* no reference to *A Shropshire Lad*, which seems a clear and influential instance of the use of contrasted rural-urban settings to reinforce an antithesis of emotional attitudes and values.) XXXIX ('’Tis time, I think, by Wenlock town') echoes II ('Loveliest of trees, the cherry now') but wears the exile's rue with a difference, for it is less man's morality than separation forced by circumstances that makes poignant the thought of springtime beauty; the 'cherry hung with snow' is no longer seen but dreamed of:

> Lie long, high snowdrifts in the hedge
> That will not shower on me.

As for the 'air that kills' in XL, this is a development of the almost Metaphysical punning of XXXVIII, where the 'sighing air' is first the west wind linking home with the place of exile, then the breath of life and the spoken words of lost friends, and finally the exile's own sighing. (An earlier pair of poems, XXXI–II, has used the wind as both literal force and rich metaphor, and the same image recurs in XLII, 'The Merry Guide'.) London exile is also the theme of LI–LII. Death is the end of exile (in LXI: 'Hughley Steeple', the reunion with lost friends is found only in the grave), but it is also the final exile. XI ('On your midnight pallet lying') is a short poem that brings together the themes of unsatisfied love, departure, and death in a distant spot.

This discussion has already, and inevitably, begun to blur the thematic categories proposed earlier – love, nature, exile and death – as well as the personae Housman uses (for example, the lover, like the soldier, may suffer exile and go to his death), and it will certainly not do to suggest that there is anything schematic about Housman's use of these themes and figures. B. J. Leggett has argued that, by his arrangement of poems composed piecemeal, Housman gave his first collection of verse an elaborate structure: 'the dominant pattern in the Shropshire poems is the growth of awareness and sophistication in the persona which eventually brings about his departure from the pastoral land'.* I think Professor Leggett exaggerates, among other things, the structural sophistication of the volume: I find a simple though strong structure in which characters and viewpoints shift somewhat as they do (far-fetched though the comparison may seem) in *The Waste Land*.

The soldier, as I have said, is a type of exile; but separation can take many forms, and one of the most prominent figures in *A Shropshire Lad* is the unhappy lover: the victim of rejection or faithlessness, he may resort to suicide as an escape that is also a form of exile. V ('Oh see how thick the goldcup flowers') is a light-hearted poem, the lyric for a coyly comic song, in which the young man's blandishments are prudently rejected; but its companion-piece (VI: 'When the lad for longing sighs') more soberly instructs us that if one of a pair is not made unhappy by love, the other will be. X–XVIII is a group of poems about the varied faces of love: among them, the sadness of being unloved at a time of loving (X), the exchange of innocence for experience (XIII), the folly of loving that produces only misery (XIV), the lover's suicide (XVI). A smaller group, this time of variations on the theme of faithlessness, is formed by XXV–XXVII.

That Housman's lovers should so often be country lads and lasses suggests a debt to Shakespeare (it has often been noted that the 'Dick' of *LP* XX bears a suspicious resemblance to his namesake in 'When icicles hang by the wall') and to a long tradition of English pastoral; but it is also part of a widespread interest in 'folkways' that represents a response, scholarly and creative as well as sentimental in its manifestations, to the late-nineteenth-century awareness of a vanishing England. *Tess of the d'Urbervilles*, almost exactly contemporary with *A Shropshire Lad*, is a major monument to that awareness; and one wonders whether Housman – whose favourite novelist, according to Pollard, was Hardy – had that novel in mind in his references to the nettle on the grave, most strikingly in *ASL* XVI (cf., in Chapter 14 of *Tess*, Hardy's reference to 'that shabby corner of God's allotment where He lets the nettles grow, and where all . . . suicides, and others of the conjecturally damned are laid', which amounts to a prose gloss on Housman's poem). There is also a striking chronological

closeness between Housman's early verse and the rise of the
English folksong movement: Cecil Sharp was born in the same
year as Housman, Vaughan Williams was absorbing the folksong
idiom in the early nineties, the English Folksong Society was
founded in 1898, and in due course, and neatly enough, Vaughan
Williams, George Butterworth, Ivor Gurney, and other members
of the English school of composers showed themselves eager to set
Housman's words to music.

The lover, like the soldier, is destined for the grave; and in some
of the poems mortality becomes a central theme. In VII ('When
smoke stood up from Ludlow'), the blackbird's message is less like
that of Hardy's darkling thrush than that of Tennyson in *Tithonus*
('Man comes and tills the field and lies beneath'). XIX ('To an
Athlete Dying Young') finds consolation in death as a preserver of
youth; Housman, we recall, 'admired athletes greatly', and Moses
had won a challenge-cup – did Housman perhaps feel that he
might have been less unhappy if his friend had died young? XLIV
('Shot? so quick, so clean an ending?'), based on the newspaper
account of a Woolwich cadet's suicide, finds nobility in the act, a
theme pursued more briefly in XLV ('If it chance your eye offend
you'). XLVIII ('Be still, my soul, be still') recalls Housman's
phrase in a letter to Gilbert Murray, 'the resourceful malevolence
of nature', and presents life's turmoil as 'but for a season' between
two stages of oblivion; its burden, however, is not consolatory but
deeply pessimistic, though it is immediately followed by advocacy
of 'carpe diem' (XLIX: 'Think no more, lad; laugh, be jolly').

Some of the poems briefly mentioned, and some unmentioned,
call for fuller comment. The opening item in the volume ('*1887*')
suggests that, for all Housman's reputation for transparent
simplicity, it is possible to misread particular poems. His decision
to place this at the head of his collection is very striking; for the
expectations it creates are not immediately gratified. This ironic
and ambiguous poem, subversive of Victorian patriotic pieties,
gives way to the straightforward lyrical melancholy of II
('Loveliest of trees') and the fervent balladry of III and IV. For all
that, one does not have to be doggedly determined to unearth
something to explicate at all costs to find '*1887*' a subtle poem that
introduces many of Housman's most prominent ideas: a local
setting and the contrast with the remote (Shropshire and Asia);
youth and age (young men, the old Queen); time; the soldier's life

and death; religious orthodoxy in a Godless world; a conventional and a real morality.

The seven-fold reiteration, with variations, of the shibboleth 'God save the Queen' takes on a cumulative irony: merely conventional in the second stanza, it quickly becomes something more in the reference to those who 'shared the work with God', where we are compelled to think about the meaning of the cliché; and by the fourth stanza the Queen is forgotten, or dismissed, in the poignant reference to those who died far from home (the reference to Christ is to be taken up again in XLVII: 'The Carpenter's Son'). The initially simple concept of 'saving' is now played upon by the near-blasphemous collocation of 'saviours': the young men, like Christ, have been God-forsaken in their hour of need (cf. *LP* XXXVII, 'What God abandoned, these defended . . .'). By the end of the poem, 'God will save her' has become a smooth fiction that ought to deceive no-one: God saves those whom others die for.

The last line of the poem repeats almost exactly a line in the second stanza; but in the meantime it has taken on a different, more ruthlessly honest meaning. (A slighter and neater example of the same device occurs in XXV ('This time of year a twelvemonth past'), where the phrase 'the better man,' used twice but with ironically shifting meanings in the exact middle of the poem, serves as a pivot on which the whole poem turns.)

Hardy's poem of 1899, 'Drummer Hodge', offers an instructive contrast to '*1887*': Hardy, like Housman, is haunted by the notion of a country boy lying eternally in the soil of an exotic clime; but his wartime poem is less bitter. There is less of passionate indignation than of a detached fascination with the sheer oddity of life's accidents, and it seems to me, though fine in its way, a less human poem than Housman's. A similar contrast between Hardy's preoccupation with a kind of conceit or ingenious and beguiling reflection, and Housman's more personal and tragic response, is to be found by setting *ASL* LI ('Loitering with a vacant eye') beside Hardy's 'In the British Museum'.

Emphasis on the recurring themes and characters of *A Shropshire Lad* ought not to be taken as implying that the collection maintains a uniformity of poetic style and tone. The contrast between the sceptical irony of I and the undesigning simplicity of the poems that immediately follow has already been noted; and

comparison between XI and XIX will reinforce this point. XI
('On your midnight pallet lying') is not one of the best poems in
this volume, but it is representative of Housman's fondness for
reducing a dramatic situation to a few essential features – a
characteristic that recalls the Border ballads to which he
confessed his indebtedness. The young man asks his lover to take
pity on him, for he is about to leave for a distant land where death
awaits him. There is some ambiguity, however, whether the
envisaged journey is actual or metaphorical: the Shakespearean
'darnel' suggests an English rather than a foreign grave, and
perhaps the poem should be interpreted as a plea for the requiting
of love before separation – from whatsoever cause, death or exile –
makes it impossible. (There is a similar ambiguity in the final
stanza of XXXIII ['If truth in hearts that perish']: is the
supposed journey to another part of this world, or to the next? If
the 'town' in that poem echoes the 'stiller town' of XIX, the latter
interpretation seems possible.)

As in so many of Housman's poems that express the tragedy of
unfulfilled desire, the verse-form with its frequent feminine
endings is song-like, almost dance-like, feeling and form seeming
to work in opposite directions to produce a curiously bitter-sweet
tone. But if XI resembles a Shakespearean song (and the 'sigh no
more' of line 4 inevitably recalls 'Sigh no more, ladies'), XIX ('To
an Athlete Dying Young') is much closer to a seventeenth-century
Metaphysical poem: the pun on 'shoulder-high', the octosyllabic
couplets and the frequent trochaic rhythms recall Marvell's 'To
his Coy Mistress', and

> Eyes the shady night has shut
> Cannot see the record cut,
> And silence sounds no worse than cheers
> After earth has stopped the ears

is very close to

> The grave's a fine and private place,
> But none, I think, do there embrace

though *ASL* XII ('When I watch the living meet') perhaps comes
even closer to Marvell in sentiment if not in the movement of the
verse:

Lovers lying two and two
  Ask not whom they sleep beside,
And the bridegroom all night through
  Never turns him to the bride

To evoke the poignant actuality of death by speaking of highly specific earthly activities is to exploit that Metaphysical variety of wit that, as Eliot said, allies levity with seriousness; and I cannot see that, except insofar as he is derivative, Housman's lines are inferior to Marvell's. (Compare also the Marvellian couplets of *ASL* LXII.)

As my earlier comments have suggested, almost any individual poem in *A Shropshire Lad* has a total meaning that is partly supplied by its relationship to other poems in the collection. This relationship may be thematic or it may be a matter of recurrent diction or imagery. One of Housman's favourite images, for instance, is that of the wind: its richness of meaning includes the literal winds of heaven, human passion, the spirit of life, connection with one's origins (the wind blows from one place to another), and destruction (as in Shelley's ode, the wind as 'destroyer' as well as 'preserver'). The wind is also part of Housman's pervasive geographical sense: for him, exile and separation are concepts indivisible from the idea of movement in this or that direction, usually, and for good reason, on an east-west axis. Within a single poem, the wind may be evoked punningly; and the image links poems at different points in the collection. XXXII ('From far, from eve and morning'), for instance, moves rapidly from the 'twelve-winded sky' to 'the stuff of life' blown by the wind, then to the 'breath' that, Beckett-like, Housman sees as man's portion, finally back to the 'wind's twelve quarters' that disperse the fleshly envelope after death. In XXXI ('On Wenlock Edge the wood's in trouble'), the wind blows not just through a human life but through history: an actual wind becomes 'the old wind in the old anger' – the wind of the distant past; then the 'gale of life', blowing through 'the tree of man', that links dead Roman and Victorian Englishman. (The archaeological imagination again suggests an affinity with Hardy.) The wind reappears in the 'sighing air', blowing from west to east, of XXXVIII ('The winds out of the west land blow'); by the end of that poem, the sighing of the wind merges into the sighs of the exile. Later appearances of the image are as 'the air that kills' in XL and 'the wind of morning' in XLII ('The Merry Guide').

What is in question, it seems, is not simply a recurring image but a playing upon various meanings and associations, literal and metaphorical, that attach themselves to that image. So far from being uniformly a poet of simplicity or *simplesse*, that is to say, Housman – himself a professional student of language, including its shifts and multiplicities of meaning – is prepared to exploit the rich suggestiveness of language. A minor example is to be found in XLIII ('The Immortal Part'):

> . . . 'Tis that every mother's son
> Travails with a skeleton

where the unexpected word *travails* readily suggests the more obvious and still relevant *travels*.

Interpretation of *LP* VIII ('Soldier from the wars returning') must take account of the ambiguous 'here' in the third line: only in the final line of the poem ('inn of night') is the ambiguity resolved. *MP* IX ('When green buds hang in the elm like dust') closes with an exquisite pun: '. . . where cuckoo-flowers/Are lying about the world' (for collocation of flowers and lies, compare *MP* XVIII). In *LP* XXVII ('The sigh that heaves the grasses'), the 'tears of morning' are also the tears of mourning (cf. the 'morning rose' of Keats's 'Ode on Melancholy'). Even the apparent simplicity of *ASL* XVI ('It nods and curtseys and recovers') harbours ambiguities that have been exposed in an analysis by Randall Jarrell. In this, at once one of the least pretentious and one of the finest of all Housman's poems, language and meaning work together in intimate and harmonious alliance: the reader's voice 'curtseys' even as he offers the word for consideration; the delicately poised ambiguity in the haunting final lines ('the lover of the grave') echoes in the mind after the voice has ceased.

There is some evidence that Housman arranged the contents of *A Shropshire Lad* to form a series: T. B. Haber notes, for instance, that at the head of XIII in the printer's copy of his manuscript he wrote 'Another Series'. But while there are certainly a number of sub-groups of two or more poems (several of which have been identified in the above discussion), there are difficulties in the way of seeing the collection as a continuous series as well as in grasping the aptness of the original title *Poems of Terence Hearsay*. Thus, though the speaker in II declares himself to be twenty years old, the persona of I had seemed an older, more experienced man; and it is hard to identify the simple ploughman of VII with the mythologically well-informed dreamer of XLII ('The Merry Guide'). At times the shift of viewpoint is more obvious and readily explicable: in VIII and IX, Terence first listens to a young man's tale of fratricide and then replies. But Terence, ruminating on the nature and function of his verses, has the last word in the final two poems of the volume.

Professor Leggett's claim that the poems constitute a sequence does not altogether carry conviction, and his suggestion that *A Shropshire Lad* has 'the unity almost of a single poem'* goes too far, even after due weight has been given to that prudent 'almost'. Leggett admits that 'the poems were not composed in the order in which they were finally arranged', so that any element of sequence seems likely to have been introduced at the stage after piecemeal composition, when Housman was selecting and arranging his poems for publication. We know that he took considerable pains over the arrangement of *Last Poems*, and it seems likely that the earlier volume underwent a similar process; indeed, Haber's revelation that several poems were deleted and others added at a late stage seems to support this idea, and Leggett is probably right in suggesting that the purpose of these changes was to 'strengthen the sense of relocation in setting'* from Shropshire to London. As he also suggests, Housman's disinclination to have his poems anthologized may be explained by his fear that, divorced from their context, they might be deprived of some of their force, though it is not difficult to propose other explanations. There is an element of overall structure in *A Shropshire Lad*, but the structure seems to me no more than a fairly loose one.

Last Poems resembles Hardy's collections of verse in representing no striking development over its predecessor, and for the same reason: it includes many old poems, including some rejected from the earlier volume. (We know, for instance, that *LP* III and XXIII originally stood in the 1896 collection.) For all the care Housman took over the arrangement of its contents, there can be no question of regarding it as a tightly ordered sequence. The themes of *A Shropshire Lad* recur, and the world of redcoats, beer, the hangman's noose, woman's fickleness, is evoked, or recalled, in the first few pages. One suspects, in fact, a conscious shunning of modernity: V–VI, according to Housman, were written at the time of the Boer War, and their publication in 1922 seems intent on abolishing twenty years of history (H. W. Garrod called V 'jaded Kiplingese'); XVII ('Astronomy'), also written at the beginning of the century, was prompted by the same war and recalls the opening poem of the earlier collection.

Some of the poems are known to be patchworks: the first stanza of XXXVI ('Revolution'), for instance, was added in 1922 to two stanzas written earlier; the final stanza of IX ('The chestnut casts his flambeaux') was added at the last moment to a poem some twenty-five years old; and XIII ('The Deserter') was, again according to Housman, begun in 1905 and finished in that same productive month of April 1922. Perhaps this feature helps to account for an unevenness that is sometimes evident, and nowhere more evident than in IX, in which both the first and the last stanzas begin magnificently and end wretchedly, with the repeated and extraordinary banal 'pass the can' jingling in a pun for once pointless and presumably unintended ('Bear them we can, and if we can we must').

But *Last Poems* also contains what is perhaps the finest of all Housman's longer poems (thirty lines being, for Housman, a longer poem): XL ('Tell me not here, it needs not saying'). This, again, is a poem of April 1922. Immediately behind it is the long late autumn of 1921, but its roots lie deep in Housman's experience; and it derives its strength from that quality of controlled passion – an intensity held in check by lexical precision and the formal discipline of verse – that is characteristic of his best poems. It starts, urgently, with an imperative, 'Tell me . . .'; but its force is quickly qualified by a repeated negative, so that, in its simultaneous thrusting forward and firm withdrawal, the first line gives us in little the tension that energizes the whole poem, the literal meaning of which involves both an impassioned celebration of nature's beauty and a renunciation of or farewell to that beauty. In the event, of course, the initial injunction is disobeyed: for all that 'Tell me not', most of the poem comprises an exquisitely particularized catalogue of seasonal sights and sounds, with some implicit contrast between early ('blanching mays', 'The cuckoo') and late ('September', 'autumn'), with progressively greater insistence on the latter (in stanza three, 'seeded grasses', 'moons of harvest', storms stripping the beeches 'for winter'). The language is of great subtlety. 'Blanching mays' has been misquoted by at least one critic (or compositor) as 'branching mays', and the error may be inspired: we may feel one word working upon us behind the other, just as 'mays' (the hawthorn blossom) inevitably also suggests 'Mays' (the month, later opposed to 'September').

The verbal music of 'The pine lets fall its cone' resembles that of the opening lines of Tennyson's *Tithonus*: as Francis Berry has shown, Tennyson reinforces the idea of sinking or falling with vowel-sounds of descending pitch, and in his placing of pine/fall/cone Housman does precisely the same; note, too, how 'pine' echoes 'idle', and 'fall' echoes 'floors', not with the obviousness of internal rhymes but with a delicate interlacing of sound. The simple and bold 'shouts' for the cuckoo's song was, we find from Housman's notebooks, arrived at only after other possibilities had been considered and rejected.* 'Traveller's joy' starts as a precise piece of nature-observation and turns into a heart-rending pun in the line that follows. The Tennysonian plenitude and delicacy seem a real presence in this poem: apart from the instance already noted, Christopher Ricks finds in Housman's use of 'burnish' a suggestion of *Locksley Hall*, where Tennyson has 'the burnish'd dove'.*

As we have seen, most of Housman's poetry is poetry of indirection, expressing his secret feelings through metaphor: the preoccupation with soldiers going to the wars, rustics dying of love, and criminals awaiting execution allegorizes his own unuttered, unutterable anxieties and yearnings. In 'Tell me not here', the situation is curiously reversed, or reversed and then reversed again, so that a kind of double bluff operates. Instead of speaking of his love through the medium of other preoccupations, he here seems to be speaking of his feeling for nature in terms of a love affair, the love affair being now a source of metaphor rather than a hidden truth; but then, by another turn of the screw, we sense by the end of the poem that it may after all be about another kind of love as well as (not instead of) love of nature. (Professor Ricks notes the 'remarkable erotic force' of the poem, and adds: 'Not that the poem is "really" erotic and not about nature; it is about both.')* It resembles the Shakespearean tension in which both idea and image have their own kind of intense reality. The language is, in detail, that of a carnal infatuation: punningly (again), it is the Circe-like 'enchantress' as well as the 'pillared forest' that 'would murmur and be mine' (lovers murmur as well as trees); the repeated 'possess' conveys a strong sense of physical union, as in the phrase 'in possession' in Shakespeare's great 'expense of spirit' sonnet (129); the stranger's 'trespass' – another partially submerged pun – is both a topographical or legal straying and a moral lapse of the kind we ask to be forgiven, an infidelity. Ultimately, though, the love is one-sided and unrequited, the loved one indifferent. Superficially this places the poem in a long tradition of wry jesting about woman's inconstancy, but our knowledge of Housman hardly allows us to see it as other than a comment, by 1922 resigned rather than bitter, on his own experience of love.

Professor Ricks quotes with approval (a 'superb insight') William Empson's comment on this poem; part of that comment runs thus:

> I think the poem is wonderfully beautiful. But a secret gimmick may well be needed in it to overcome our resistances, because the thought must be about the silliest or most self-centred that has ever been expressed about Nature. Housman is offended with the scenery, when he pays a visit to his native place, because it does not remember the great man; this is very rude of it. But he has described it as a lover, so in a way the poem is only consistent to become jealous at the end . . .*

'A visit to his native place' seems to be gratuitously imported, 'very rude of it' inaccurate, 'the great man' a poor joke, and I find not jealousy at the end but a dignified resignation to the inevitable. That which is, literally, 'heartless' and 'witless' can hardly be 'rude'; here and elsewhere it seems to me that Housman's use of language is more precise than Professor Empson's. He is surely saying – not as a complaint, but as a fact registered without self-pity – that he has loved nature devotedly, but that his time for loving nature has run out (that being the nature of time) and now it is another's turn. He declines the easy consolation of the pathetic fallacy: the fact is that nature will not mind or miss him – a truth long known but now felt on the pulses. Neither Empson's strictures ('silliest or most self-centred') nor Ricks's less intemperate verdict ('an attitude that is almost silly or absurd') seems justified. But the final stress ought to fall on the marvellous economy and rightness of Housman's language: such lines as

> On acres of the seeded grasses
> The changing burnish beaves;
> Or marshalled under moons of harvest
> Stand still all night the sheaves; . . .

and

> On russet floors, by waters idle,
> The pine lets fall its cone; . . .

have a Keatsian strength in their matching of exact observation with words perfectly chosen – one might say, for music as well as meaning, were it not that the music is part of the meaning (a judgment on Housman's practice that contradicts, of course, his preaching in 'The Name and Nature of Poetry').

More Poems, which adds a further forty-eight poems to the canon, was assembled by Laurence Housman very soon after his brother's death; there can, therefore, be no question of its being more than the sum of its parts. The systematic fictionalizing process that we have seen at work in *A Shropshire Lad* – the creation of a dramatic world as a device for truthtelling not otherwise to be contemplated – has no counterpart, or at best a counterpart only vestigal. One result of this is that, to the reader unacquainted with what Housman calls obscurely 'this cursed trouble' (XXI), many of the poems must seem to express a mood of despair in excess of any revealed cause. And yet there are poems in this volume as close to the major landmarks of Housman's emotional life as anything he ever wrote – as close if not closer. (XXXIV has been cited earlier in this study as a possible comment on the events of May 1881.)

Moses Jackson's presence is often a potent one: among other examples, XXIII, XXX and XXXI are fragments from an autobiographical account of Housman's feelings towards him, and, as if to confirm the surmise, the attitude expressed in the last line of XXX is movingly echoed in Housman's final letter to Mo. Although they are of considerable biographical interest, though, it needs to be remembered (even axioms bearing occasional repetition) that these are poems and not letters or diary entries, and are therefore subject – one had better say, pedantically, even more powerfully subject than letters or diary entries – to the kinds of fictionalizing and dramatizing processes that we have seen at work elsewhere in Housman's verse. Moreover, their lack of explicitness means that, though often haunting, they are sometimes tantalizing and ultimately unsatisfying – a category instanced by the Kafkaesque vision of XXXVII.

The poem also prompts reflection on the variety of Housman's metrical forms, a variety that includes a large element of the unpredictable and even the disconcerting. It is true that a good many of the most familiar anthology-pieces are cast in more or less traditional stanza-forms, most commonly the four-line stanza (though there are some interesting variations such as the five-line stanza used in 'Bredon Hill' and elsewhere). But the familiar form of 'Loveliest of trees' and the like is far from invariable, and the standard iambic line itself undergoes frequent modifications. One feature of Housman's metrical style is a fondness for trochaic rhythms; another is the use of feminine endings to give lightness to what might otherwise be a somewhat plodding beat, as in the second and fifth lines of the six-line stanzas of 'The Night is freezing fast' (*LP* XX). In this poem of remembering, where the word 'remember' itself exemplifies the use of feminine endings, the effect seems to be an enactment of the process of unbidden memory: the voice presses against the word for a moment before relieving the pressure, just as the memory presses with a momentary pang upon the heart. The delicacy and subtlety of *ASL* XVI ('It nods and curtseys and recovers') also owes something to the feminine endings in alternate lines. Though the octosyllabic line is Housman's normal maximum length, and many of his lines are shorter, he will sometimes move into pentameters, weighty by contrast with the verses that form their context, as in the Gray's *Elegy* stanzas of 'The chestnut casts his flambeaux'' (*LP* IX).

What can be disconcerting is Housman's use of metres in which a high proportion of unstressed syllables produces an effect of jauntiness very much at odds with the statements made by the poem. Consider *MP* XXXVII, already cited for a different reason:

> I did not lose my heart in summer's even,
> When roses to the moonrise burst apart; . . .

Metrically, this recalls, or more properly is recalled by, John Betjeman's

Oh sun upon the summer-going by-pass
  Where ev'rything is speeding to the sea . . .

Again, 'Illic Jacet' (*LP* IV):

Oh hard is the bed they have made him,
  And common the blanket and cheap; . . .

has the same metrical form as Praed's 'Goodnight to the Season'
and Betjeman's 'Arrest of Oscar Wilde at the Cadogan Hotel'; of
these two, the latter is closer to Housman's poem in enlisting a
form that suggests Victorian *vers de société* to serve serious ends.
'Lancer' (*LP* VI) narrows the gap between Housman and
Betjeman still further, with a fundamental seriousness that does
not exclude the wit of the punningly recurring phrase 'sleep with
the brave' – another example of the pious cliché revivified for
ironic purposes.

Housman's diction includes words that attract attention on
account of their strangeness, and what is probably the densest
cluster of these is to be found early in *A Shropshire Lad*, as if giving
early warning of a style that in the event never becomes dominant:

Up, lad: thews that lie and cumber
  Sunlit pallets never thrive; . . .

(IV)

For the actual proportion of such words is very small, Housman
habitually favouring a 'language really used by men'. Such a
poem as *ASL* XVI ('It nods and curtseys and recovers') includes,
after the first line, no word not in daily conversational use; even
there, 'curtseys' was less unfamiliar in 1896 than today, and the
specialized sense of 'recovers' ('rises again after bowing or
curtseying') coexists with a familiar sense ('gets well after an
illness') that is also present in the poem. To cite another of
Housman's best poems, *MP* VII ('Stars, I have seen them fall')
ventures beyond colloquial limits only at one point of heightened
solemnity, 'primal fault' recalling the Wordsworthian use of
'diurnal' in the otherwise starkly plain style of 'A slumber did my
spirit seal'; and the final powerful image of Housman's poem is
conveyed in language of uncompromising starkness:

> It rains into the sea,
> And still the sea is salt.

Some of the rarer lexical items in Housman's verse illustrate the contemporary taste for Saxon plainness in reaction against Tennysonian and Swinburnian ornateness – a taste that has its counterpart in the poetry of Hopkins and Hardy and (a more extreme case) William Barnes. As well as *thews* and *cumber* just cited, we find *handselled*, *shaws* (Housman's translation of Horace's *arboribus*), *oakenshaws*, and the Hopkinsian *reave*. Other lexical oddities show more specific literary influences: *frore* and *league*, for instance, are Miltonic, and the use of the latter work in *LP* XVIII ('The rain, it streams on stone and hillock') may involve an ironic recollection of *Paradise Lost*: 'Linkt in happie nuptial League'. One or two words are very rare: *OED* cites Housman's use of *sain*, which he may have remembered from Browning's 'In a Gondola' ('sains and saves') but which also, in the particular sense he bestows upon it, probably has the Latin *sanare* pressing upon the English word. Such instances, however, tend to convey a misleading impression of a poet's vocabulary: it is easier to talk about caviare than about bread and butter, yet it is not after all the oddities that constitute his staple working wordstock.

Housman's acknowledgement, in his reply to Pollet, of his debt to such remote poetic ancestors as the Border ballads and Shakespeare's songs has been eagerly taken up by source-hunters and influence-mongers. Whatever local and specific debts may be traced, however, two considerations ought to remain paramount. We must remember that he was a late-Victorian poet whose notions of the form and language of poetry were largely shaped by the practice of his immediate predecessors. What we know of his tastes as a reader of poetry contains few surprises. He admired Matthew Arnold greatly (and Arnold's 'The Last Word' has to a remarkable extent the flavour of a poem by Housman, if the paradox may be forgiven); he praised Coventry Patmore; among later poets he admired Edmund Blunden, Wilfrid Blunt and Robert Bridges. (His verdict that Edna St Vincent Millay's dreary sonnet-sequence 'Fatal Interview' was 'mighty good' remains baffling, especially since its mediocrity is combined with her dual disqualifications as an American and a woman.)

Philip Larkin* has examined Housman's copy of Palgrave's *Golden Treasury: Second Series*, acquired on publication in October

1897 or very shortly afterwards, in which he exercised his independent editorial judgment by deleting forty-one poems deemed unworthy of inclusion. Many bad poems are struck out, but also some good ones, including Tennyson's 'In the Children's Hospital', Browning's 'Prospice', and Clough's 'Say not, the struggle naught availeth'; and Larkin raises the question whether this suggests that Housman's taste was erratic. His tentative conclusion is that 'perhaps there was more of a mid-Victorian in Housman than is generally realized', and the hint seems worth pursuing and likely to yield more useful results than comparisons with the Border ballads and the like, where resemblances can at best be only very limited.

The other major influence on Housman's creative practice was his more persistent occupation and preoccupation as a student of classical texts and especially of Latin poets. The relatively narrow range of his major classical publications, in which editions of didactic and satirical poetry loom so large, ought not to carry too much weight; for his Cambridge lectures and minor publications embraced a considerably wider scope, including some poets (Martial and Catullus, for instance) whose kind of poetry is much closer to his own than is that of Manilius or Juvenal. What is here in question, of course, is not 'borrowings' or 'echoes' but an instinct, partly natural but also highly developed by intensive and protracted engagement with verse written in the Latin language, for precision and economy of verbal means. It is manifested, to take a conveniently small-scale instance, in Housman's choice and placing of epithets and especially in his favourite attaching of two unco-ordinated epithets to a single noun: 'scorned unlucky lad'. Sometimes the epithets contrast with each other in their reference to different areas of physical or mental perception ('blue remembered hills', 'sad uncoloured plain'); sometimes they seem to tug in different directions to produce an impression of a tensely complex emotional state ('brisk fond lackey': cf. Auden's 'urgent voluntary errands'); but always there is a sense of language highly charged and of a delicate balance between the predictable (reinforced by metrical regularity) and the unexpected. Possibly Housman's use of this stylistic mannerism owes something to Arnold, in whose verse the stacking up of epithets – 'unplumbed, salt, estranging sea'; 'wet, bird-haunted English lawn' – is responsible for some of his most memorable phrases.

Like Mark Ambient, the novelist in Henry James's story 'The

Author of Beltraffio', Housman is an example of 'the artist . . . who felt . . . the desire to resolve his experience of life into a literary form' (I omit the phrase 'for ever' from James's sentence since in Housman's case the desire was not continuous but intermittent). But like Ambient – and like John Addington Symonds, whom James seems to have had in mind and with whom this study has already had occasion to compare Housman in one or two minor respects – it could be said of him that 'in his books he had uttered but half his thought, and that what he had kept back – from motives I deplored when I made them out later – was the finer and braver part'. And yet we may be less prompt to deplore than James, for in the existing combination of temperamental and social realities it could hardly have been otherwise.

Christopher Ricks has made the illuminating suggestion that 'much of Housman's serious verse uses a method – of indirections, disparities, and emotional cross-currents – that is at its clearest in nonsense verse. What is said is not what is meant, but something is certainly meant.'* I have suggested in this chapter that different poems can represent different degrees of indirection, and on such a spectrum the nonsense verse stands at one extreme (the other extreme probably stands empty). In the nonsense poems Housman could outrage convention as he could not or would not either in his serious poetry or in real life. He brings together there propriety and impropriety, placing the scandalous in the context of the ultra-conventional, as if one were to plant an aspidistra in a chamber-pot. In his serious poems, the strategy is necessarily and self-protectively devious: the aspidistra is an orchid, or perhaps a green carnation, in disguise. On the other hand, the reticence ought not to be exaggerated: Housman could have remained silent, but he chose to break the silence, and it cannot be said of him, as Arnold said of Gray, that 'he never spoke out', even if some of the loudest of his speeches were posthumous. Since he spoke out relatively little, however, his output is small and the best of it much smaller – though to have left at least a dozen perfect lyrics and epigrams as well as others flawed but unforgettable is not such a common achievement that it ought to be undervalued.

Epilogue

In his review, reprinted in *Partial Portraits*, of J. W. Cross's *Life of George Eliot* – a biography that has been described as a reticence in three volumes – Henry James declares that

> the creations which brought her renown were of the incalculable kind, shaped themselves in mystery, in some intellectual back-shop or secret crucible, and were as little as possible implied in the aspect of her life.

There are writers the 'aspect' of whose lives seems all of a piece with their work: Dickens, say, or Lawrence, or Byron. And there are others, such as Jane Austen and Hardy and George Eliot herself, in whom the man or woman who lives and the mind and imagination that create seem to inhabit the same body almost uneasily and to our constant surprise. It is to this latter category that Housman the poet belongs: the 'secret crucible' was tended in solitude, and the poems emerged, if not from 'some intellectual back-shop', from the foul rag-and-bone shop of the heart.

But there was, of course, another Housman: holder of high academic office, lecturer and controversialist, scholar of the front rank, lover of food and wine and good company – in another of Yeats's phrases, a 'public man'. If any connection can be traced between the poet about whom we know so little and the public man whose life, especially in the later years, is quite fully documented, it is perhaps to be found in a phrase of Housman's quoted earlier in this book: 'seeing things as they are'. Whether it was a matter of removing errors from the text of Manilius, ascertaining the precise date on which a bud broke into blossom, determining the merits of a vintage, or recording the hour and minute of an emotional crisis, Housman can be said to have spent a lifetime in pursuit of certainty; and his poetry is, in its most important and moving aspect, a means of knowing and telling truths about himself. *Why* he should have pursued the knowable so singlemindedly can hardly be answered: perhaps the painful example of his father's self-deceptions had something to do with it; perhaps he came to realize early – he who had been shocked and bewildered first by his mother's death and then by the discovery of his own sexual nature – that not to be taken by surprise was the surest defence against the onslaughts of a universe that was at best indifferent. Such at least is the sombre boast of one of his finest poems:

> The thoughts of others
>   Were light and fleeting,
>   Of lovers' meeting
>   Or luck or fame.
> Mine were of trouble,
>   And mine were steady,
>   So I was ready
>   When trouble came.

Bleak and dispiriting as such a philosophy may sound, it seems to have worked for Housman, who extracted a good deal of enjoyment, intellectual, sensual and social, out of a world into which, like Hardy, he often wished he had never been born. For us, a life passionately and perseveringly devoted to the banishment of error and the strenuous effort to see things as they really are, even if we do not feel inclined to emulate it (as, without Housman's great gifts, we could scarcely do), must command our admiration and respect.

Notes and References

(The place of publication is London unless otherwise stated.)

ABBREVIATIONS

ASL   *A Shropshire Lad* (1896)
LP   *Last Poems* (1922)
MP   *More Poems* (1936)
AP   'Additional Poems', first printed in *A.E.H.* (see below)
AEH   A.E. Housman
A.E.H.   Laurence Housman, *A.E.H.* (1937)
BL   British Library
Classical Papers   *The Classical Papers of A.E. Housman*, ed. J. Diggle
   and F. R. D. Goodyear (Cambridge, 1972)
Gow, *Sketch*   A. S. F. Gow, *A.E. Housman: A Sketch* (1936)
Graves   Richard Perceval Graves, *A.E. Housman: The Scholar-Poet*
   (1979)
LC   Library of Congress
Letters   *The Letters of A.E. Housman*, ed. Henry Maas (1971)
LH   Laurence Housman
Richards   Grant Richards, *Housman: 1897–1936* (1941)
Selected Prose   *A.E. Housman: Selected Prose*, ed. John Carter (1961)
Trinity   Trinity College, Cambridge
Unexpected Years   Laurence Housman, *The Unexpected Years* (1937)
Withers   Percy Withers, *A Buried Life* (1940)

INTRODUCTION   'ALL THAT NEED BE KNOWN'

PAGE
1   'All that need be known':   *Letters*, 309. Less than two years later, however,
   Housman unexpectedly provided fuller autobiographical information
   than on any previous occasion. A French research student, Maurice
   Pollet, sent him a list of twenty questions (given in Richards, 267–9);

209

Housman 'thought that for the sake of posterity I might as well answer some of the young man's questions'. The reply, which is of great interest, was published by Pollet in *Etudes Anglaises* (September 1937); see *Letters*, 328–9.

1　'I have sometimes thought': *Letters*, 313.

2　J. A. Symonds: *Memoirs of John Addington Symonds Written by Himself*; the two-volume typescript copy now in the London Library gives the date as 1893.

2　G. L. Dickinson: *The Autobiography of G. Lowes Dickinson & Other Unpublished Writings*, ed. Dennis Proctor (1973).

2　'dreadful mistake': LH to Maude Hawkins, 8 November 1949 (LC).

2　'he must have guessed': *Letters*, 393.

2　'it says something': *A.E.H.*, 213.

2　'to let me know the secret': LH, 'A. E. Housman's "De Amicitia"', *Encounter*, 29 (October 1967) 39.

2　'I have known for many years': LH to Gow, 2 June 1936 (Trinity, Add. ms. a. 71. 188).

3　'what they say': G. L. Dickinson to AEH, 22 November 1922 (LC). Dickinson's friend E. M. Forster (who 'had loved *A Shropshire Lad* since Cambridge days', and wrote to Housman in 1907 expressing his great admiration for the poems) came to a similar conclusion: he told J. S. Phillimore that 'he thought the poems concealed a personal experience; and when Phillimore agreed, he became certain that the author had fallen in love with a man' (P. N. Furbank, *E. M. Forster: A Life* (1979) 152–3).

3　'Is it a coincidence': *New Statesman*, 15 (1 January 1938) 19; quoted in Richards, 297.

3　'I have a queer feeling': LH to Gow, 13 July 1936 (Trinity, Add. ms. a. 71. 115).

3　'It is strange': *The Sunday Times* (25 October 1936) 8.

4　'That Alfred's heart': H. W. Garrod, 'Housman: 1939', *Essays & Studies*, 25 (1939) 11–13.

4　'one of the wittiest writers': D. R. Shackleton Bailey, reviewing *Classical Papers* in *Cambridge Review*, 94 (1973) 190.

5　'How mean a thing': Coleridge, 'A Prefatory Observation on Modern Biography', *The Friend*, no. 21 (1810).

5　'No one, not even Cambridge': Auden's sonnet was first printed in *New Writing* (Spring 1939) and was collected in *Another Time* (1940). I quote the revised version, which appeared in *Collected Shorter Poems 1927–1957* (1966), and which, apart from slight changes in the punctuation, incorporates two revisions: in the original version, line 4 reads: 'The leading classic of his generation', and line 13, 'Where purely geographical divisions.' Auden's poem may have been prompted by his reading of *A.E.H.*, which he reviewed (under the title 'Jehovah Housman and Satan Housman') in *New Verse* in 1938. A reference to Housman in the original version of Auden's *Letter to Lord Byron* – in the poets' heaven, 'Housman, all scholarship forgot at last,/Sips up the stolen waters through a straw' – was subsequently dropped.

PAGE

6 'I have always thought': W. H. Auden, 'Straw without Bricks', *New Statesman*, 53 (18 May 1957) 643–4 (review of Watson's biography).

9 'biographies will continue': Richard Ellmann, *Golden Codgers* (1973) 15.

10 'Housman remarked dryly': Graves, 209.

11 'his emotional life': Gow to LH, 26 September 1936 (LC). Gow (1886–1978) became a Fellow of Trinity in the same year (1911) that Housman moved to Cambridge, and was in residence from 1925.

11 something of an activist: As well as being involved in the pacifist and feminist movements, LH (1865–1959) seems to have campaigned for homosexual freedom. He was a friend of Oscar Wilde and Edward Carpenter, and was Chairman of the British Society for the Study of Sex Psychology and a 'prominent member' of the Order of Chaeronea, a homosexual secret society that worked for law reform (Jeffrey Weeks, *Coming Out: Homosexual Politics in Britain* (1977) 118, 124). Mr Weeks suggests that AEH 'was possibly also a member of the Order'; this strikes me as highly unlikely. He tells me that his suggestion is based on information supplied by a former owner of the diary of George Ives, the chief luminary of the Order. Until recently, the diary was in private hands and not freely available for consultation; it now reposes in the Humanities Research Centre of the University of Texas, and the point awaits checking (though the diary's use of code-names may make it difficult or impossible to check).

14 'the faintest of all human passions': Preface to *Manilius I* (1903) xliii.

14 'perhaps the reader will do well': Preface to *Manilius V* (1930) xxvi.

1 A WORCESTERSHIRE LAD

PAGE

17 'caught in his youth': Graves, 2.

17 'witty and wrote skits'; LH to Maude Hawkins, 24 October 1950 (LC).

17 'a tiny scattered hamlet': Katharine Symons to Gow, 2 August 1936 (Trinity). Mrs Symons (1862–1945), the younger of Housman's two sisters, corresponded extensively with Gow while his memoir was in course of preparation.

18 'Was there ever such an interesting family': *Unexpected Years*, 19–20; see also *A.E.H.*, 22.

19 'At eight or earlier': *Letters*, 328.

20 'his youthful adoration': A. C. Benson, diary for 26 January 1923 (Magdalene College, Cambridge).

20 'My father': LH to Maude Hawkins, 24 October 1950 (LC).

21 'I became a deist': *Letters*, 328.

21 Graves: Graves, 7.

22 'I think the woman': LH to Maude Hawkins, 6 August 1950 (LC).

22 'deprived him of a guide': Katharine Symons, Introduction to Richards, xii.

22 talked freely of her: *A.E.H.*, 24.

PAGE

22   'every scrap of writing':   Katharine Symons, 'Boyhood', *Alfred Edward Housman* (Housman Memorial Supplement of *The Bromsgrovian*, 1936) 10.

22   'a very mixed character':   LH to Maude Hawkins, 6 August 1950 (LC).

23   The school: see J. D. Collis, *A Short History of the Grammar School of King Edward VI, Bromsgrove, Worcestershire* (Bromsgrove, 1960); H. E. M. Icely, *Bromsgrove School through Four Centuries* (Oxford, 1953) 81, 89.

24   'Excellent for those':   *Unexpected Years*, 87.

24   'He was absolutely in love':   Icely, op. cit., 93–4.

24   'took no part in games':   Katharine Symons, 'Boyhood', 8.

24   'used to tread on him':   *A.E.H.*, 23.

25   'but I think, of all I have seen':   *Letters*, 6.

25   'the rough sailors':   Phyllis Grosskurth, *John Addington Symonds* (1964) 20. Symonds' unpublished autobiography (see above) makes the same point with greater wealth of picturesque detail.

25   'Yesterday I went':   *Letters*, 7.

25   'has in it the authentic note':   *A.E.H.*, 27.

25   'commented severely':   *Unexpected Years*, 62.

26   'As regards work':   ibid., 71.

26   'streaks of puritanism':   ibid., 97.

26   'two of our quite "respectable" domestics':   LH to Maude Hawkins, 9 September 1950 (LC).

26   'in arm-in-arm pairs':   Katharine Symons to Gow, 28 February 1937 (Trinity).

26   daily Bible-readings: Lucy Housman, diary for 24 July 1882. Quotations from this diary are reproduced from a typescript document titled 'Extracts from the diaries of Mrs. Edward Housman' (Trinity); some of the entries are evidently summaries of the original made by Katharine Symons, presumably for Gow's benefit.

26   secular reading aloud: *Unexpected Years*, 76–7.

27   word-games and play-acting: ibid., 97, 99–100; *A.E.H.*, 36–7.

27   'a way of making things':   Katharine Symons, 'Boyhood', 16.

27   'subject to gloom':   ibid.

27   'quick to see humour':   ibid., 20.

27   'in a very quarrelsome family':   *Unexpected Years*, 382.

28   'saying that his English':   *A.E.H.*, 39.

28   'they considered':   J. M. Edmonds to LH, 28 November 1937 (LC).

28   'Alfred went to Oxford':   Lucy Housman, diary for 15 January 1877.

28   Herbert Millington later claimed: in a letter to the *Journal of Education* (1 February 1888), quoted by Gow, 'A. E. Housman at Oxford', *Oxford Magazine*, 56 (11 November 1937) 150.

2   OXFORD

PAGE

29   'The great and real troubles':   *Letters*, 363.

PAGE

29 Oscar Wilde: quoted by H. Montgomery Hyde, *Oscar Wilde* (1976) 15; Philippe Jullian, *Oscar Wilde* (1969) 33.

29 'By the third quarter': Ruth Fasnacht, *A History of the City of Oxford* (Oxford, 1954) 189.

30 'on Sunday': Sir Charles Oman, *Memories of Victorian Oxford* (1941) 86.

30 But even Oxford: see V. H. H. Green, *A History of Oxford University* (1974); W. R. Ward, *Victorian Oxford* (1965).

31 'the time for minute criticism': E. Abbott and L. Campbell, *The Life & Letters of Benjamin Jowett, M.A.* II (1897), 143 (letter of 16 February 1878).

32 'knowledge for its own sake': quoted by N. C. Chaudhuri, *Scholar Extraordinary: the Life of Professor the Rt. Hon. Frederick Max Müller* (1974) 2. The reference to places of emolument echoes, consciously or otherwise, the delicious observation made in the 1830s by Gaisford, Dean of Christ Church, that the study of Greek 'not only elevates above the vulgar herd, but leads not infrequently to positions of considerable emolument'.

32 young men who read classics: see *Oxford University Calendar*; J. Foster, *Alumni Oxonienses, 1715–1886* (Oxford, 1888); *Merchant Taylors' School Register, 1561–1934*, ed. E. P. Hart (1936).

33 'the restriction of many fellowships': E. L. Woodward, *The Age of Reform* (Oxford, 1962) 489.

33 'if the College had looked after Housman': A. W. Pollard to Gow, 15 July 1936 (Trinity, Add. ms. a. 71. 166).

33 'the tuition at St John's': E. W. Watson to Gow, 25 May 1936 (Trinity, Add. ms. a. 71. 169).

34 the famous quatrain: Geoffrey Faber, *Jowett: A Portrait with Background* (1957) 22.

34 an Oxford guide-book: *Oxford University & City Guide* (n.d.: c.1860) 21.

34 His letter to Lucy Housman: *Letters*, 11–12.

34 an Oxford story: Hugh Last to Gow, 28 October 1937 (Trinity).

34 'from the single lecture of Jowett's': Gow, *Sketch*, 5.

34 'getting up quietly': quoted by William Hayter, *Spooner: A Biography* (1977) 158.

35 Thomas Herbert Warren: see Laurie Magnus, *Herbert Warren of Magdalen* (1932).

35 a testimonial: printed in *Testimonials in Favour of Alfred Edward Housman . . . A Candidate for the Professorship of Latin in University College, London* (Cambridge, 1892).

35 'a genial but somewhat eccentric divine': David Hunter Blair, *In Victorian Days* (1939) 72.

35 'a man on whom he had done his best': Hugh Last to Gow, 1 November 1937 (Trinity, Add. ms. a. 71. 162).

36 'perfectly useless': Oman, 78. Oman found his first year at New College 'only a continuation of my last Winchester years of study, under less inspiring supervision'.

37 'This afternoon': *Letters*, 13.

37 'commenced operations': *Letters*, 18.

38 'He said nothing': *Letters*, 16.

38   'the best sermon': undated letter quoted in Sotheby & Co. Sale Catalogue, 15 December 1970, item 811.

38   'used to leave out': LH to Gow, 27 July 1936 (Trinity).

39   'among the first six': *Letters*, 19.

40   'Iona': printed as Appendix A in John Pugh, *Bromsgrove and the Housmans* (Bromsgrove, 1974).

40   'Oxford left little mark': Gow, *Sketch*, 5.

40   'He lived a quiet student's life': J. T. Nance to Grant Richards, 8 February 1939 (LC).

41   Vale Academy: information kindly supplied by Mr C. E. Busson, Branch Librarian, Ramsgate Library. Vale Academy, now demolished, was a large house on the corner of Vale Square and Crescent Road; Moses Jackson senior rented or leased it from 1857, and by 1869 had purchased it and turned it into a school.

41   'a perfect Philistine': E. W. Watson to Gow, 25 May 1936 (Trinity).

42   'often lively': A. W. Pollard to LH, 25 October 1936 (Sotheby & Co. Sale Catalogue, 8–9 July 1968, item 804).

42   'admired athletes greatly': LH to Gow, 27 July 1936 (Trinity).

43   'all the law and the prophets': Pollard, 'Some Reminiscences', *Alfred Edward Housman (Bromsgrovian* Supplement) 31.

43   'would challenge us': E. W. Watson to Gow, 25 May 1936 (Trinity).

43   *Ye Rounde Table*: six numbers of the first volume of this periodical appeared between February and June 1878. LH stated in the *Manchester Guardian* on 5 February 1957 that his brother contributed to it 'under a pseudonym which I promised never to reveal'. The pseudonym, 'Tristram', was attached to thirteen items in the six numbers. See John Carter's note in *The Book Collector*, 6 (1957) 404.

43   'a picturesque old house': Pollard, 'Some Reminiscences', 31.

43   'enjoyed idling': Pollard to Gow, 17 July 1936 (Trinity). Pollard adds, 'I think he underrated the standard for Greats.'

44   'He did once in talk': Percy Withers to Gow, 27 November 1937 (Trinity).

44   'I rather think': Pollard to Gow, 25 May 1936 (Trinity).

44   'practically nothing': Pollard to Gow, 17 July 1936 (Trinity).

44   'short and scrappy': J. T. Nance to Grant Richards, 8 February 1939 (LC).

44   'terribly ill for weeks': from Katharine Symons' summary of entries in Lucy Housman's diary for 1881 (Trinity).

45   a letter to his sister Kate: dated 4 April and printed by Pugh, *Bromsgrove and the Housmans*, lxxiv. This kind of correspondence was a family tradition: a letter from Kate to Housman (February 1878) now at University College, London, is full of jokes, wordplay and affectionate teasing, and delightfully evokes a lively, articulate, close-knit family life.

45   'exceptionally able': Pollard, 'Some Reminiscences', 31.

3   THE YEARS OF PENANCE

47   'years of penance':   the phrase is used by Katharine Symons in a letter to
E. H. Blakeney, 25 January 1942 (BL).
47   'He very much lived':   Katharine Symons to Gow, 17 December 1937
(Trinity).
47   'We were frightfully poor':   LH to Gow, 15 June 1936 (Trinity).
47   'very morose':   Katharine Symons to Gow, 31 July 1936 (Trinity).
47   'he withdrew':   LH to Gow, 15 June 1936 (Trinity).
47   'he would see':   Katharine Symons, summary of 1881 diary of Lucy
Housman (Trinity).
48   'returned to Oxford':   Lucy Housman, diary for 14 December 1881
(Trinity). Why did Housman not bring his 'things' with him in the first
place? Graves (p. 57) posits a father–son confrontation on the evening of
the 13th; but this can be no more than surmise, and it is not difficult to
think of more prosaic reasons for a double journey.
49   'investigating the claims':   Ralph Griffin to A. F. Scholfield, 19 June 1936
(Trinity).
50   'was an outspoken critic':   E. W. Hulme to Stephen Gaselee, 8 June 1936
(Trinity).
50   'lived on most friendly terms':   Ralph Griffin to A. F. Scholfield, 19 June
1936 (Trinity).
50   'His most familiar friends':   F. W. Hodges to Gow, n.d. (Trinity).
50   'His most intimate friend':   E. W. Hulme to Stephen Gaselee, 8 June 1936
(Trinity).
51   'He neither looked nor talked':   William Rothenstein, *Men and Memories*
(1932) 39.
51   'most delightful companion':   W. H. Eyre to Gow, n.d. (Trinity).
51   'the great and real troubles':   *Letters*, 363.
51   'I abandoned Christianity':   *Letters*, 381.
52   'became a deist':   ibid.
53   '*shied away*':   LH to Maude Hawkins, 19 June 1958 (LC).
53   'I have *no* doubt':   LH to Maude Hawkins, 21 July 1958 (LC).
54   'the most amiable nature':   Sotheby & Co. Sale Catalogue, 8–9 July 1958,
item 802.
55   'rather amusing':   *Letters*, 25.
55   'as we parted':   LH to Maude Hawkins, 29 May 1958 (LC).
55   'AEH held us':   LH to Maude Hawkins, 9 September 1950 (LC).
56   'the first book':   *Letters*, 26.
57   'The time lost':   *Classical Papers*, I, 55.
58   Housman's record: The British Library possesses Housman's diary for
1888–90, with a single further entry for 1898. 'Diary' is, however, a
misleading term: what Housman did was to use pocket diaries in order
to set down a skeletal record of certain events and observations,
apparently writing many of the entries at a sitting and presumably
making a fair copy from notes subsequently destroyed. The diaries are
described and partly reproduced in the *Encounter* article referred to
below. The entries fall into two categories on different levels of interest.

One category comprises references to the Jackson brothers, mainly Moses. The other consists of botanical and meteorological notes for certain periods: for example, between 27 June and 10 July 1889, Housman noted the temperature daily as well as the appearance of various types of flowers; on 2 October 1889, a walk in Epping Forest revealed 'one honeysuckle bloom' and other discoveries. There is an evident interest in ascertaining and preserving the precise date on which buds, leaves and flowers make their appearance in a given a locality (the cherry, ready to flower on 28 March 1893, is in flower three days later). The 1891 diary contains nature notes relating to several subsequent years. There are also records of daily expenses. Long stretches of the diaries are blank.

Laurence Housman deposited the diaries in the British Museum 'to remain *unopened* till the year 1967'; he also wrote an explanatory essay, published as 'A. E. Housman's "De Amicitia"', *Encounter*, 29 (October 1967) 33–41, with annotations by John Carter.

60 'I experienced':   quoted by Enid Starkie, *Flaubert: the Making of the Master*, (Harmondsworth, 1971) 40.

61 'to return to the rule':   the report is at University College, London. Earlier occupants of the Latin chair had been J. R. Seeley, the historian (1863–70), and Robinson Ellis (1870–6).

61 'conservative in politics':   *Dictionary of National Biography*, article on Ker by R. W. Chambers.

61 'in 1881 I failed':   *Letters*, 30.

61 a printed booklet: *Testimonials in favour of Alfred Edward Housman* . . .

63 'As a rule':   John Maycock to A. E. Housman, quoted in *A.E.H.*, 92.

4 'PICKED OUT OF THE GUTTER'

64 'He said':   R. W. Chambers to Gow, 31 October 1936 (Trinity).

65 'scholarships enough':   Report of Committee on Greek and Latin Chairs at University College, London, May 1892; adopted by Council on 11 June 1892 (University College, London).

66 'scholarly gaiety':   R. W. Chambers, *Man's Unconquerable Mind* (1939) 362.

66 'Philology was tame':   quoted by Chambers, ibid.; originally published in *The Times* (9 November 1936).

66 'the students in Classics':   R. W. Chambers, *Philogists at University College: Centenary Address* (1927) 29–30, 32.

66 'a place of learning':   David Taylor, *The Godless Students of Gower Street* (1968) 33–4.

67 'the work of the College':   University College, London: Annual Reports of Council, 1905–6, 832.

67 the lecture: privately printed in 1892 and 1933, published in 1937, and included in *Selected Prose*. Housman refused to publish it himself because 'it contains a statement which I cannot verify' (*Letters*, 285); he sent

Withers a copy of the 1933 private printing by 'a couple of besotted admirers' (*Letters*, 349), John Sparrow and John Carter, but refused to autograph it.

71 'so caustic':   Chambers, *Man's Unconquerable Mind*, 368.

71 'a tall, slender, serious-faced man':   quoted in Richards, 330, from an article in the *Birmingham Post*, 22 June 1937.

72 'we did not mind':   Chambers, *Man's Unconquerable Mind*, 368.

72 'we thoroughly appreciated':   G. H. Savory to Grant Richards, 11 December 1940 (LC).

72 'professing Latin':   Mortimer Wheeler, *Still Digging* (1955) 31.

72 'friendly and cordial':   Richard Aldington, *A. E. Housman and W. B. Yeats* (1955) 6–7.

72 'very kind and helpful':   Annette M. B. Meakin to Grant Richards, 22 June 1943 (LC).

73 'always friendly and considerate':   Lawrence Solomon to Gow, 30 October 1936 (Trinity).

73 'was at his best':   F. W. Oliver, 'A. E. Housman: Some Recollections', in Richards, 438 (originally published in *University College Magazine*, March 1937). Oliver was professor of Botany at UCL.

73 'an incomparable after-dinner speaker':   F. W. Oliver to Gow, 23 November 1936 (Trinity).

73 'lay an adversary low':   R. W. Chambers, 'A London Memoir', in *Alfred Edward Housman* (*Bromsgrovian* Supplement), 43.

73 papers on Arnold, etc.:   the paper on Swinburne has survived and was published in *Cornhill Magazine*, 177 (1968–9) 380–400. A fragment of the paper on Arnold is given in *Selected Prose*, 196–8.

74 'Housman's reading':   R. W. Chambers, letter in *John o' London's Weekly*, 24 October 1936.

74 'Towards the end of it':   S. C. Roberts, *Adventures with Authors* (1966) 124.

74 'things must come right':   R. W. Chambers, 'A London Memoir', 43.

74 'the feeling we had for him':   R. W. Chambers to Grant Richards, 6 July 1938 (LC).

75 'power of leadership':   F. W. Oliver, 'Some Recollections', 439.

75 'lay on the open veldt':   Corporal B. Hobden to Mrs Edward Housman, 1 November 1901, in Pugh, *Bromsgrove and the Housmans*, lxviii.

75 'buried on battlefield':   in a family chart drawn up in 1908 and reproduced in Richards.

76 'When I got into Italy':   *Letters*, 44.

77 'just after sundown':   A. E. Housman to J. G. Frazer, 17 May 1913 (typescript copy, Trinity).

78 'I did not begin':   *Letters*, 329.

78 'I have hardly ever written':   ms. of Leslie Stephen Lecture, 'The Name and Nature of Poetry' (Cambridge University Library).

79 'nearly everything':   Sydney Cockerell, diary for 10 November 1911 (BL).

79 'about one third':   Tom Burns Haber, *The Manuscript Poems of A. E. Housman* (Minneapolis, 1955) 16.

79 chronology of individual poems: LH gives dates for sixty-three poems

218 *Notes and References*

PAGE

(*A.E.H.*, 273–5), and states that he has taken twenty-five of these dates from Housman's notebooks and most of the others from a list made by Sir Sydney Cockerell. Cockerell had discussed *Last Poems* with Housman on 28 October 1922, and on that occasion Housman dictated to him a list of dates of composition of the poems in that volume; Cockerell published the list, in which many of the dates are (as he says) 'only approximate', in *The Times Literary Supplement* (7 November 1936), and it is reprinted as Appendix 4 to Richards. Revised dates for 'at least the early drafts' of fifteen items have been suggested by J. M. Nosworthy (*TLS*, 11 January 1968).

81 '1895 disturbance': Katharine Symons to Gow, 30 October and 5 November 1936 (Trinity).

82 'Its emotional effect': Richards, 313.

82 'my family': *Letters*, 390.

82 'the poor man': LH to Maude Hawkins, 24 October 1950 (LC).

82 'ill and depressed': Richards, 312.

83 'touched off a process': Kenneth Quinn, *Catullus: An Interpretation* (New York, 1973) 5.

83 the Wilde case: the Wilde affair was not an isolated phenomenon: at earlier stages of Housman's time in London, the Dublin Castle affair of 1884 and the Cleveland Street scandal of 1889–90 had made a variously shocked or eager public aware of the prevalence in their midst of homosexual behaviour and male prostitution. England had been slow to modify its archaic legislation – indeed, legal sanctions became more rather than less severe in the nineteenth century – and public tolerance in this area of conduct had lagged behind the general humanitarian advance. In the 1820s, when more than a hundred offences were removed from the list of capital crimes, the death penalty for sodomy instituted in the sixteenth century was re-enacted. In 1859, one learns with astonishment, more men were sentenced to hang for consensual sexual relations with other men than for killing them; Louis Crompton, though conceding that 'it is probable that no executions took place [for this reason] in England after 1835', comments that the record 'indicates a level of homophobia possibly higher than in any other country in the world' (*Victorian Studies*, 22 (1979) 212). In 1885, under a Criminal Law Amendment Act primarily directed against female prostitution, *all* male homosexual acts became illegal. Public hostility to the male homosexual deepened; and when Wilde was committed for trial in April 1895, the magistrate, Sir John Bridges, told him that 'there is no worse crime than that with which the prisoners are charged'. Jeffrey Weeks has suggested that the Wilde trials 'created a public image for the homosexual, and a terrifying moral tale of the dangers that trailed closely behind deviant behaviour' (*Coming Out*, 21). Havelock Ellis commented that the trials seemed 'to have generally contributed to give definiteness and self-consciousness to the manifestations of hostility' (quoted by Weeks, 22). More profoundly, a legacy of the Wilde case to homosexuals was an intensified awareness of their condition. Hitherto, the language had scarcely furnished terms in which it was possible for the homosexual to reflect soberly on his own nature. There was, of course, a vocabulary for

homosexual acts (or, rather, two vocabularies, one classical, the other demotic), as well as a vigorous argot descriptive of the flourishing homosexual underworld. But, as John Addington Symonds wrote in 1891, 'the accomplished languages of Europe in the nineteenth century supply no terms for this persistent feature of human psychology, without importing some implication of disgust, disgrace, vituperation'. In the years immediately following the Wilde case, the language expanded to fill this need. The *Oxford English Dictionary* records *inversion* as appearing in 1896 – the year of *A Shropshire Lad* – and *homosexuality* in 1897. Housman's reaction to this sad episode in the history of intolerance is undocumented. On his contact with Wilde, see *Letters*, 267; Laurence Housman, *Echo de Paris* (1923) 14.

84 'from Wenlock Edge': *New Statesman*, 15 (1 January 1938) 19 (review of *A.E.H.*).

84 Woolwich cadet: see *A.E.H.*, 103–5; J. M. Nosworthy, 'A. E. Housman and the Woolwich Cadet', *Notes & Queries*, n.s. 17 (1970) 351–3.

85 'As in 1895': *Letters*, 223.

86 'during these periods': M. A. Jackson (sister of Moses), notes on Moses Jackson (typescript copy, Trinity).

86 'said goodbye': AEH, diary (BL).

87 eighteen-page report: at University College, London.

89 'a couple of hundred times': Richards, 145.

90 'I think you are now': *Letters*, 99.

90 'catapulted himself': David Cecil, *Max* (1964) 64.

91 'discouraged any show': William Rothenstein, *Since Fifty: Men and Memories 1922–1938* (1939) 6.

91 'never failed to tell me': William Rothenstein to Gow, 13 August 1936 (Trinity), Add. ms. a. 71. 283.

91 'you are much too great an artist': *Letters*, 260.

91 'I am told': AEH to Grant Richards, 30 November 1922, quoted in Richards, 205.

91 'such infatuation as yours': *Letters*, 347.

92 'I value the good opinion': AEH to Geoffrey Wethered, 13 September 1933 (Trinity).

92 'My chief object': *Letters*, 65.

93 'I once attended': T. R. Glover, *Cambridge Retrospect* (1943) 86.

94 'he had been zealously active': W. R. M. Lamb to Grant Richards, 6 May 1942 (LC).

94 'hadn't the ghost of a chance': Grant Richards, *Author Hunting* (1943) 29; Richards, 97–8.

94 'I remember Robinson Ellis': Leonard Whibley to Gow, 19 November 1936 (Trinity).

94 'Macaulay used to rank': AEH to H. M. Innes, 21 January 1911 (Trinity, Add. ms. c. 1. 192).

94 'Satisfaction is general': 'Cambridge Letter', *Oxford Magazine* 56 (2 February 1911) 171.

95 'the jokes': Winifred Husbands to Grant Richards, 21 October 1942 (LC).

95 'smallish', 'dapper': Katharine Symons to Gow, 17 July 1936 (Trinity).

Housman once admitted to being 'very susceptible to comments on my personal appearance', and recalled how 'one day when I was just turned forty, I was walking along and brooding on the fact, when a passing carter of some twenty-five summers said, "What's the time, young fellow?" A spring of joy gushed from my heart and I blessed him unaware' (AEH to J. J. Thomson, 27 March 1929; quoted by Lord Rayleigh, *The Life of Sir J. J. Thomson, O.M.* (Cambridge, 1942) 264). For an example of the tricks played by memory in recalling anecdotes, see the version of this story in J. J. Thomson, *Recollections and Reflections* (1936) 315.

95   'if drinking nothing':   R. W. Chambers, *Man's Unconquerable Mind*, 380–1.

95   'Cambridge has seen':   an oft-quoted story: see, *inter alia, A.E.H.*, 101; *Unexpected Years*, 365; *The Times*, 5 May 1936, 21; R. W. Chambers, *Man's Unconquerable Mind*, 380–1; Chambers to Gow, 28 and 31 October 1936 (Trinity). The version given here obviously belongs to an occasion in London, before the move to Cambridge, and there seems no reason to doubt Chambers' declaration that the remark was first made at the farewell dinner given by Housman's colleagues at University College. A version that concludes, 'A better scholar than Wordsworth, a better poet than Porson, here stand I, betwixt and between', suggests a Cambridge setting.

95   'We felt the loss':   R. W. Chambers to Gow, 31 October 1936 (Trinity).

95   'in his right setting':   Chambers, *Man's Unconquerable Mind*, 381.

5   CAMBRIDGE I

96   'identified himself':   R. W. Chambers to Gow, 2 February 1937 (Trinity).

96   'joy does predominate':   *Letters*, 115.

96   'she could not entirely':   Richards, 99.

97   'because at Trinity':   ibid.

98   'small, crowded, smoke-laden cell':   Mortimer Wheeler, *Still Digging*, 31.

98   'to have less work':   *Letters*, 115.

98   'was notoriously not easy':   G. M. Trevelyan, *Trinity College: An Historical Sketch* (Cambridge, 1946) 112.

98   'I shall most likely spend':   *Letters*, 115.

98   'the only professorial function':   *Letters*, 117.

99   'social duties':   *Letters*, 118.

99   Inaugural Lecture: on AEH's reasons for refusing to publish this in his lifetime, see *Letters*, 285; Gow, *Sketch*, 33n; John Carter, *TLS*, 6 September 1963, 680; John Carter and John Sparrow, *TLS*, 21 November 1968. The manuscript was destroyed after his death, but a typescript copy turned up in 1968 and was presented to Cambridge University Library by Mr Robert E. Symons. Most of it was printed in *TLS* on 9 May 1968, and it was published complete as *The Confines of*

PAGE

Criticism: the Cambridge Inaugural 1911, with notes by John Carter (Cambridge, 1969); the title is not Housman's. See also TLS, 27 November and 4 December 1969.

99 'a crowded and curious audience': Gow, *Sketch*, 33.

99 'Splendidly fine': Sydney Cockerell, diary for 9 May 1911 (BL).

99 'Brilliant is the only epithet': J. M. Image to W. F. Smith, 9 May 1911; quoted by John Carter, *The Confines of Criticism*, 8.

99 'Housman's discourse': R. St John Parry, *Henry Jackson, O.M.* (Cambridge, 1926) 164.

102 'stark and comfortless': Withers, 15.

102 'bleak': William Rothenstein to Grant Richards, 5 December 1941 (LC).

102 'bare and grim': A. C. Benson, diary for 22 November 1913.

102 'narrow and austere': Richards, 265–6.

102 'I often wondered': Sydney Cockerell to Richards, 7 December 1941 (LC).

103 'one of several': Gow, *Sketch*, 16.

103 'being a new-comer': *Letters*, 121.

103 'I also have over-eaten': AEH to Grant Richards, 13 December 1911.

103 'when he first came to Cambridge': Gow, *Cambridge Review*, 57 (8 May 1936), 367.

103 'sat next to A. E. Housman': A. C. Benson, diary for 18 May 1911.

104 'far more genial': ibid., November 1911.

104 'but all the time': Gertrude Stein, *The Autobiography of Alice B. Toklas*, (New York, n.d.) 145; Alice B. Toklas, *What is Remembered* (1963) 90.

104 The Family: see S. C. Roberts, *The Family: The History of a Dining Club* (Cambridge, 1963).

104 'he was very seldom absent': J. J. Thomson, *Recollections and Reflections*, 114–15.

104 'Housman . . . told me': A. C. Benson, diary for 26 January 1923.

104 M. R. James's recollections: in M. R. James, *Eton and King's* (1926) 247.

105 'one of my best boon-companions': *Letters*, 364.

108 'if you ever have to examine': *Letters*, 128–9.

109 'in style and diction': ms. report on C. R. Haines's edition of the letters of Fronto (Cambridge University Library).

109 'he simply dictated arguments': L. P. Wilkinson, 'A. E. Housman, Scholar and Poet,' *Housman Society Journal*, I (1974) 32.

109 'he had commonly': Gow, obituary of AEH 'prepared with the help of Sir S[tephen] Gaselee', sent to a German journal in 1939, but never published (Trinity).

109 'exactly like a coiled spring': E. L. Franklin to Gow, 13 May 1936 (Trinity, Add. ms. a. 71. 253).

110 'I attended': D. S. Macnutt to Gow, 12 October 1963 (Trinity).

110 'immaculate': quoted by T. E. B. Howarth, *Cambridge Between Two Wars* (1978)89.

110 'The severity': ibid.

111 'I hear that I am lecturing': *Letters*, 389.

111 lecture-courses: Housman's notes are now in Cambridge University Library.

PAGE

111 ' "That," he said hurriedly':   Mrs T. W. Pym, letter in *The Times*, 5 May 1936; quoted by Richards, 289.

111 'the events of that reign':   Address to King George V on the occasion of his 'so-called jubilee' (*Letters*, 368), published in *Cambridge University Reporter* on 14 May 1935; reprinted in *Selected Prose*, 165–7.

111 'completely transformed':   S. C. Roberts, *Introduction to Cambridge* (1934) 25.

111 'normal undergraduate life':   Trevelyan, *Trinity College*, 115.

112 'a Hospital':   J. R. M. Butler, *Henry Montagu Butler* (1925) 200.

112 'The thirst for blood':   *Letters*, 136.

113 'Hitherto I have always':   *Letters*, 138.

113 'Providence, for my benefit':   AEH to J. G. Frazer, 7 March 1915 (Trinity, Add. ms. b. 36. 83).

113 'Whewell's Court':   ibid.

113 'Above the soldier's grave':   Leonard Whibley to Gow, 19 November 1936 (Trinity). The Woodbine, it may be necessary to explain, as well as being a kind of honeysuckle, was a brand of cheap cigarettes particularly favoured by the lower classes.

114 'to harmonise the sadness':   *Letters*, 141.

114 'cannot have made much change':   *Letters*, 329.

114 'not on account of mines':   *Letters*, 145.

114 'I never discharged':   Butler, *Henry Montagu Butler*, 216.

115 'Russell is a great loss':   AEH to Henry Hollond, quoted by Howarth, *Cambridge Between Two Wars*, 29. See also G. H. Hardy, *Bertrand Russell and Trinity: A College Controversy of the Last War* (1942; reprinted, with foreword by C. D. Broad, 1970).

116 'a mainly disillusioning experience':   E. M. W. Tillyard, *The Muse Unchained* (1958) 14.

116 'minute and pedantic studies':   *Letters*, 228.

116 'disapproval writ large':   H. G. Wood, *Terrot Reaveley Glover: A Biography* (1953) 68.

117 'he held no Seminar':   Gow, unpublished obituary of AEH.

119 'I have known certainly':   *Letters*, 332.

119 'looking neither to right':   Mr L. P. Wilkinson (personal communication).

119 'They were joint examiners':   Professor Glyn Daniel (personal communication).

120 'His favourite afternoon walk':   Rex Salisbury Woods, *Cambridge Doctor* (1962) 93.

120 'settled down to work':   *Letters*, 163.

120 'on the return journey':   *Letters*, 180.

121 casually remarking at dinner: Professor Glyn Daniel (personal communication).

121 'in search of illicit pleasures':   jacket-description of Graves, referring to a passage on p. 155 of Graves's book and to note 18 on pp. 282–3. The 'document' in question (10 × 6.5 cm), which is neither reproduced nor quoted by Mr Graves, was given considerable prominence in many of the reviews of his book; not all reviewers made it clear that his

interpretation is expressed with some tentativeness. Housman's notes are far from explicit; I myself find it difficult to accept that they include 'a note of the price paid on various occasions' for the services of male prostitutes. They consist of a list of fifteen consecutive days of the week (from one Monday to the Monday a fortnight later); beside each is written a numeral, the only numerals employed being 0, 3, 9, and 10; beside all those except the ones with a 'zero' notation is a French noun indicating some masculine avocation or attribute – sailor, boxer, dancer, negro. (In one case *danseur* is queried.) In the margin the phrase '10 in 15 days' is written. I am grateful to Mr Martin Higham for supplying me with photocopies of this document, to which Mr Paul Naiditch has assigned an approximate date of May 1932 (personal communication).

121   'the annual holiday':   Peter Levi, review of Graves in *New Statesman*, 7 December 1979, 906.

121   'I probably should not be free':   *Letters*, 214.

121   'Housman after dinner':   Richards, 243.

121   'cannot offer you':   *Letters*, 320.

121   'disappointed of a companion':   *Letters*, 336.

121   'a French companion':   *Letters*, 339.

121   'a French companion, though not':   *Letters*, 338–9.

122   'a nice young man':   *Letters*, 339.

122   helpful companion: AEH to Lady Frazer, 26 September 1935 (BL).

122   E. M. Forster: in a review of *MP* and Gow, *Listener*, 16 (1936) 922.

122   'love-affair':   Graves, 150.

122   'falling out of love':   Graves, 152. Another specimen of Mr Graves in speculative vein: 'Now, rather to his surprise, he tasted some of the pleasures which he had longed for so intensely since childhood' (151). The surprise is not confined to Housman.

122   'on a romantic evening':   *Letters*, 238.

122   'my gondolier':   *Letters*, 58, 237.

122   'where my poor gondolier':   *Letters*, 237.

122   On the flight back: see E. V. Lucas, *Reading, Writing and Remembering* (1932) 86.

123   'a poem about his gondolier':   Graves, 152.

123   'I suppose he will go':   *Letters*, 238.

123   a phallic symbol: 'The tower that stood and fell/Is not rebuilt in me' echoes an earlier poem: 'the house is fallen/That none can build again' (*LP* XVIII).

124   'the Platonic amorist':   Swinburne, *Studies in Prose and Poetry* (1894) 34. On Symonds and Venice, see Phyllis Grosskurth, *John Addington Symonds*, 241–3.

124   'cheaper to indulge':   *Letters*, 159–60.

124   'sold in Paris':   *Letters*, 151.

125   fifty titles: see *Register of Collections Presented, 1929–44* (Cambridge University Library).

125   'did not inflame my passions':   *Letters*, 291.

125   'I have been more amused':   *Letters*, 264.

125 to write to Sir Henry Stuart-Jones: information kindly supplied by Mr Richard Palmer; the letter is in archives stored at the office of the Oxford Latin Dictionary in Oxford.

126 'a typical Cambridge don':   Wilfrid Scawen Blunt, *My Diaries* II (n.d., [1919]) 371–2.

126 'had a "disconcerting way"':   Edith Finch, *Wilfrid Scawen Blunt 1840–1922* (1938) 325.

126 'very pleasant talk':   Viola Meynell, *Francis Thompson and Wilfrid Meynell: A Memoir* (1952) 80.

126 'very precisely dressed':   Joseph Hone, *Life of Henry Tonks* (1939).

126 'the deplorable sex':   *Unexpected Years*, 358.

127 'emotion terrifying in its strength':   Joan Thomson, 'Biographical Reminiscences', given as Appendix VII to Richards. Typescript at Trinity.

127 'I never heard Housman':   Mary Anderson de Navarro, *A Few More Memories* (1936) 263.

127 'reserved, chivalrous friendliness':   R. W. Chambers to Richards, 2 December 1941 (LC).

127 'an avowed misogynist':   Withers, quoted by Richards, 395.

6   CAMBRIDGE II

128 'I wrote the book':   *Letters*, 65.

128 'The other day':   *Letters*, 108.

128 'none even of my few unpublished poems':   *Letters*, 135.

128 'Last year':   *Letters*, 171.

129 'Suppose I produced':   *Letters*, 179.

129 '"My new book"':   *Letters*, 183.

129 'It is now practically certain':   *Letters*, 192.

130 'I want you to note':   *Letters*, 199.

131 'a faint pleasure':   *Letters*, 209.

131 'as ill as I have ever been':   *Letters*, 211.

131 'better, but not well':   *Letters*, 215.

132 *Punch*: the issue for 25 October 1922 contains (p. 392) a cartoon depicting the Muse emerging from a building clearly labelled 'Temple of the Muses' and greeting Housman (shown dancing and playing a pipe, with the familiar centre parting and drooping moustache, and with a copy of *Last Poems* protruding from his knapsack) with the words: 'Oh, Alfred, we have missed you! My Shropshire Lad!' The issue for 24 January 1923 included (p. 78) a parody in a series titled 'Shocking Travesties': supposedly sent to AEH by the French statesman M. Poincaré, it begins, 'When treaty time was over/At Essen on the Ruhr . . .'.

132 'list of presentation copies':   Percy Muir to Richards, 2 July 1942 (LC).

132 'very badly off':   Katharine Symons to Gow, 7 February 1937 (Trinity).

133 'I long ago resolved':   *Letters*, 77.

134 'it would give me more trouble':   *Letters*, 318.

134 '"I'm damned if I will"':   Richards, 275–6.

134 'I do not think highly':   letter of 1 July 1933, in *Thirty Housman Letters to Witter Bynner*, ed. T. B. Haber (New York, 1957).

134 'until I have broken':   *Letters*, 331.

134 'for alleged weakness':   AEH to Lady Frazer, 12 July 1933 (BL).

134 'in a very low nervous condition':   ibid.

134 'my disagreeable tour':   *Letters*, 344.

134 'a form of influenza':   ibid.

135 'you could have heard':   Mr L. P. Wilkinson (personal communication).

135 'a slight stir':   S. C. Roberts, *Adventures with Authors* (1966) 126.

138 'glad you were amused':   *Letters*, 334.

138 'its success here':   *Letters*, 335.

138 'surprisingly, almost naughtily simple':   *The Times*, 10 May 1933, 15.

138 'the greatest poetry':   quoted by Noel Annan, *New York Review of Books*, 19 July 1979, 20.

138 '"Did he really mean"':   G. H. Hardy, *A Mathematician's Apology* (1940; reprinted 1967 with an interesting introduction by C. P. Snow), 62–3. There are some striking resemblances between Hardy and Housman, and the former's defence of his life's work in his *Apology* recalls Housman's defence of textual criticism. Pure mathematics in its higher reaches, he argues, is useless (relatively little mathematics being needed for engineering and other practical pursuits), but it is intellectually and aesthetically satisfying. Of ambition, he writes that it 'is a noble passion . . . but the noblest ambition is that of leaving behind one something of permanent value' (77); he concludes that 'the case for my life . . . is this: that I have added something to knowledge' (151). He remarks of Housman that he 'would have refused to be Lord Simon or Lord Beaverbrook . . . because of his ambition, because he would have scorned to be a man to be forgotten in twenty years' (83).

139 'He is a terribly industrious humourist':   AEH to J. G. Frazer, 7 March 1915 (typescript copy, Trinity).

139 'worshipped as a god':   *Letters*, 344.

139 'It has long been known':   T. S. Eliot in *The Criterion*, 13 (1933) 151–2.

140 'The commentary':   *Selected Prose*, 46.

140 'Works of this sort':   *Classical Papers*, II, 797.

140 'Mr. Merrill':   ibid., III, 1092.

140 'half the ship's cargo':   ibid., III,1090.

140 'To read attentively':   *Selected Prose*, 51.

141 'If a man will comprehend':   ibid., 31.

141 'A textual critic':   *Classical Papers*, III, 1059.

141 'Mr. Bailey':   ibid., II, 524.

142 '"Scholars will pardon"':   ibid., II, 517.

142 'hardly a page':   Preface to *Lucan* (1926), xxxiv. The reference is to Francken's edition.

142 'It was a fine August morning':   *Classical Papers*, II, 815.

142 'moral integrity':   Preface to *Lucan*, xxvii.

143 'the average man':   *Selected Prose*, 43.

143 'How the world': ibid., 36.

143 'that habit': ibid., 53.

143 'the sloth': ibid.

143 'the faintest': ibid., 43.

143 'emendators': Preface to *Lucan*, xxvii.

143 'an aristocratic affair': *Classical Papers*, III, 1069.

143 'the reader whose good opinion': *Selected Prose*, 53.

144 'The names': Preface to *Lucan*, xviii.

144 'were in perpetual contact': *Selected Prose*, 45.

144 'the inhumanity of humanism': H. W. Garrod, *Scholarship: its meaning and value* (1946) 28.

144 'in verbal scholarship': AEH to J. G. Frazer, 22 October 1927 (Trinity, Frazer 1. 41).

144 'Sciatica': *Letters*, 174.

144 'Death and marriage': ibid., 229.

145 'Pattison': ibid., 236.

145 'He may be consoled': ibid., 271.

145 'stored ammunition': *A.E.H.*, 88. LH had earlier used the phrase in a letter to Gow dated 20 December 1937 (Trinity). He writes (*A.E.H*, 77): 'there can be no doubt that [AEH] did greatly enjoy writing and saying bitter and contemptuous things about people who seemed to him to deserve them; and he had in his notebook a whole stock of phrases which were apparently waiting till opportunity came for him to use them . . . in the notebooks I found five pages of them obviously awaiting application . . .' LH's 'apparently' becomes 'obviously' within a few lines; the latter adverb has perhaps been taken rather too readily on trust. A surviving typescript (Trinity, Add. ms. a. 71. 20) of eleven pages is headed 'From the A.E.H. notebooks' and appears to represent LH's transcription of the 'phrases' before destroying the original. 'Phrases' is an understatement: while some of the entries consist of only a few words, others run to five or six lines and most are complete sentences. If there were indeed only 'five pages' they must have been very closely written. The example I quote referring to Meredith suggests that the collection includes material from a wide span of years (Meredith died in 1909).

147 'epigrammatic and witty': J. H. Monk, *The Life of Richard Bentley, D. D.* (1830) 34–5.

147 'he had about the happiest *laugh*': LH to Maud Hawkins, 30 March 1951 (LC).

148 'every action': Angus Davidson, *Edward Lear* (1938) 229.

148 'his plans were never elastic': Richards, 153. Withers (69–72) gives a very striking account of Housman's curiously tormented behaviour on leaving at the end of a visit.

148 'stickler for exactitude': Elizabeth Sewell, *The Field of Nonsense* (1952) 38. Some of the observations made by one of Carroll's biographers could be applied with equal force to Housman. For instance: 'he . . . was incessantly engaged in *a struggle for perfection* . . . from one aspect he might appear fussy, difficult, touchy; from another . . . he would be all generosity and kindness . . . He was almost fanatically anxious to secure

artistic perfection and the best possible printing for his readers . . .' (Derek Hudson, *Lewis Carroll* (1954) 112, 117).

148 'Did Sir Stanley': R. W. Chambers to Gow, 6 August 1936 (Trinity, Add. ms. a. 71. 271).

149 'Arthur Benson told me': Edward Marsh, *A Number of People* (1939) 221.

149 'commended the custom': *Unexpected Years*, 365.

150 '*First don*': E. Marsh, *A Number of People*, 222.

150 'I proceeded': John Fothergill, *My Three Inns* (1949) 74.

151 'There was only one toast': H. J. Chaytor to Richards, 6 January 1941 (LC). See also *A.E.H.*, 100.

151 'the kindest action': Richards, 324.

151 'Mr. A. E. Housman': Richards, 199.

151 'no nonsense': *Letters*, 79.

152 'shy, proud, reserved': LH to Maude Hawkins, 3 March 1950 (LC).

152 'a laugh which betokened': *The Times*, 2 May 1936, 9.

152 'unsociable and decidedly sour': William Plomer, 'The land of Lost Content', *Listener*, 61 (1959) 545.

152 'an undertaker's mute': Richard Middleton, *Monologues* (1913) 219.

152 'he was like an absconding cashier': David Cecil, *Max* (1964) 262.

152 'most unclubbable man': Thomas Jones, *A Diary with Letters, 1931–1950* (1954) 93. I owe this reference to Mr Paul Naiditch.

152 'underneath the dry asperity': William Rothenstein to Gow, 25 November 1936 (Trinity).

152 'strange that he should be': J. D. Duff to E. H. Blakeney, 16 March 1931 (BL).

153 'at all times': O. L. Richmond to Richards, 20 December 1941 (LC).

153 'a genial person': R. W. Chambers, *Man's Unconquerable Mind*, 362.

153 'of long talks I had': Mrs Lily Thicknesse to Richards, 7 April 1940 (LC).

153 'not even Moses': A. W. Pollard to LH, 25 October 1936 (Sotheby & Co. Catalogue, 8–9 July 1968, item 804).

153 'There was a pause': A. C. Benson, diary, June 1912.

153 'extremely witty': Alan Ker to LH, 15 December 1937 (LC).

154 'in Platt's company': *Classical Papers*, III, 1267.

154 'knows everything': *Letters*, 50.

154 'a dear and wonderful creature': ibid., 258.

154 'For Hardy': ibid., 329.

155 'an amazing old man': ibid., 217.

155 'I write to offer': ibid., 294.

155 'my favourite': ibid., 326.

155 'an almost ascetically slight figure': Joan Thomson, quoted in Richards, 446.

156 'I have grown older': *Letters*, 333.

156 'after five or six miles': AEH to Katharine Symons, 22 December 1932, in Pugh, *Bromsgrove and the Housmans*, lxxxiv.

156 'My life is bearable': *Letters*, 363.

156 'illish': R. S. Woods to Gow, 31 July 1936 (Trinity, Add. ms. a. 71. 269).

156 'nervous depression': *Letters*, 336.

156 'the real bother': AEH to LH, 15 June 1933, in *A.E.H.*, 186.

156 'My companion':   *Letters*, 340, 341.

156 'neither strong nor comfortable':   ibid., 352.

156 'he was ill':   ibid., 363.

157 'showed signs of definite failure':   R. S. Woods to Gow, 31 July 1936. Later in the year he was 'very distressed with dyspepsia, and oedema [swelling due to accumulation of fluid] of lower limbs', according to Dr Woods' notes.

157 'You probably know':   *Letters*, 372.

157 'sudden and painless end':   Withers, 99.

157 'My life ought to have come':   AEH to Lady Frazer, 26 September 1935 (BL).

157 'going downhill':   *Letters*, 378.

158 'unable to write a cheque':   ibid., 385.

158 'I am now':   ibid., 386.

158 'The material was as austere':   L. P. Wilkinson, 'A. E. Housman, Scholar and Poet', 33.

158 'All his many previous visits':   Withers to Gow, 27 October 1936 (Trinity).

158 'the extreme and undeserved kindness':   *Letters*, 387.

159 'a considerable number of honours':   ibid., 389.

159 'In philosophy':   ibid., 390.

159 'reading to fill my hours':   *Letters*, 391.

159 'great turn for the better':   *Letters*, 391.

159 'I fear I shall live':   ibid., 390.

160 'He was terribly ill':   J. J. Thomson, *Recollections and Reflections*, 318.

160 'Back to Evelyn nursing home':   *Letters*, 392 (original reproduced opposite p. 203).

160 'no public announcement':   Sydney Cockerell to Richards, 15 January 1942 (LC).

160 'rather too Christian':   LH to Gow, 27 July 1936 (Trinity).

161 'passion for perfection':   G. B. A. Fletcher to Richards, n.d., in Richards, 385.

161 'I have to admit':   LH to Maude Hawkins, January 1950 (LC).

7   THE SCHOLAR

162 'sacred mystery':   'The Application of Thought to Textual Criticism', *Classical Papers*, III, 1058.

162 'although we Germans':   reported by Annette M. B. Meakin, *The Times*, 7 May 1936; quoted in Richards, 84. Richards also quotes E. H. Blakeney's report (*The Sunday Times*, 4 October 1931) of Wilamowitz's remark that 'we in Germany are fully aware that Housman is the leading living Latinist.'

163 'my notorious arrogance':   Preface to *Manilius V*, xxxv.

163 'he was very sensitive':   W. H. Temple to Gow, 15 May 1936 (Trinity, Add. ms. a. 71. 299).

PAGE

163 'guilelessly':   Withers, 64.

163 'I have read':   D. R. Shackleton Bailey, 'Bentley and Horace', *Proceedings of the Leeds Philosophical Society* (1963) 110.

164 'If the next Bentley':   *Letters*, 429.

164 'no critic will get far':   D. R. Shackleton Bailey, 'Bentley and Horace', 107.

165 'The very notion':   E. J. Kenney, *The Classical Text* (Berkeley, 1974) 23–4.

166 'was founded less':   Gow, unpublished obituary of AEH.

166 'posterity':   *Classical Papers*, I, vii.

166 'peculiarly rich':   H. H. Huxley in *Fifty Years of Classical Scholarship*, ed. M. Platnauer (Oxford , 1954) 414.

167 'Housman's philological persona':   D. R. Shackleton Bailey, review of *Classical Papers* in *Cambridge Review*, 94 (1973) 189.

167 'deliberately and grimly':   Edmund Wilson, 'A. E. Housman', in *The Triple Thinkers* (1938); reprinted in *A. E. Housman*, ed. C. Ricks (New Jersey, 1968) 19.

167 'no hope':   *Classical Papers*, I, 29.

168 'he writes on astronomy':   *Letters*, 222.

168 'If you prefer Aeschylus':   *Letters*, 144.

168 'perhaps the most ingenious':   D.R. Shackleton Bailey, review of the Loeb edition of Manilius in *Classical Philology*, 74 (1979) 158.

168 'by the canons':   H. Lloyd-Jones, review of Graves, *London Review of Books*, 22 November 1979.

168 'to read it closely':   D. R. Shackleton Bailey, review of Loeb Manilius, 168–9.

168 about 1894:   P. L. Hedley, *Times Literary Supplement* (30 June 1937) 76; Gow, *TLS* (6 February 1937) 92.

169 'produced at my own expense':   Preface to *Manilius V*, v.

169 'I am taking great care':   *Letters*, 283.

169 'the last volume':   AEH to Katharine Symons, 29 December 1930 (Trinity).

170 'an edition of Manilius':   L. P. Wilkinson, 'A. E. Housman, Scholar and Poet', 40.

170 'the supreme glory':   T. E. Wright, in *Fifty Years of Classical Scholarship*, 333. G. P. Goold notes in his Loeb edition of Manilius (1977) that 'Manilius is a difficult author. His text is unusually corrupt, his subject-matter highly specialized, and his Latin style . . . bizarre and bewildering' (vii). He pays tribute to Housman's edition: 'There cannot be a page of this book untouched by his influence . . . if time has opened my eyes to [Housman's] fallibility, it has also brought me a fuller awareness of his scholarship, for which my respect has grown and not diminished' (viii). Professor Goold adds that, in addition to his more familiar qualities, Housman was 'a consummate astrological scholar' (ix).

170 'a monument of scholarship':   C. J. Fordyce, *Classical Review*, 53 (February 1939) 40 (review of the 1937 edition of the five books).

170 'equalled by no other':   Blanche B. Boyer, *Classical Philology*, 35 (April 1940) 223 (review of 1937).

PAGE

171 'that a man of taste': K. M. Abbott and W. A. Oldfather, *Classical Journal*, 35 (February 1940) 297 (review of 1937).

171 'is based on an inadequate number': Gilbert Highet, *Juvenal the Satirist* (Oxford, 1954) 343.

171 'Lucan would do you no good': *Letters*, 263.

171 'Emendators': Preface to *Lucan* (1927) xxvii.

171 'justly elicited superlatives': H. H. Huxley, in *Fifty Years of Classical Scholarship*, 420. J. D. Duff's Loeb edition of Lucan (1928) owes much to AEH, whose lectures on that poet Duff had attended.

172 'The statutes of Cambridge': L. P. Wilkinson, 'A. E. Housman, Scholar and Poet', 41.

172 'it has been perhaps': J. P. Sullivan, 'The Leading Classic of his Generation', *Arion* (1962); reprinted in *A. E. Housman*, ed. Ricks, 161.

173 'to isolate': D. R. Shackleton Bailey, 'A. E. Housman as a Classical Scholar', *Listener*, 61 (7 May 1959) 795–6.

8 THE POET

PAGE

179 'the fewer there are': Derek Hudson, *Lewis Carroll* (1954) 291, 293.

179 'very amenable': Katharine Symons to Gow, 19 November 1940 (Trinity).

180 'the genius': Harold Williams, *Modern English Writers* (1918) 69.

180 'At the beginning': George Orwell, *Inside the Whale* (1940).

181 'he might have thrown': Stephen Spender, review of *Collected Poems*, *Horizon*, 1 (1940) 300.

181 'I don't know': W. H. Auden, review of *Letters*, *New Yorker* (19 February 1972) 332; reprinted in *Forewords and Afterwords*, ed. E. Mendelson (1973).

182 'Despite an apparent': J. P. Bishop, 'The Poetry of A. A. Housman', *Poetry*, 56 (1940) 141; reprinted in *Collected Essays* (1948).

183 'the limits': ibid., 139.

187 Hardy: *A Shropshire Lad* antedates the publication of Hardy's poems, the first collection of which (*Wessex Poems*) appeared in 1898. AEH admired Hardy's novels as well as his poetry; Hardy's favourite from *A Shropshire Lad* was 'Is my team ploughing?'.

187 'exposure': Richard Ellmann, 'Romantic Pantomime in Oscar Wilde', *Partisan Review*, 30 (1963) 352.

188 'not a descriptive writer': *Letters*, 386.

188 'almost entirely of death': R. P. Blackmur, *The Expense of Greatness* (1940) 202.

188 'desire for all the manly types': Jean Genet, *The Thief's Journal*, trans. by Bernard Frechtman (Harmondsworth, 1967) 33.

189 'over a beautiful': Michael Levey, *The Case of Walter Pater* (1978) 129.

191 'the dominant pattern': B. J. Leggett, *Land of Lost Content* (1970) 101.

197 'the unity': ibid., 69.

197 'strengthen the sense': ibid., 93.

PAGE

199 'shouts': Earlier versions of the line ('The cuckoo shouts all day at nothing') are (1) 'The April cuckoo shouts at nothing'; (2) 'The cuckoo shouts for glee at nothing' (manuscript in LC).

199 Tennyson: Christopher Ricks, 'The Nature of Housman's Poetry', *Essays in Criticism*, 14 (1964) 283; reprinted in Ricks, *A. E. Housman*.

199 'remarkable erotic force': ibid., 282–3.

200 'I think the poem': William Empson, 'Rhythm and Imagery in English Poetry', *British Journal of Aesthetics*, 2 (1962) 40–1; quoted by Ricks in the article cited.

204 Philip Larkin: 'Palgrave's Last Anthology: A. E. Housman's Copy', *Review of English Studies*, n.s. 22 (1971) 312–16.

206 'much of Housman's serious verse': Ricks, op. cit., 279.

Index